**GETTING HITLER
INTO HEAVEN**

had its origins in the 267 pages of ....
in English, that formed the me........ ..ei.iz Linge who,
throughout World War II, was the personal valet of Adolf Hitler.

John Graven Hughes has written a compelling narrative of events
in Germany, beginning with the rise to power of Adolf Hitler and
ending on that fateful day when, faithful to the last, Linge carried
out his master's last wishes. Many of the events are well-known,
but the viewpoint of Linge is paramount and brings a new
perspective to the portrayal of the Fuhrer, who is seen to be an
inwardly tormented man with little more than an uncanny instinct
and the energy to apply it; and with a childlike belief in the
workings of Providence.

GETTING HITLER INTO HEAVEN will appeal to all those who
are intrigued by the nature of evil as personified by Adolf Hitler,
whose power and influence affected millions of people throughout
World War II.

GETTING HITLER INTO HEAVEN

John Graven Hughes

CORGI BOOKS

GETTING HITLER INTO HEAVEN

A CORGI BOOK   0 552 99285 2

First publication in Great Britain

PRINTING HISTORY

Corgi edition published 1987

Copyright © 1987 John Graven Hughes

This book is set in 10/11pt Paladium

Corgi Books are published by Transworld Publishers Ltd.,
61-63 Uxbridge Road, Ealing, London W5 5SA, in Australia by
Transworld Publishers (Australia) Pty. Ltd., 15-23 Helles
Avenue, Moorebank, NSW 2170, and in New Zealand by Transworld
Publishers (N.Z.) Ltd., Cnr. Moselle and Waipareira Avenues,
Henderson, Auckland.

Made and printed in Great Britain by
The Guernsey Press Co. Ltd., Guernsey, Channel Islands.

INTRODUCTION

'Memory is our shield. Our only shield'
Elie Wiesel, Holocaust survivor

As you read this, a woman may be giving birth somewhere to a baby who may some day attempt to destroy the world. Elsewhere another baby may be born capable of preventing it. Do you believe in the random nature of chance, or the mathematical logic of rise and fall? Or the proposition which suggests we are all linked to the pulse of a primal supernatural life force; planetary systems controlling fundamental energies? Or in God and the Divine Principle of the universe?

'God, like a gardener, sows people as they are,' wrote Frederick the Great in 1760, '. . . leaving them to grow without interfering here on earth.'

The birth of a baby boy on April 20, 1889 in the frontier village of Branau-on-Inn would have passed without comment by the three thousand inhabitants. How could any of them have known that the son of a minor customs official was destined one day to destroy a nation and change the face of Europe?

Was he perhaps born as a reaction against the forces of anarchy, or sent by Providence to save a world threatened by Bolshevism?

A single fertilised cell implanted in a sickly, flawed womb by an obdurate, blood-tainted patriarch, growing in an ordered pattern, with the heart as nucleus and internal organs arranging themselves for specific functions; the brain receiving impulses stimulating instinctive responses; dominating the waking and sleeping cycles of the adolescent's life; inheriting a fixity of purpose, a force of mind; wilful, tough, shrewd, with the memory of an elephant and a latent ability to group aggressions in a coherent bundle; aggressions which, according to Freudians, resulted from a death wish blocked by erotic and self-preservative instincts.

Unable to free himself from himself, the man develops a schizoid dualism: on one side, an intimidating nonchalance and a cold-

5

hearted impersonality, later resulting in an unnatural calm in the face of insurmountable difficulties; on the other, grandiose rages and a romanticism which seeks an outlet in a stubborn attachment to an unsophisticated girl twenty-three years younger, and in the music of Wagner. Wagner mirrors the range of his emotions, a tumultous disregard for others and ultimately a willingness to hurl the world into chaos, typified by Wotan's fury:

> 'In whatever I do, I find always only myself
> and I loathe it . . . I must leave what I love;
> I must murder what I woo; deceitfully I must
> betray whoever trusts me . . . what I built I
> must break down. I abandon my work. One
> thing alone I demand, the end, the end.'
>
> (*Die Walkure*; Act II Sc. 2)

The leader, in a hypnotic trance, longs for release from the restrictions of life and whatever frenzied lusts possess him.

Some of his followers welcome him as another Siegfried, the sun god in *Nibelungen*, Wagner's likeness to Christ the son of God, who died, was mourned and avenged; he who would return on the day of judgement — the faithful rewarded with eternal life.

The rising politician subscribes to the Providence theory: all history is providential. As nationalism is its principal motive force, its record of crimes and genocide is simply the expression of divine will. Employing an elementary knowledge of philosophy, a gift for bizarre oratory and a caustic contempt for the masses, he justifies his national-socialist dogma, reinforcing it with a potent racism; and is wholeheartedly endorsed by a nation traditionally susceptible to the dark forces in the universe. The original *vandals* who sacked Rome in 455 AD came from East Germany.

Raucous demands for *rohstoffe* (raw materials) and *lebensraum* (living space) pave the way for malign activities of indiscriminate henchmen. Inevitably, unfettered by human or spiritual laws, his deputies become responsible for initiating unparalleled depths of human suffering; and the apocalyptic *Endlossung*, the Final Solution. Man in the end is capable of anything.

At the beginning of World War II, dynamic, charismatic, powerful, by the spring of 1945 the Fuhrer is the victim of his own uncontrollable dictatorship, answerable to no outer or inner laws. Prescribed an inordinate quantity of drugs for too many years, the diseased mind's mechanism for handling stress erodes, finally ripping apart the frail psychological armour. Preferring a voluptuous self-destruction

6

to a slow decline into decrepitude, he decides on a macabre *Gotter-dammerung*: resigned to a place in Teutonic mythology alongside Barbarossa; ready to rise again when urgently needed back on earth.

Frederick I (Barbarossa), 1121-1190, was buried in *Thuringia*: 'He never died and sits at a stone table with his six knights waiting for the fullness of time when he will rescue Germany from bondage and give her the foremost place in the world . . . his beard has already grown through the stone slab but must wind itself thrice around the table before his second advent.'

Hitler's empire, destined to last a thousand years, perished with him in the ruins of Berlin twelve years, three months and one week from his rise to power. And as a result of his defeat at the hands of the Allies, 'the western frontier of Russia has been advanced from the Pripet Marshes to the *Thuringerwald*, a distance of 750 miles. As in the days of Charlemagne the Slavs stood on the Elbe and the Bohmerwald. A thousand years of European history has been rolled back.' (Fuller)

Those who believe in the 'second helping' theory of reincarnation will be heartened to read the findings of an acknowledged clairvoyant: 'It has been said on high, in the spiritual realms, that Hitler may never be allowed to reincarnate. He must stay in purgatory for at least a thousand years, possibly even two thousand. Refusing to accept that he has passed on, he cannot admit or face up to the evils and crimes which have resulted from his actions. Therefore he will not have the opportunity to live on earth again, not until he is truly repentant. This may be never.'

* * *

What became of Hitler's personal valet, Heinz Linge?

After he was released by the Russians in 1955, the former SS *Obersturmbannfuhrer* (Major) went home to Schenefeld in Hamburg. He earned a living as a salesman for Nordmark, manufacturers of prefabricated houses.

His favourite tavern was in the Lurup district of Hamburg: the *Treffpunkt* (meeting-place). The regulars knew him well and they were familiar with his background. Whenever he visited the bar he talked quite openly about his years with Hitler. He found that most of the women were curious about Eva Braun. He told them that 'Eva was just a simple girl who loved the Fuhrer. The Fuhrer loved her too. He liked her innocence — he had a dreadful fear of venereal disease. She was truly the right one for him.' He would conclude by stating that 'they were just normal people.'

7

In most interviews the valet, repository of so many secrets, the one who opened doors, served meals, put on records and invited girls to coffee, comes across as a rather stereotyped SS man. This is probably what he was — his manner most of the time being one of faintly bewildered gravity.

In 1975 a journalist suggested to Linge that he must have been 'a 150 per cent Nazi in his former occupation.'

Without hesitation, the valet replied in a loud, cheerful voice, 'Yes, I was.'

Aware of a feeling of superiority which he never attempted to disguise, he stayed *Fuhrertreu* until he died in 1981.

'History,' says Barbara Tuchman, 'is the record of human behaviour, the most fascinating subject of all, but illogical and so crammed with an unlimited number of variables that it is not susceptible of the scientific method nor of systematising.'

*   *   *

There are two enduring lessons we can learn from a fresh appraisal of Hitler and his regime: absolutism, or a dictatorship, has no place in the world — we all have rights and corresponding duties; and the interest of a state ought to be in the many, not in the few who seek to monopolise money-creation for personal gain.

History began long before the birth of Hitler and since his death, perhaps as part of his legacy, many of the problems seem to be insurmountable, particularly the nightmare of nuclear destruction.

Bearing in mind the events that led to World War II and the 'peace at any price' diplomacy of the 1930s, there is a continuing need for dialogue between East and West, providing the West recognises the anxieties of a vast country that has been — since the days of Stalin — one gigantic dungeon. Western leaders, rather than wasting time in party rancour, must not cease, using all the means consistent with courage and common sense, to negotiate.

In a democracy we have a choice of representatives. We must choose well. They are, in the end, all we have to work with — whether we like it or not.

There will be other contenders for Hitler's baton. Fortunately television, while seeming on a supercificial level to encourage image-making, makes it easier to recognise the irrelevant ambitions of intransigent militants and the naked self-interest of the meretricious few who pose as political heavyweights by hurling random insults at convenient targets in oratorical flights of fancy.

John Graven Hughes 1987

ACKNOWLEDGEMENTS

The reconstruction of historical events is a relatively simple matter. Careful research assists accuracy. Historical generalisations tend to be unreliable, differing according to the nationality of the historian. If there is a departure from fact in the book I hope it only occurs in passages containing Linge's personal opinions. 'The first quality of a biographer,' wrote Cyril Connolly, 'should be humanity, the second wonder, and the third a passion for truth'.

Having spent some time in Germany in 1982-83, I am indebted to the following for assistance with the German research:

Barbara Distel, Dachau Museum Archives; Simon Wiesenthal, Dokumentationszentrum, Vienna; the staff of the State Library, Ludwigstrasse, Munich; the head waiter at the *Osteria Bavaria*, Hitler's favourite restaurant (still on Schellingstrasse, Munich, albeit under another name); and the many people in Munich, Hamburg and Berchtesgaden who talked to me but who wish to remain anonymous.

Part of the book was written in France and I wish to express gratitude to the late Jacqueline Bourguignon Frank for her help: she spent her adolescence in Nazi-occupied France, and worked as a courier for the Resistance.

I gratefully acknowledge the co-operation of Frau Redden, Nymphenburger Verlagshandlung, Munich; and the assistance of Diana, Lady Mosley; Michael Brown (former Chief Reporter, *Daily Express*); Einzi Stolz, widow of the late composer Robert Stolz (who spent the years from 1924 to 1936 in Berlin); Terence C Charman, Imperial War Museum; Christine Shuttleworth, London (for translation services); Alex Law, Sherborne (for photographic assistance); The British Newspaper Library staff, Colindale, London and Alan Earney, Editorial Director of Corgi Books, for his skilful editing of the final typescript.

I particularly want to express thanks to my friend, Freddy Clayton who, despite a severe illness over the years, has been a never-failing source of encouragement and inspiration.

For permission to include copyright material I must thank the following:

Ambassador's Wife by Elisabetta Cerruti: Allen & Unwin, London 1952; *Before She Met Me* by Julian Barnes: Jonathan Cape, London 1982; *Germany 1866-1945* by Gordon A Craig: Oxford University Press, Oxford 1981; *Heil and Farewell* by Pierre J Huss: Century Hutchinson, London 1942; *Mein Kampf* by Adolf Hitler: Century Hutchinson, London 1933; *Men Under Fire* by R W Thompson: Macdonald, London 1945; *Practicing History* by Barbara Tuchman: Alfred Knopf Inc., New York 1981; *Skorzeny's Special Mission* by Otto Skorzeny: Robert Hale, London 1957; *The Decisive Battles of the Western World* by Maj-Gen J F C Fuller: Eyre & Spottiswoode, London 1956; *The Mind of Adolf Hitler* by Walter C Langer: Secker & Warburg, London 1973; *The Rise and Fall of the Third Reich* by William L Shirer: Hamish Hamilton, London 1947; *The Murder of Rudolf Hess* by Hugh Thomas: Hodder & Stoughton, London 1979 and *Unity Mitford: A Quest* by David Pryce-Jones: Weidenfeld, London 1976.

Brief extracts from *Hitler the Pawn* have been included with the knowledge of the publisher, Victor Gollancz, London. All efforts at tracing the present copyright holder proving unsuccessful I trust this will be sufficient acknowledgement.

I want to thank the following literary agents (and copyright negotiators) for permissions as follows: A D Peters for extracts from *The Berlin Bunker* by James P O'Donnell: Dent, London 1979; Elaine Greene for *The Last Battle* by Cornelius Ryan (copyright © 1966 Cornelius Ryan): Collins, London 1966; A P Watt for two extracts from *A Tale of Ten Cities* by George Sava: Faber & Faber, London 1942. The James Rusbridger quotes are used with the permission of *Encounter*, London.

ILLUSTRATIONS

1922: 'The masses are so obtuse, they . . . will remember the simplest idea only if it is repeated a thousand times.' Hitler

1929: Eva Braun met Hitler for the first time at Hoffman's studio. He was forty; she was seventeen.

1929: A rare photograph taken on Martin Bormann's wedding day, showing (l-r) Hess, Herbert Blank, von Pfeffer (head of Munich SA), Walter Busch (Bormann's father-in-law and Head Party Judge), Hitler, Albert Bormann (younger brother), Bormann and wife.

1932: The 'Bohemian Corporal' meets the Prussian Junker, Field Marshal Hindenburg.

1933: Hitler marching with the SA Chief of Staff, Ernst Rohm.

1934: Hitler, Goring and Rohm. After the purging of June 30, Hitler 'foamed with rage' at Rohm's homosexuality.

1934: Unity Mitford (r) with her sister, Diana Lady Mosely, at a pre-war Nazi rally.

1934: Hitler and Goebbels greeted outside the Prinz Albrecht Hotel, Berlin.

1940: Linge (extreme left) looks on as Hitler and Mussolini seal the Berlin-Rome Axis, a few days after Il Duce declared war.

Linge checks the menu for dinner at the Fuhrer's wartime headquarters. The stripe on the valet's sleeve indicates he joined the Nazi Party before 1933.

Dedicated to
my daughters, Theresa, Eileen and Siobhan

PART ONE

In Hidalla, *produced in Munich in the 1890s, Frank Wedekind foreshadowed the future.*

With typical, tongue in cheek symbolism his play was built around a man so obsessed with the idea of human perfection he founded a society of pure bred, physically perfect human beings. Only those in possession of a superb physique and natural beauty qualified for membership.

When the man himself made his first entrance the audience was taken by surprise — he was an ill-featured hunchback.

On the one hand there is truth, on the other there is personality. And if we think of truth as something of granite-like solidity, and of personality of rainbow-like intangibility, then reflect that the aim of biography is to weld these two into one seamless whole, we shall admit the problem is a stiff one.

Virginia Woolf

ADOLF HITLER
Born 6.30 pm on April 20, 1889 at Branau, Austria

Abridged birth chart analysis

URANUS: Rising planet in 12th House makes subject secretive; attracted to the unusual; conflicts in the unconscious could be serious.

SATURN: In 10th House generally means subject is ambitious, demands recognition, can be ruthless — even cruel — in realising ambitions.

VENUS: In Martian conjunction — exact conjunction with Mars — makes subject irrational and inclined to overreact to minor problems.

MOON: In 3rd House indicates unsettled childhood/education; in conjunction (2°) with Jupiter, self-important and vain; inner need for change; enormous energy.

SUN: In (5°) conjunction with Mercury; stubborn, dogmatic, prejudiced; inflexible of mind.

SUMMARY: No unusual groupings of planets apart from cluster between Aries and Gemini where there are several conjunctions — both positive and negative aspects but negative conjunctions: Sun/Mercury, Venus/Mars are analysed above and could give subject irrational behaviour patterns.

Absence of water element in chart can indicate lack of emotion; an uncaring attitude, an absence of genuine intuition.

Hitler was impulsive, self-motivated, (the head is the part of the body correlating to Aries) able to call on reserves of energy when pursuing goals. His courage and disregard for danger were legendary; dangerous situations, requiring leadership and initiative, appealed to him; keen to start new projects, he tended to lose interest when they became humdrum.

Quick-tempered, aggressive, able to recover a good mood rapidly; abrupt, impatient, tactless, pragmatic, he performed well

17

under pressure; prepared to study energetically if interested in a subject; inclined to be childish if frustrated; when in a good mood a stimulating conversationalist; his sexual nature was ardent, not devoid of romance.

CHAPTER ONE

Today it's a museum piece made mawkish by repetition. A travesty restated, reprinted, reissued; the theme of a thousand documentaries.

A guard of honour, bronzed, invulnerable, ramrod straight behind the barriers.

The green police lining a dusty street keeping crowds at bay: faceless men carved in stone sporting party badges; buxom women with their children shouldered aside by goodnatured young men in coffee-coloured shirts with bright red armbands and rattling collecting boxes — not the sort to beat up Jews or kick dissidents to death.

A blaring of brass, a rat-a-tat of drums under scarlet bunting whipping in the wind, heralding an endless line of soldiers, steel helmeted in full field kit, tramping in jackboots to a Potsdam goosestep rhythm.

'*Deutschland! Deutschland, uber Alles!*' A muted roar and the hymn of victory, *Heil dir im Siegerkranz,* as a large black limousine moves slowly beneath a solid salute of outstretched arms, proclaiming the arrival of their beloved Fuhrer — *Der Chef* himself.

'Heil Hitler! Heil Hitler! Heil Hitler!' A forest of flags is raised, each displaying the swastika, the 'fire whisk' in German mythology which had twirled the primal substance at the creation of the universe, now the symbol of *volkisch,* racist nationalistic fervour.

It is 1934 and Bremen's turn to celebrate some National Socialist anniversary or other. Party uniforms proliferate, black and silver, chocolate, pale cream, proclaiming loyalty to the man invested with absolute power, the leader — *der Fuhrer* — failed decorator turned dictator, Charlie Chaplin alias Arturo Ui wielding a crooked cross, a simple man with a silly moustache and the fanatical eyes of a mystic.

The voice at first pitched a shade too high, faltering, finding a rhythm, switching from smirking sarcasm to frenzied rhetoric, an insistent thudding eloquence, rigid, precise, bitter. Drawing on imperfectly understood dark-age myths, bedazzled and tainted by Clausewitz, Bismarck, Frederick the Great and Barbarossa — hard men of blood and iron infected with an anti-semitic Wagnerian virus.

Using a kind of derisive irony, calling for the end of just about everything, employing statements of staggering dubiousness. Against catholics, Jews, gipsies, profiteering, communism, unemployment and the Treaty of Versailles.

He is for the fight that was not yet won. He is for Germany, the land of Germans. He is for never allowing Germany to submit again to intrigue by other nations.

He is scornful, domineering, omniscient, the mass orator, the war lord, exerting his strange magnetism on the susceptible; designating outsiders as victims fit only to flesh the claws of his youthful, eagle-swift adherents — creating a jagged excitement; his listeners baying and swaying, jaws erupting, muscles taut, rising and praising and chanting his name; case-hardened, obedient, lusting for blood and power and conquest — responding to the leader's hypnotic balderdash.

For him natural laws, politics, religious beliefs, even erotic compulsion — none of them were as overwhelming as his instinct to be the incarnation of an idea, able to inspire a fanatical following.

It was a new German dream directed against the social evils of the industrial revolution; directed against races lacking political power; transcending boundaries; a lever against any state containing German elements — a programme of Aryan solidarity. With the Fuhrer as programme maker.

The destiny of Germany, and that included Bremen, would be to pluck the trident from the spineless inheritors of the Anglo-Saxon empire; to dominate the world. A National Socialist world that would be a heaven on earth. And anyone foolish enough to reject it could go to hell.

'From now on,' warned the Fuhrer, 'we shall attack such elements with brutal ruthlessness and, if we cannot win them by kindness, we shall not fight shy of fitting and adapting them to the general interests of the nation by means of the concentration camp.'

The crowd, aroused, inspired, yelled themselves hoarse. One young man in the front rank, a section leader with the Hitler Jugend, felt his heart bursting with pleasure and pride.

He was a student, Heinz Linge, one of Baldur von Schirach's best and finest, sworn to service, ardently believing that under such a leader anything was possible. The young man went home from the meeting yearning to cooperate more wholeheartedly in the rebirth of the Fatherland.

A few days later he volunteered for the SS.

*   *   *

Heinz Linge grew up in a middle-class home in Bremen, staying at school until his late teens. Hoping to qualify as an engineer he studied at the technical college from 1929 to 1933. Most of his spare time was dedicated to the Hitler Youth.

Being clear-eyed and strong, with perfect teeth — and able to prove his ancestry was above reproach — Linge was accepted for an intensive course of training in the SS before being sent to a specialist unit.

Because of his splendid physique and height — he was well over six feet tall — Linge was no sooner into his trim black uniform than he was selected for the *corps d'elite*, the Leibstandarte Adolf Hitler.

This entailed rigid medical and genealogical examinations and an appearance in front of the 'racial commission'. No matter how pure his racial origins might have been, Linge would have been rejected if his appearance had not been of the pure German type.

By such careful grading of its members, the SS, an 'Order of Men with a Nordic Vocation', which signed itself with the runic sign as a symbol of its conscious insistence on racial purity, would produce a body of German supermen.

And girls who wanted to marry SS men, which they were allowed to do only after being examined for racial and biological suitability, had to attend special SS brides' schools.

After weeks of drilling, marching, parading, Linge was plucked from the ranks once again, this time to train with the *Fuhrerbegleit-Kommando*, composed of ten officers, veterans of World War I and thirty brawny life guards. Their job? To protect Hitler twenty-four hours a day; to keep their eyes wide open, their ears pricked and bodies instantly available to act as shields in the event of any attempt on the life of the chief. And they were to act not only as flesh and blood guardian angels but as stewards, tasters, cup-bearers, valets and grooms of chamber.

Still dazed by his good luck, Linge underwent intensive training at a Berlin catering college before putting in a prolonged tour of duty at the Chancellery. Detailed to report to the Fuhrer personally, his cup ran over. He had been shortlisted for selection as one of Hitler's manservants.

Three valets covering each twenty-four hour watch accompanied the Fuhrer everywhere, and in many ways they enjoyed a privileged relationship. His aloofness and reserve setting him apart from other men, the chief would always be more at ease with his personal staff than with government officials.

It seems that Hitler took a partiuclar interest in twenty-two year old Linge, later appointing him number one manservant.

And the valet made very few mistakes. He soon realised that the direct approach was the way to the Fuhrer's heart. Hitler admired loyalty and truth above all other qualities. If things went wrong it was better to tell him straight away rather than wait for some mealymouthed informer to spill the beans.

Linge recalls a certain mannerism of the chief's; the way he stared at a fellow unblinkingly as though able to read his thoughts. 'His clear blue eyes could penetrate the depths of your soul.'

Naturally, even in a tight ship like the Reich Chancellery, things could go wrong. When they came to light, Linge, at the centre of operations, manfully bore the brunt of the chief's disdain.

'That's why you're here, Linge, so I can vent my spleen on you. You're a fine, sturdy young fellow, well able to stand a tonguelashing — even when you've done little to deserve it.'

Frequently, at the end of a successful dinner party, Hitler would lift a limp hand and indicate his loyal valet hovering at the door. 'This man,' he'd say, 'defies me to punish him for his shortcomings. He always jumps in first to confess his mistakes, taking the wind out of my sails.'

Later, during World War II, he made similar remarks at military discussions — perhaps hoping his generals might take the hint and follow the valet's example.

*   *   *

As an advocate, Linge deferred to none in his regard for Hitler. As a leader, he found him straightforward, considerate and impartial;

very often indulgent with people he had every reason to despise.

If there had been infamous excesses then it was the fault of subordinates.

Some, like Heydrich, went too far. Others, like Himmler didn't know when to stop.

From their point of view National Socialism had brought about a revolution. Revolution inevitably ends in extremes of one kind or another — the result of too much misplaced enthusiasm.

Years after he had helped dispose of the ravaged remains in the Chancellery garden, Linge was inclined to make a stronger case for the Fuhrer than the facts warranted. This worthy servitor of his master, enslaved by the incontestable brilliance of the man he served, needed to paint a portrait, not of the rabble-rousing demagogue of 1935, nor of the shambling vacant-eyed puppet of 1945, but of a dynamic human being with an implicit belief in the theory of providence and his own destiny.

To humanise the master might be to falsify him. This perhaps was the valet's aim. What Hitler was defies scientific analysis; attempts in the past at analysis of his character have raised as many questions as they have answered.

Nowadays, psychiatrists, opening the sluicegates of cause, motivation and interpretation advise us to absolve all manifestations of sickening behaviour, as long as acceptable frailties of the psyche can be dredged up to excuse them.

An astute physician might point the finger of responsibility at the Fuhrer's malfunctioning colon. Like Luther before him, Hitler was plagued for most of his life by chronic constipation.

Linge clung stubbornly to his own article of faith: the pattern of events had been preordained; therefore the catalogue of barbarities and insanities were simply an expression of divine will. Hitler, while prepared to profit from the slightest change in the wind, had acted at all times upon the dictates of a force beyond himself. This justified his belief that war was a good thing, fulfilling the will of providence.

And as supreme commander in World War II he needed every scrap of power, every ounce of drive, every bit of cunning he had acquired in his embattled career.

Rationalising the dictator's coldhearted ruthlessness in the name of exceptional powers, the valet remained convinced that such a life could be lived in no other way.

Like the rest of humanity he should finally be left to the judgement of Heaven.

*   *   *

Some years ago Einstein was asked what the weapons of World War III would be. 'I don't know,' he said, 'but I know what the weapons of World War IV will be — rocks.'

*Twelve commandments for political leaders in 'the coming struggle'
were handed out by vice-district leader Nippold at a meeting of
gauleiters in Munich.*

They were:

1. *I believe in the leader not with my intellect but with my heart
   and soul.*
2. *In me lives the love of my German fatherland.*
3. *I will act in love to all my comrades.*
4. *I believe in unconditional obedience to my superiors.*
5. *I believe in comradeship to the last.*
6. *I believe in unconditional fulfilment of my duty.*
7. *I will be a good National Socialist, inwardly and outwardly.*
8. *I must preserve the confidence of the people in the
   movement.*
9. *I must be aware of the relationship between state and party.*
10. *Between the party and its organisations.*
11. *Between the party and the armed forces.*
12. *The National Socialist does not think in hours — but in
    centuries.*

Voelkischer Beobachter August 1935

*Hitler might have been a different sort of man if he had been
a bowler — he might have been less biased.*

President : Barnstaple Bowling Club 1939

CHAPTER TWO

On Wednesday, January 16, 1935 a number of officials arrived one by one at the Chancellery. Members of the inner cabinet, they had been summoned by their Fuhrer to an important meeting; to listen to the voice of authority outline plans for the complete military and economic mobilisation of the Third Reich.

The prudent von Neurath was the first to arrive. Followed by Blomberg, soon to be dismissed as war minister — he had made an unfortunate marriage with a former prostitute; Fritsch — to die in mysterious circumstances in the Polish campaign; Admiral Rader; Frick; Schacht the banker; Bormann and Goebbels. Goring then appeared, the collar of his heavy overcoat up around his ears — and finally Hess.

As snow began to fall outside, the party leaders stood around in the main hall, chatting quietly, smoking their cigars and cigarettes. There'd be no smoking in front of Hitler, an unbroken rule to be observed as carefully as an equally stringent one: never to take alcohol before an audience with the Fuhrer.

The Fuhrer played his usual cat and mouse game; making the men wait until exactly one minute to twelve. Then he sent SS man Schaub, his closest shadow, to check that everyone was present. The adjutant limped back to the office. *'Mein Fuhrer, die herren warten,'* he said. (The German equivalent of 'All present and correct'.)

Hitler nodded curtly, handing a folio of papers to a bloated giant of an *obergruppenfuhrer* (general). He was Wilhelm Bruckner, original personal adjutant, captain in World War I, associated with the chief since their imprisonment together at Landsberg. One of Germany's finest tennis players in his youth, Bruckner, at 6 ft 7 ins., towered like a wall over Hitler, as protective in the good days as he was in the bad.

He fell from grace three years later in 1938, not only because of his addiction to drink, but as a result of a liaison with a married

26

woman in Munich which made his own wife an object of malicious Bavarian gossip. Although he eventually divorced his wife and married his mistress, Bruckner had left it too late. The Fuhrer had already decided to pension him off and Bruckner dropped from public view.

Schaub had also been with Hitler since 1923; a former postal clerk in Munich, he had approached the chief in Landsberg jail, offering to serve him in any capacity without pay — he was with the Fuhrer until the end.

It was Schaub who brought the party officials up the flight of stairs to the cabinet room. And Heinz Linge, erect in his black uniform, marched forward to open the doors before Hitler. 'Der Fuhrer!' he said loudly. The subdued conversation stopped abruptly.

Hitler loped in, the right hand describing a kind of half circle before it flopped back to his side. Staring straight into the eyes of each man he shook hands, beginning with Goring and ending with von Neurath. Then they all grouped themselves around the highly polished table in the centre of the room. The Fuhrer's chair was in the middle, dominating the rest.

Linge hurried back to his quarters, about to put in motion a resolution he had made at the beginning of the year, to record day-to-day events in his diary.

Because of his inclination to present a picture of bland domesticity, to portray a master on democratic if not downright affectionate terms with his personal servant, his story tends to be perfunctory, his sense of chronology distorted and his conclusions somewhat suspect. He obviously knew his place. And as a member of the Lifeguard he had been trained to dispense with sentiment, to ignore truth and to cultivate detachment.

However, if he achieves nothing else, he does manage to destroy quite a few myths by rounding out the character of the Fuhrer. He also gives the lie to the saying that no man is a hero to his valet.

*   *   *

Once the formalities had been observed the meeting got under way. The Fuhrer was in an expansive mood, taking four hours to put forward, solely on the basis of his own intuition, a few central ideas.

27

Outlining his plans for the future, he pointed out that Germany, going from strength to strength economically, was almost ready to free herself from the chains of Versailles. There were two immediate aims. Austria must become part of the Reich. And Czechoslovakia, the 'bone in the throat of Germany', must be detached from its links with France and Rumania. An unnatural creation of the Treaty of Versailles, Czechoslovakia was nothing less than a dangerous springboard for the Soviets. Therefore the vital sphere of influence was the east. Russia was the mortal foe.

'National Socialism,' — the words were rapped out harshly, marked by abrupt emphasis — 'came into being to expand Germany, to destroy Jewry, to eliminate Bolshevism. Quite soon the German people will have the capacity to fight the world — if called upon to do so.'

'*Richtig, mein Fuhrer!*' That was the beefy, flamboyant Goring, staccatissimo.

Finally Hitler stood, pushing back his chair. He concluded by reminding the group that before adjustments could be made to the map of Europe some sort of detente with England would have to be arranged. 'Better to lose a few regiments *with* England rather than against her.'

It was dark when the meeting broke up and the men began talking volubly among themselves as they walked down the corridor, relighting cigars and cigarettes. Schacht, accompanying Neurath, expressed doubts about Hitler's intentions. If the Fuhrer attempted a move into Czechoslovakia then the rest of Europe would prepare for war.

Neurath held his tongue. If he didn't go along with the policies, Hitler would quickly replace him with his 'ambassador at large', the odious Ribbentrop.

Goring, puffing on his cigar, also had reservations despite his enthusiastic endorsement of the Fuhrer's programme. 'The idea of an agreement with England is sound but they'd hardly stand aside while we broke up the Little Entente. We must cultivate France as well as England.'

The hubbub of voices faded as the group reached the ground floor. There was a great deal of boot-stamping on marble and the metallic clicking of rifles presented as the death's head bodyguard recognised the leaders.

Upstairs in his study, Hitler sat at his desk beneath the bronze head of Hindenburg, leafing through the leather-bound copy of *Sulla*, autographed with a fond personal message from Mussolini. Bruckner sorted some documents; Linge hovered near the door.

The Fuhrer asked the adjutant for his views on the possibility of England's agreeing to stand back in the role of silent partner. Bruckner felt that England had to be dissuaded from forming alliances with France and Russia.

Hitler reminded him he had friends in England.

'They must first come to power, then everything will work out.'

He was referring to the widespread diffusion of sympathy for National Socialism which, in England, was spearheaded by Viscount Rothermere, who had built a large, enduring newspaper group, and also by members of the January Club, a pro-fascist group formed in 1934 and supported by an assortment of members of the House of Lords.

Capitalising on the fear of communism among his circle of business associates, Rothermere was able to convert several of them to his belief that an endorsement of National Socialism would serve their interests more profitably.

'Good,' said Bruckner, 'then it won't be necessary to spend so much on making our army more powerful than it is.'

'You don't understand,' said Hitler. 'Positive military strength is essential. Diplomacy must be supported by a strong war machine. There will be only one war we will be called upon to fight — a total war that will mean the complete and final disappearance of the world enemy number one, Bolshevism.'

Two months later he re-introduced conscription. One year later the Rhineland was reoccupied.

For the once powerful Left in Germany it signified that the revolutionary initiative had been seized by the forces of reaction.

For Jews — one German in a hundred was Jewish — it was time to feel for their watches and count their small change. Those who felt apprehensive were justified.

*   *   *

Linge, leaving aside for the most part the methods employed by the party, concentrates on presenting Hitler as human being.

Constantly on call, his valet had all the time in the world to study his chief.

29

He was there first thing in the morning. He was there last thing at night. He was still there at the end — when the Fuhrer mournfully forecast, just before his death, that the world would brand him a monster.

Hitler's working day began late — usually after ten in the morning. Newspapers, including his own *Volkischer Beobachter*, and official documents were placed on a chair outside his bedroom.

A light tap on the door; Linge's greeting never varied: 'Good morning, my Fuhrer. Are you ready for breakfast?'

Hitler was always awake when the valet entered the room, an apartment plainly furnished with a white metal bed, a chest of drawers, and two or three easy chairs. A small lamp stood together with books and files on a trolley to the right of the bed.

In the adjoining bathroom, Linge ran the hot water before placing fresh underwear on the chair. Hitler wore cotton underpants and singlet, never silk. Next, the outfit for the day: mostly a well-cut brown shirt fitted with moisture-absorbing pads under the collar and the arms, tailored black breeches in fine gaberdine, highly-polished boots of soft leather.

Breakfast was served in the saloon: pumpernickel bread, oatmeal, cheese, honey, milk, some fresh fruit. During the meal Hitler would discuss the luncheon menus, checking guest lists and their preferences; selecting simple dishes for himself, soup, eggs, vegetables, occasionally a slice of ham, some caviar, peaches, chocolates and mineral water.

Before Hitler left his apartment, Linge held out a jacket for him; before World War II, a light brown unbelted tunic, displaying the Fuhrer's decorations, wound stripe, gold party badge and swastika armband. The peaked cap which tended to obscure the upper half of Hitler's face was heavier than it looked. Lined with armoured steel, it weighed 3½ lbs.

The valet was personally responsible for two other essential items in the chief's wardrobe; his hippopotamus-hide whip and his automatic pistol.

Linge believed Hitler was a far better marksman than many of the top army and SS sharpshooters. He had studied most of the technical books on guns and ballistics, making it a point to know more about weapons than the various arms instructors in his services. There was a standing order for the latest books on the subject and the chief frequently spent the night absorbing information on both German and foreign arms.

Moving as silently as a shark in shallow water, the valet was never far from the Fuhrer throughout the working day. In white mess jacket and black breeches he was on hand during heart-to-heart chats with the party potentates; close enough to overhear off-the-cuff exchanges; not quite out of earshot during historic squabbles; recording everything, saying little.

Familiar with Hitler's idiosyncrasies; his fastidiousness; the manner in which he would wash his hands thoroughly several times a day; his aversion to tight clothing. Most of his jackets sat uneasily, being a couple of sizes too large and he hated formal or evening dress, because of a belief that tails made him look comical.

Then there was his phobia with the time it took to change clothes. 'Take the stop watch, Linge,' he used to say, 'check how quickly we can do it this time.' Standing before a full-length mirror Hitler, eyes closed, ticked off the number of seconds it took, impatiently waiting for the valet's 'All done, my Fuhrer.' If the previous record, eight seconds, was beaten, Linge received an approving pat on the shoulder. If he overran the time Hitler stared unblinkingly at him through narrowed eyes. 'Come along, man, are you going to take all day to knot a simple tie?'

The Fuhrer had little time to spare his tailor and almost none for the barber. The characteristic lock of hair, said Linge, came into being through neglect rather than studied effect. Once established as part of the chief's public persona it was maintained with care. The moustache, contrary to rumour, was not grown to hide a facial blemish. Hitler grew it in the army; later he trimmed it down to a more manageable toothbrush shape.

For his staff, it acted as a barometer. When it began to twitch, foul weather was on the way, warning them to prepare for squalls.

Hitler hated moonlight, the heat of the sun and tobacco smoke. Without success he had tried to persuade Linge to give up cigarettes. His dislike of the habit stemmed from earlier days in Munich just after World War I. Then an ex-soldier, he used to relax at night in his room with a meerschaum pipe. Smoking in bed one night, he dozed off. Ash fell to the rug, setting it alight, destroying bolster, eiderdown, sheets and mattress as well as severely damaging the carpet. Forced to a face-to-face confrontation with his enraged landlady, he was so shattered he swore to put away the pipe forever. Years later, as Chancellor, he took the trouble to call on the good frau, bearing a bouquet of flowers and a bottle of eggflip — her favourite drink. He had never smoked since.

As late as 1936, the Fuhrer still kept on his apartment at 16 Prinzregentenplatz, Munich. It was cared for by Herr and Frau Winter, located on the second floor of the block and maintained at Hitler's own expense.

The Fuhrer avoided alcohol. If he took a glass of beer it was of a special brew, low in alcoholic content, and bottled for him by the Holzkirchen brewery. He rarely ate meat, referring to those who did as 'corpse eaters', and quoting Tacitus; 'In time of war when hunger strikes, these people will eat one another'.

But his own austere style of living was never imposed on guests at the Chancellery. His closest lieutenants would sit at his table wolfing pork chops and quantities of other meats without incurring scathing remarks. Occasionally employing heavy irony, he might make a joke at their expense. One night during dinner, Linge recalled, he watched Goring noisily gulp down whole platefuls of asparagus before turning to Admiral Rader on his left and remarking, 'Some people believe pigs eat only peelings and swill. Who would credit that so great a porker could appreciate such a delicacy as asparagus?'

Linge's main concern at mealtimes was to check that Hitler's food was properly prepared, ideally free of such toxic additives as cyanide or hemlock, and that it was not served too hot. The Fuhrer had undergone surgery for persistent throat trouble and was unable to swallow anything unless it was lukewarm.

Hitler hated eating alone. There were always cronies gathered around his table, at lunch and at dinner. They consisted mostly of high-voltage loyalists whose politics had been spawned in the beercellars of Munich, survivors of sundry purges, adept with the fist, the boot, the bottle — sluggers turned avuncular, having traded punches for paunches; they who had risen to the top of the heap through jungle law, the survival of the toughest through a process of elimination: such sophisticates as the thick-necked, alcoholic Ley, head of the Labour Front; the sleek Weber, former racecourse tout and political hit man; the scarfaced Wagner, gauleiter of Bavaria, and the epileptic sex-maniac, Streicher.

'Frankenfuhrer' Streicher's outrageous activities reached such a pitch that in 1940, Hitler was forced to put him in his place. This, for six months, turned out to be a private room in a top-security psychiatric clinic. Streicher was finally exiled to his farm outside Nuremberg, still hallucinating.

Hitler was always more at home with the hard men of the party; old comrades with authority downwards and responsibility upwards — the essence of the Fuhrer principle, and handpicked for the job. His bad choices, and there had been many, found their careers and usually their lives abruptly terminated for causes varying from overt homosexuality to embezzlement of party funds.

Dinner was usually a jokey, foot-stomping knockabout affair and served late. On one occasion noted by Linge, two female guests were arguing over which of them was more skilled in the preparation of Bavarian dumplings. The Fuhrer settled the argument by packing them off to the Chancellery kitchens to try out their skills. The finished products appeared and it was left to the men to decide the winner. Unfortunately the orderly serving the dish tripped over the carpet and sent the dumplings careering down the table. Hitler, snatching up the nearest weapons to hand, a knife and fork, pretended to stalk them in the manner of a big-game hunter on safari. Everyone joined in the hunt and the evening ended, said the valet, in high good humour.

Another time, with Bruckner in the lead, the laughter was even louder. Before twenty guests at an informal luncheon, Hitler's aide hoisted his bloated bulk out of his chair to prove that — despite polishing off two litres of champagne — he was an expert at performing the *schuhplattler*, the Bavarian courtship dance in which thighs, buttocks and knees are slapped to waltz time. Bruckner managed the thigh and the buttock pat, but bending towards the knee he fell heavily. Grabbing at the table he slipped to the floor, helplessly enmeshed in cloth, cutlery and several ornate floral arrangements. Swearing to himself, he managed to stagger back on his feet before bowing towards the head of the table and rushing from the room.

Linge went pale, waiting for the storm to break. But Hitler, Goring, Goebbels and Hess were sprawled back in their seats, helpless with schoolboy glee. With relief, the rest of the table joined in the raucous applause.

As the servants began to clear up the mess, the Fuhrer tapped his glass to attract attention. 'Look around the table,' he commanded, 'and see how relaxed and contented we all are. Yet there are a number of hostile *scheisskerls* (shitheads) in the world who believe the most powerful nation in Europe is in the hands of a pack of wild animals. To show them what nice people we truly are, it might be a good idea to change the name of the Chancellery to the Happy Hotel.'

Despite his attention to detail, Linge's attempts to invest such scenarios with significance wilts in the face of their intrinsic shallowness, in the seediness of the main participants and in the knowledge that too many of them shared full responsibility for the universal catastrophe of World War II. While the cutting edges of their antagonisms may have been temporarily blunted by success, their thinking became increasingly flawed.

On January 30, 1933, when Hitler became Chancellor of the Reich, Berlin, already throbbing with passion, dark emotion and bad taste, went lightheaded with happiness. Hysterical party members ran through the streets in outbursts of wild enthusiasm.

That night the lights remained on in all the embassies and legations until dawn as officials and diplomats dictated feverishly, sending out cables and reports to every corner of the world. In the general anxiety one man understood the true position. Francois-Poncet, the French Ambassador, sent a telegram to his government in Paris, *'Hitler est chancelier. N'hesitez pas un instant. Mobilisez.'*

As we were to discover, France failed to heed his warning. The first time Hitler's name appeared in an English newspaper (November 9, 1922) Reuter's incorrectly spelt his name. It stated that 'The Bavarian National Socialists are beginning to don uniforms consisting of a tam-o'-shanter, grey blouse, and a black, white and red armband with an anti-semitic swastika. Their leader, Herr *Hittler*, is said to be desirous of becoming a Bavarian Mussolini . . .'

A year later following the abortive Munich putsch, Hitler was in jail. Three weeks after he had been sentenced, Herr Hittler became Hintler. According to *The Times*: 'Adolf *Hintler* started a monster campaign against the French in case they occupied the Ruhr.'

Many papers were misinformed about his background. One said 'he had fought in Cuba against the Spaniards. And in June 1900, he was the last man out of Daspoort Fort, Pretoria before Lord Roberts arrived. He stood by the Boer flag until the last, then hauled it down and barely got away in time.' (In 1900 Hitler was eleven years of age) Another paper described him as 'forty-eight years old, active and well-preserved. In the Great War he transferred to Germany's junior service, serving as a naval officer'.

He was described in *The Times*, May 22, 1923, as 'one of the three most dangerous men in Germany. This is probably a rather flattering estimate . . . his rise to prominence is mainly due to his gift for oratory. It has yet to be proved that he has any ability as a constructive statesman . . . by many he is regarded as a useful tool to be discarded in case of success and disowned in the event of failure . . .'

A reported attempt to assassinate him in 1923 meant little to English newspaper readers, who were more interested in the wedding of the Duke of York (later King George VI) to Lady Elizabeth Bowes-Lyon. Theatre-goers were wondering how much longer *The Beggar's Opera* would run at the Lyric, Hammersmith.

Hitler finally made the front page of the *Daily Chronicle*, which described him as 'the German Mussolini', in November 1923, when the paper carried the story of the Munich putsch. Misspelt again as Hittler, he was overshadowed by the better-known Ludendorff, also implicated in the conspiracy. A leader in the *Evening Standard* the same day neglected to mention Hitler's name; the names of two other rising politicians involved, Goring and Goebbels, were also omitted.

A foreign correspondent in an interview with Herr Hitler described him as 'scarcely seeming to fill the part, this little man in the shabby waterproof with a revolver at his hip, unshaven and with unruly hair; so hoarse he could scarcely speak'. He was dismissed as just another troublesome agitator richly deserving of imprisonment.

Upon his release from prison a year later, *The Times* reported the National Socialist party's 'loss of prestige' and the failure of the Munich uprising. Hitler was regarded as a spent force.

Over the next six years his name appeared now and again: upon his return to the political arena in March 1925; at the time of the ban on his entry into Austria and after a speech made at Essen in 1926; and a report of a meeting in May 1927, when 'his impresario Dr Goebbels' had his name misprinted 'Gobbler' in *The Times*.

In September 1930, again according to *The Times*: 'Hitler and his party are likely to give rise to ridicule and perhaps a certain irritation rather than any real alarm outside Germany'. That same month he polled six million votes out of twenty-four million. Three years later the vote was tripled.

In 1933 he became the leader of Germany. But it wasn't until August 1935 that he achieved international prominence.

The Morning Post reported that 'Munich's storm troops rolled through the streets in heavy lorries in a vigorous repetition of Sunday's (August 11) attack on Jews and Catholics from a propaganda point of view.

'Churchgoers were confronted by lorryloads of troopers shouting "Down with political catholicism"; "Rome for all papists"; "Palestine for the Jews"; "Germany for us".

'Slogans and banners on the sides of the trucks read "Thou shalt love thy neighbour — not foreign currency", a reference to the arrest and conviction of three brothers of the catholic order of Merciful Brothers in Montaubar, found guilty of treason for breaking currency regulations. Brother Ottomar Vey was sentenced to four years in a labour camp and fined £4,000; another brother was given two years and fined £1750; a third, a Dutch subject, received twelve months and was fined £250.

'The lorries toured the streets, horns blaring, distributing large cartoons depicting nuns selling "the keys of heaven" for sacks of money and fat priests sheltering behind clasped hands from deformed babies, bearing the caption "No! No! Government sterilisation is a Sin!"

'Other banners read: "The Jew is our misfortune"; "Who knows the Jew knows the devil" and "Out with the Jews". Anti-catholic choruses alternated with shouts of "Let's stand for no more Jewish swinishness". There were also large drawings showing spiders with semitic features clutching women and children in their webs and large-nosed Jewish villains pawing beautiful but helpless young blonde girls.

'As a climax to the six-hour parade the storm troopers drove past the Brown Shirts Monument, arms raised in salute.'

* * *

There were few outside Germany in 1935 who were able to foresee the consequences of Hitler's rise to power.

But Goebbels, his propaganda minister, (goat's hoof concealed in a clubbed boot) spoke for Germany when he stated that 'It is the rising of a nation — the revolution has begun'.

It was Marx who, some years earlier, defined revolution as an art that required the insight of an artistic genius to recognise the moments of its vital opportunities.

Hitler was no artistic genius.

And what, above all, the final decade of his life from 1935 to 1945 illustrates is the inexorable outcome of absolute authority. As Fuhrer, Hitler was an island universe of private experiences maintaining a belief in his superiority over submissive subordinates, many of them subnormal, slack or given to the bottle.

Once his homemade revelations had been accepted as gospel truths by his followers; once the German people had been converted into unquestioning instruments of his preposterous policies, he placed himself in the hands of Fate with a capital F.

Fate, as it usually does, took its revenge, transforming him into 'the most squalid and petty medieval baron reborn'; into a schizoid, deeply melancholic fanatic with an eye resolutely fixed on things invisible to ordinary sight, who believed he could create — through organised insanity and sanctioned crimes — a nation that would last a thousand years.

Historians, lethargic buggers at the best of times, had finally arrived at a filtered awareness of Freud. Suddenly it all boiled down to sex. Did Balfour deliver the goods? Was Hitler monorchid? Was Stalin a Great Terror in bed? As a research method it had as much chance, Graham judged, of turning up the truth as did wading through boxes of state papers.

Julian Barnes 1982

The ancient human lusts pick up men and women and dash them screaming on the rocks of their own desires.

John Cheever

CHAPTER THREE

In the early days of his captivity in Russia, Linge was closely cross-examined about the Fuhrer's sex life.

The Soviets already had reliable information that Hitler was far from the celibate portrayed by his propaganda bureau. As a rising politician had he not been supported, with heavily sexual undertones, by the wives and widows of wealthy industrialists? Surely Eva Braun wasn't the only mistress? Was it true that Hitler always remained fully dressed when attempting intercourse? Or did he prefer watching simulated sex? Did he suffer from constriction of the foreskin? Was he a masochistic sadist? A monorchid pederast? And what about his vast collection of pornographic books and films?

Linge told his interrogators that while Hitler may have had a penchant for decorative nudes, it was simply an artistic interest. He admired decently painted female forms, but frauleins who posed provocatively meant nothing to him. Enjoying the company of well-endowed women, he treated them all impersonally. The Fuhrer was fond of small girls and little boys, but only in a warm, protective way. He was not lecherous, neither was he sexually impaired in any way.

The commissars, expressing dissatisfaction with Linge's answers, implied that the valet might at least have had the decency during his years of service to have recorded every rut, jiggle and pant.

Linge stayed stolidly unmoved. Whatever he knew about the rum couplings that took place in the Fuhrer's quarters, whatever sexual secrets he had stumbled upon, he had no intention of revealing them to the men in the Kremlin.

Did he keep his mouth shut through shame? Or fear? Or was he telling the truth? He knew little about Hitler's personal life before he joined the staff, but if anyone was familiar with his sexual proclivities from 1935 until his death, it was Linge.

Hitler's sex life has always been the subject of a great deal of conjecture. Those closest to him: Julius Schaub, Otto Strasser, Putzi Hanfstaengl and the photographer Hoffman, have all published their own theories.

In 1943, Dr Walter Langer prepared a psychological appraisal of the Fuhrer for the American Office of Strategic Services. While working on the project he discussed his research notes with a psychoanalyst, Dr Jenny Waelder Hall. As he revealed little known facts about Hitler's childhood, about the badly disturbed parental relationship, she said: 'I know what his perversion is.'

How had she so quickly arrived at her conclusion, Langer asked.

'It came out of my clinical experience,' she told him. With many similarities between the dictator's character traits and case histories she had dealt with herself, she was able to diagnose his compulsion.

Langer believed it was probably true that Hitler was impotent, but he was not homosexual in the ordinary sense of the term. 'His perversion has quite a different nature, which few have guessed. It is an extreme form of masochism in which the individual derives sexual gratification from the act of having a woman urinate or defecate on him'.

As Langer accurately predicted Hitler's suicide, it is possible that his analysis, working back to childhood experiences, was more than guesswork.

Perhaps before Hitler was born his fate was sealed in his parents' mind. He could certainly have inherited some abnormalities from his father.

Father Alois, that 'mass of contradictions' married three times. The third wife Klara, Hitler's mother, was twenty-three years younger and his foster-daughter (his grandfather was her great-grandfather).

Klara, the former maid, was tall, pretty and delicate. Pregnant before her marriage to Alois, she lost the child; a son born in 1885 died two years later; a second son born in 1894 died at six years of age; a daughter born in 1886 died in 1888; another daughter, older than Adolf, was born an imbecile. Klara's sister had two sons, one a hunchback with a speech impediment. This gave rise to the probability of a congenital taint in Hitler's ancestry, possibly syphilis.

Alois, remote, domineering, was fifty-one when Adolf was born. He tended to ignore the children most of the time but as a stern disciplinarian, he insisted on unquestioning obedience and absolute silence during meals. Alone with Klara he was by turns whiningly lachrymose and, when in drink, gratingly hearty. As a provider, he was reluctant to accept anything that threatened to diminish his domination over the unfortunate drudge who shared his bed.

In 1889, when Adolf was born, discrimination against women had reached a peak. They were regarded as inferior and sinful, fit only for servile domesticity and sexual indulgence. Fornication was a furtive business performed in the dark. Sodomy, fellatio, cunnilingus and anal intercourse were criminal offences; masturbation caused madness. Foreplay in conventional sex was nonexistent.

Dr Langer, carefully rewinding the tape of Hitler's life, stopping it, playing it back, saw a sickly child, exceptionally attached to his mother, bullied by his father, a victim of Freud's 'major source of potential neuroses'. He probably accidentally stumbled on his parents in the throes of love-making, was repelled by the obscenities, the stark ugliness of sex; all of it helping to create a lopsided personality with a lifelong contempt for women's extreme wantonness. Childhood memories are visual, like snapshots, moments held captive in the imagination: glimpses of a mother undressing, full breasts pendulous, body hair emphasising nakedness; the father unclothed, examining the secret parts by the light of an oil lamp, roughly penetrating her naked lower half; a shocking sense of betrayal when the child realises the shy and gentle mother loves the brute duration of contact, submitting passively then rapaciously accepting, retaining, uttering half-stifled animal grunts of encouragement, groaning, gasping. All of this filled the childmind with images of monstrous ugliness, blood red, night black, full moon white, leaving him limbless, fleshless, blind, buried in darkness and longing for light, mired in a foul stench of bowel and bladder, an ancient ooze falling away, burrowing beneath blankets, lamentably shame-faced, an urge like a clenched fist in the gut to kill the father, sabotaging the libido, stimulating deep, instinctive response.

A hatred for the father would inevitably follow, generating further abnormality, creating greater anxieties, culminating in a regression to an infantile stage of sexual development, a diffusion of the normal sex instinct into voyeurism which, in a later stage of semi-impotence would substitute for sexual intercourse. At four or five, too young to go hunting around for a solution to his problems, Hitler would have resorted to sulking, to throwing an occasional tantrum; flying into explosive rages, all substitutes for the emotional events of his adult life.

Once his conflicts reached an unbearable pitch, they would vanish from his conscious mind to simmer away quietly in the subconscious until ready to be activated as the blind hatred of adult life.

Then, just at the point when the five-year-old Adolf is experiencing all kinds of identity problems, what happens? A baby brother arrived to claim most of his mother's attention, so creating further fat maggots of anxiety.

At the age of seven, he was ready to form relationships outside the home, but received no guidance from the cantankerous father as to how he might deal with the world. And he was unable to look to his mother for security or direction, as her timid submissiveness to his father repelled him.

As a teenager, Hitler found the crushing morality of his teachers absurd and contemptible. Born and brought up a Catholic, confirmed in Linz Cathedral in 1904, he eventually rejected religion. Instead, he leaned towards pessimism and nihilism: German philosophy from 1900 onwards prophesied the spread of nihilism throughout Europe; Schopenhaur, Hegel, Bohme, Eckhart and Stirner spoke of little else; Nietzsche foresaw 200 years of it. Nationalism was a growing issue, while the influence of religion was on the wane.

At school, among the hostile ragtag and bobtail of boys more privileged, Hitler grew mistrustful, secretive, showing little aptitude for anything except physical training and art. He was aggressive while inwardly hoping for acceptance, constantly trying to convey the impression he came from a socially superior background. The outsider, unemotional on the surface, suffering the puzzling pain of life, finally seeing it as a suspended sentence until the death penalty was irrevocably pronounced. Heart and mind had been shaped by the childhood events that affected him — added to whatever adolescent traumas he was later subjected to.

As a young man, when stirrings in the loins are normally triggered off by the hectic fantasies of puberty, he was forced to take the road less travelled, achieving manhood via the magma of excrement and vile juices; able to obtain release only in the dispassionate destruction of a woman's spirit and self-respect.

The one experience Hitler dreaded, led only to self-disgust and utter dejection. So he was obliged to repress his instincts by compromising with less degrading actions.

To Langer, Hitler's perversion was an attempted compromise between psychotic tendencies and a need to appear normal. As 'an extreme form of masochistic degradation', most individuals who require such gratification only find it getting out of control in circumstances where a strong love relationship exists: when the need for such a sexual outlet becomes overwhelming.

The onetime SA chief of staff, Ernst Rohm, said once that 'Hitler thinks about peasant girls, the way they stand in fields and bend down at their work so that you can see their behinds. That's what he likes, especially when they've got big, round buttocks. That's Hitler's sex life.'

In the Fuhrer's own words: 'Decadence originates in the stomach, causing constipation and the poisoning of juices.' It was important for him to know what went into his mouth and what passed out of his anus.

His niece, the buxom, blue-eyed Geli Raubal, with whom he had an incestuous love affair, is reported to have said that it was necessary for her to crouch above Hitler's face in such a position that he was able to fix his gaze on her hindquarters.

'When Hitler liked a girl,' said Hanfstaengl, 'he would grovel at her feet in a disgusting manner; telling her he wasn't really fit to kiss her hand, never mind to sit beside her — so he hoped she'd be kind to him.' Small wonder that Putzi fell from grace, dining out in Berlin on that sort of gossip. A favourite in the early days, independently wealthy, he was accused by Bormann of trying to pimp for the Fuhrer: 'bringing voluptuous girls to champagne parties at the Chancellery, having them parade in front of Hitler in high heels and flimsy underwear.' By 1935 Hanfstaengl, presumably having exhausted the supply of available women, was a refugee in America.

It was Otto Strasser who suggested the Fuhrer might have been an active homosexual for some time after World War I. He pointed out that Hitler's personal bodyguards were all homosexuals, many of them absorbed from radical groups like the Freikorps. And Hitler was aware of the activities of Rohm and of SA leaders like Heines, Ernst and others, which had caused the Italian *Il Messagero* to refer to the National Socialist movement in Germany as a 'gang of pederasts'.

In the event, after the blood purge in 1934, Hitler spat on Rohm's grave, referring to him contemptuously as 'an animal'. In future, he said, he required men as storm troopers, 'not ridiculous monkeys whose personal lives had become so evil I can no longer tolerate seeing them around.'

Several people close to Hitler mentioned his private collection of nude photographs, supplied by Hoffman, who also provided a series of blue films for the Chancellery cinema. His daughter Henny was one of the earliest women mentioned in connection with Hitler. Being by nature a gossipy little soul, she was happy to spread stories around Munich about the implicitly sexual aspect of their liaison. As soon as the rumours reached the ears of the top Nazis the girl was peremptorily married off to the romantically inclined Hitler Youth Leader, Baldur von Schirach.

As the Fuhrer's social contacts broadened, his name began to be linked with several women — mainly by foreign correspondents based in Berlin. Before the outbreak of war in 1939 most of them used to meet regularly in the Ristorante Taverne on the corner of Kurfurstendamm. Crowding around the *stammtisch* (table reserved for regular customers), they exchanged news and various salty scraps of scandal featuring high-ranking Nazis.

The name of Leni Riefenstahl, the film producer, was mentioned as a frequent guest at the Fuhrer's social functions. And at various times Hitler was rumoured to have had affairs with Magda Goebbels, Winifred Wagner, the pilot Hanna Reitsch, the eighteen-year-old niece of Frau Dircksen, Sigfrid von Laffert, and Annie Ondra, the Czech film actress who later auditioned for Hitchcock's *Blackmail* in Britain.

Stripped to the bare essentials, as they frequently were, the leading actresses of the time were strikingly alike. They had either flaming red, jet black or ash blonde hair, sensual bodies and an eye to the main chance — and were quick to surrender to rich and powerful men. The blonde film actress Renate Muller had, typically, the kind of looks that made the prominent members of the Fuhrer's circle want to shower her with furs.

She committed suicide, jumping from the window of a Berlin hotel shortly after spending an evening alone with Hitler in his private apartment.

Film director Zeissler later claimed in Hollywood that Renate had confided in him before her death, tormented by a degrading experience.

Seemingly, she had been more than willing to grant Hitler unequivocal pleasures, knowing what she was there for, sensing the great man's tension and preoccupation.

However, to her surprise, without a word of greeting, the Fuhrer flung himself to the floor at her feet, shamefacedly muttering explanations; how abject he was, fit only to be vigorously kicked by the beautiful woman she undoubtedly was.

Renate, confronted with the unwholesome spectacle of the most powerful man in Germany writhing on the rug, involuntarily recoiled, using sign language to point out that she preferred more conventional pleasures. To no avail. Hitler rolled nearer, begging for chastisement. Whimpering a little, the actress raised a dainty foot to put the boot in. The harder she kicked the more excited he grew, working himself into a fine fury, pulses throbbing, one fishy eye looking up at her, begging for more. Renate, averting her gaze, continued kicking until he became uncontrollably aroused, threshing about in spastic agitation. The sound he made as he climaxed was the fretful whine of a wounded fox.

Failing to appreciate her own predicament, full of a sense of horror, Renate rushed from the apartment. Having hitherto looked on such practices as the sum and substance of perverted depravity, she found it impossible to come to terms with the experience.

The whiff of scandal soon drifted into the Taverne. The question remained: did Miss Muller fling herself from the window, or was she pushed? Were there more perversions she had been too mortified to mention? Was she, like the childlike Geli Raubal, an unwilling sex object; the most common of all pornographic and masturbatory fantasies?

Geli was the daughter of Angela, Hitler's half-sister; she had married a minor tax official named Raubal. After his death, Angela worked as a cook in Vienna. In 1925 she moved to Munich to keep house for Hitler.

When Hitler rented the villa Wachenfeld at Obersalzberg — which later became the Berghof — Angela was hired as resident housekeeper. This left Geli alone in the Munich apartment with 'Uncle Alf'.

On the morning of September 17, 1931 Geli, the epitome of soiled innocence, plump and pretty, with a small peevish mouth and big blue eyes, was found dead in her room. A bullet from Hitler's Walther 6.35mm pistol had penetrated her heart. A police doctor declared it was suicide. Two days later, her body was removed to Vienna for burial.

Linge believed the Fuhrer's initial bitterness at her loss gave way to a profound grief. With the passing of time he made an effort to honour the twenty-two year old girl's memory, commissioning the artist Ziegler to paint a portrait of her from photographs. The valet had been told by Frau Winter that, after Geli's death, the Fuhrer had been unable to touch solid food for days. His customary impatience took on a more destructive form and his expression became both tentative and deliberate, suggesting an emotional vacuum.

Although it has not been established conclusively that Geli and Hitler were physical lovers, the talk around Munich at the time suggested they were; and that the girl found the sexual link distasteful. As a result of stomach trouble and rotting teeth, Hitler was reputed to have foul breath; and when the Fuhrer forced her to perform grossly abnormal acts, she was driven to suicide. Other theories were that she had been promiscuous with one or two members of Hitler's staff and had been discovered; and that she had killed herself because she was expecting 'Uncle Alf's' baby.

Hanfstaengl gave a different version of events: Geli had been enjoying an affair with a Jewish art teacher from Linz. Hitler, discovering the truth the night before her death, quarrelled with her violently. The body, said Hanfstaengl, had been found with a broken nose.

Although there is no supporting evidence for this story, it did initiate an enquiry by the Bavarian Ministry of Justice. No evidence was uncovered to substantiate a murder claim and Geli's death stayed a mystery.

Perhaps as a result of the tragedy Hitler, when he met Eva Braun a year or two later, took great pains to keep her out of the limelight.

Eva Braun was born at 45 Isabellastrasse, Munich on Tuesday, February 6, 1912 at 2.22 a.m. At the moment of her birth, wrote an astrologist, the sun and Venus were entering Aquarius and the Ram respectively, while Saturn confronted Taurus the Bull . . . all of which signifies great expectations.

In 1925, the Braun family moved to 93 Hohenzollernstrasse, Munich. The house survived the war, as did Fritz Braun, Eva's father. He died at Ruhpolding on January 22, 1964.

Eva was educated by nuns before obtaining work at Hoffman's photographic studio. Linge describes her as attractive, if slightly vulgarly so, with good legs, firm breasts and a well-rounded bottom. She was an unsophisticated girl, yet was always fastidiously groomed.

It was Hitler's custom in those days to drop into Hoffman's studio for a chat on his way to the National Socialist headquarters, and it was on the occasion of one of these visits that he first met Eva. Strategically placed high on a ladder, checking stocks of photographic plates, she caught Hitler's eye by displaying a length of thigh and a glimpse of her buttocks.

Some members of the inner circle speculated that Hoffman had used his assistant to gain greater influence with the Fuhrer by putting Eva in his way. Whatever the motive, Hitler certainly made no effort to conceal his feelings and instructed Hoffman to ask Eva to join them for coffee.

So began an affair which, although it eventually led to a last-minute marriage, was by no means a dominant part of Hitler's life. When questioned about the sexual side of the relationship, the valet would only say that, although their private quarters were out of bounds to all the staff (apart from those detailed to clean the rooms), Linge did observe evidence of a nature which suggested that their relationship was normal.

Whatever went on in the bedchamber, as Hitler's mistress, Eva lived in constant fear of being discarded and was obliged to live by stringent rules: no smoking, no dancing, no sunbathing. The Fuhrer was a jealous man who, as a result of the weight of his responsibilities, neglected her, forcing the girl to use small strategies to make manageable an almost impossible existence and making her a connoisseur of unpleasant truths about other women in Berlin.

Primarily as a result of the stress of her life, she became a habitual user of sleeping pills and, in the early hours of May 29, 1935, her sister, Ilse, found Eva unconscious. A Dr Marx, Ilse's employer, was called and treated her for an overdose of Vanodorm. After a few days' rest, Eva recovered completely.

This event was the second occasion that Eva had made an attempt on her life. In 1932, she had aimed her father's pistol at her heart and pulled the trigger. Again it was Ilse who found her lying on the bed with blood everywhere. Eva's aim had been inaccurate and the bullet had lodged in her neck. The doctor had had no difficulty in extracting it and Eva soon made a full recovery. Hitler had received a farewell note and visited her at the clinic next morning. He ordered the incident to be kept secret.

The following year, Hitler arranged for Eva and her second sister, Gretel, to occupy a small house in the Bogenhausen district of Munich. A Mercedes car was put at her disposal and she was paid a salary of 450 marks a month until the day she died.

Linge saw Eva Anna Paula Braun as a highly strung girl who yearned for a different kind of life and who became obsessed with the belief that Hitler might eventually marry her. At the same time, he said, her emotional uncertainty led her to reveal to Linge, shortly after a quarrel with Hitler, that he'd never marry her or his other women would immediately lose interest in him.

*   *   *

One young woman for whom the Fuhrer had a keen, if on the surface platonic, admiration was Unity Mitford. But was she in love with Hitler? According to her sister, Diana, she wasn't. 'Her admiration and even affection for him were boundless, but she was not in love. On his side, he was certainly very fond of her and she amused him greatly, for most of the women he met were desperately shy and overawed in his company. Unity was never awed in her life and always said what came into her head.

'She knew about Eva Braun. At a *parteitag* we were given seats next to Fraulein Braun and thought her pretty and charming. There again, if Unity had been in love she would have been jealous of Eva and this she quite obviously was not. She had a boyfriend in Munich named Erich. His surname, if I ever heard it, I have forgotten. She also had innumerable friends and was constantly on the move.'

Whatever the nature of Hitler's relationships with other women, they had little effect on his attachment to Eva. Although he showed no particular affection for her in front of others, in private he referred to her as 'Schnacksi', an Austrian term of endearment. To the staff at Berghof she became known as *Die Chefin* — the female equivalent of *Der Chef*. Possibly as a result of her association with Hitler, several young SS officers became infatuated with her. At least three attempted suicide and Sigmund Breuer —

of the Death's Head Bodyguard — leaped to his death in a spectacular fashion after a final rejection by Eva on the parapet of Kehlstein castle.

Breuer had once worked at Hoffman's studio and had been in love with Eva for some time. When he realised he was treading on Hitler's preserves, he did the decent thing. When his body was discovered on the rocks at the foot of the tower there was a camera around his neck. The story was that Breuer had been taking pictures of Fraulein Braun and had unfortunately lost his balance.

*　　*　　*

Reflecting on the numbers of strikingly attractive women who had been drawn to the chief, Linge thought it remarkable he should have stayed so long with someone neither gifted nor particularly beautiful.

Was it because Eva had been able to provide the comfort and understanding of a wife much more than any of the others?

She always went to a great deal of trouble to choose birthday gifts for the Fuhrer. She bought him comfortable shirts for leisure wear, made from imported English cotton. In 1938, for his forty-ninth birthday, she ordered a dozen pairs of pyjamas in blue and white stripes, the colours of her native Bavaria; up to then Hitler had worn old fashioned flannelette nightshirts.

Baroness von Birkenfeld, a member of the Party, recalled helping Eva to select a gift from Friedman's, the well-known silverware shop on Unter den Linden (some time after the shop had been taken over by true-blue Germans). Fraulein Braun saw nothing suitable, explaining that what she really wanted was a tea table, glass-topped, containing an aquarium underneath. The manager, concealing his surprise, said he had nothing suitable in stock, but it could of course be specially designed.

After they left the shop, Eva confided to the Baroness 'that it was the Fuhrer's idea to have a glass tea table with goldfish swimming in the water under the glass top.' She added that she was supposed to serve him tea dressed in a see-through green negligée.

She must certainly have exercised an obscurely erotic appeal, perhaps bringing imagination as well as energy to his bed. And if his brand of sexuality precluded love, it is possible that he had

50

a longing for mutual understanding too poignant to be endured.

His record in the field of romantic conquest was unimpressive. Geli Raubal and Renate Muller: suicide or murder; Unity Mitford: attempted suicide; Eva Braun: two attempts at suicide.

'An unusual record,' comments Dr Langer dryly, 'for a man who had so few affairs with women.'

In the forty years since Langer completed his study, more information has come to light, proving if nothing else the unreliability of earlier sources.

Was Hitler out of control as a human being? Was he hopelessly flawed; in danger, once aroused, of degrading himself, unable to control coprophagous desires?

In psychiatry almost any hypothesis can be employed to explain bizarre disorders: hereditary factors, parental relationships, environment.

It is generally agreed that Hitler was psychotic. Was his psychosis a defence against personal calamity? Was he caught in an infantile dilemma with the female mystery and anal function as goads, made to quicken by the fecal core and satanist-orientated voyeurism? The mystery turning to fear, fear to rage — ending in emptiness and the need for extinction bringing in its wake a potential for destruction of every living thing?

If the perversion existed it must have been like a cancerous growth existing as a result of abnormalities capable of diagnosis.

Or to put it another way, those whom the gods wish to destroy they first make mad.

He shows most feeling in a passage in Mein Kampf, *where he describes an imaginary event as plastically as if he had experienced it. 'The blackhaired Jewboy, with satanic joy on his face, for hours on end lies in wait for the unsuspecting girl, whom he pollutes with his blood.'*

Is it perhaps not imaginary? Is it an experience? An experience in which, when he describes it, persons and situations have been mixed and confused? Was it perhaps someone else, darkhaired too, but Aryan, who 'for hours lay in wait' while the girl he awaited in vain went off 'unsuspecting' with a Jewish rival?

Why does he hate and fly from Vienna? He tells us that for him the city was 'the embodiment of blood outrage'. Here we have an undeniable, unmistakable connection.

Rudolf Olden

According to reports which Hanfstaengl, for example, repeats, Hitler contracted syphilis while he was a young man in Vienna.
Alan Bullock

CHAPTER FOUR

66-year-old Jean-Marie Loret, a French railway crossing keeper, died in February 1985 at St Quentin, northern France, haunted by a ghost from the past.

For thirty years, the man who thought he was Hitler's son tried to keep his father's identity secret. But the story came out in 1978 when a German historian, Dr Werner Maser, claimed he had proof that Jean-Marie was Hitler's son. And no one can say for certain he wasn't.

It was as a young schoolboy that Jean-Marie first learnt he was the illegitimate son of a German soldier born during World War I. It was on her death bed in 1948 that his mother Charlotte confessed that his father was Adolf Hitler. As a seventeen-year-old girl, she said, she had been seduced by him. At the time he was a German army corporal interested in art. After her death, among her belongings, was a painting of a landscape — signed 'A Hitler'. Jean-Marie, who used his mother's name, was brought up by his grandparents.

According to Dr Maser, Hitler met Charlotte Loret in April, 1916; they became lovers and the child was born in March 1918. Records at the town hall, St Quentin, stated that the father was a 'German soldier, identity unknown'.

Was Jean-Marie Hitler's son?

'Everybody seemed to think so,' said Jean-Marie, interviewed in 1984. 'All my life I've known that my father was a German corporal and records show that Hitler *was* in St Quentin in 1917. I believe he used to visit my mother on his motorbike and take her on painting trips into the country. Twice during World War II I was investigated by the Gestapo, who wanted details on my background. However, I couldn't really help them.'

* * *

54

Lance-corporal (Volunteer) Hitler, Third Company, List Regiment, was wounded twice, the first occasion during the Battle of the Somme on October 7, 1916. A shell splinter put him in hospital at Beelitz, near Potsdam, and he was away from the front until March 1917. Promoted to corporal, he took part as a dispatch rider in the Battle of Arras and in the third Battle of Ypres. His war ended on the night of October 13, 1918 during the final German offensive, when his battalion were subjected to a night-long bombardment of 'yellow-gas' shells. At seven the next morning, he says, his eyes were so badly affected he was sent down the line, ending up in hospital again, this time at Pasewalk in Pomerania.

He was awarded the Iron Cross (second class) for gallant conduct during the Battle of Wytschaete on December 2, 1914; and on August 4, 1918, he received the Iron Cross (first class).

Hitler remained in Pasewalk Hospital until November 13, when he returned to Munich to spend the rest of the winter with a reserve regiment stationed at Traunstein.

In *Mein Kampf,* he referred to World War I as 'a redemption from the disagreeable experiences of youth for which, overcome by fervid enthusiasm, I sank to my knees and thanked heaven from an overflowing heart that it had given me the good fortune to live at such a time.' During the war he had witnessed at firsthand the principle of the end justifying the means raised to the highest morality.

This was to remain a lasting influence — the morality of war becoming the guiding morality of his career as Fuhrer.

He also referred to the disability that sent him to Pasewalk, writing that he was blinded by gas — just as he had said he'd suffered 'severe lung disease' in his schooldays. Having served its purpose in a throwaway paragraph, it was never mentioned again.

Medical experts later testified that his descriptoin of the gassing in *Mein Kampf* was questionable. If the duration was correct, the symptoms should have been different. Hospital reports that might have shed light on the mystery have never been found.

Hitler's state of health has, for the past forty years, been a source of controversy. Did he suffer from Parkinson's disease — diagnosed by Dr de Crinis of Berlin's Charité Hospital? By 1943 there were continual tremors along his left arm and leg.

Were his symptoms hysterical in origin, the result of anxiety

55

catching up on his glandular network, eventually exposing him to many different infirmities?

Or was it a slow virus that, lying dormant for a number of years, finally erupted in middle age, wreaking havoc with his nervous system? Was it the sickness that had plagued so many of his contemporaries, including Mussolini?

We have the story of Felix Kersten to support this hypothesis. This 'man with the miraculous hands', a skilled masseur, treated Himmler throughout the war for persistent stomach pains. One morning towards the end of 1942, Himmler asked him if he could treat a man laid low with chronic migraine, dizziness and insomnia. Kersten reminded him that he specialised in manual therapy and that he would require medical details before suggesting treatment. The Reichsfuhrer then handed Kersten a bulky dossier, swearing him to secrecy. According to the masseur it was Hitler's medical file.

The notes stated that Hitler had caught syphilis as a young man in Vienna. Treated in the army, while hospitalised at Pasewalk, he had been discharged in November 1918 with a clean bill of health. In 1936, further symptoms suggested the disease had flared up again. The indications in 1942, when Kersten read the report, were that the Fuhrer was suffering from the tertiary phase of syphilis, progressive general paralysis of the insane.

If so, this would certainly have affected his judgement, blunting critical faculties and causing severe headaches, convulsions and problems of speech.

Years ago, general paralysis of the insane frequently occurred later in life; affecting heart and blood vessels, it could cripple or kill. In the 1930s, for example, ten per cent of all cardiac sufferers had been infected with cardio-vascular syphilis. In neuro-syphilis, the *treponima pallida* virus invaded the brain cells and damaged the spinal cord, causing degeneration of the optic and other cranial nerves, leading to blurred vision, deafness and dizziness. Other manifestations were pains in the legs, abdomen and feet, impotence, constipation and a sense of constriction about the waist.

Diagnosis of the disease was based on neurological tests and lumbar punctures to check the spinal fluid for abnormalities.

Clinical formulations are similar in congenital syphilis with 'stigmata' changes taking place in later stages. These include saddle or flattened nose, deafness, bowing of the tibia called 'sabre shin' and Hutchinsonian teeth with widespread and notched central incisors. The prognosis for the congenital form of the illness was favourable, barring reinfection, for the third generation.

For many years the disease was treated with *Salvarsan* (an arsenic compound discovered by Paul Ehrlich, who died in 1915), later supplanted by penicillin or bismuth injected intravenously.

Mussolini had undergone treatment for venereal disease for fifteen years. In 1922, samples of his blood were sent to England for testing. The result of a Wassermann test (for syphilis) proved negative. But following a talk with the Duce in 1939, Italian police chief Bocchini suggested Mussolini's restless condition was due to a recurrence of his old illness, the dreaded pox. He advised an intensive anti-syphilitic cure.

*   *   *

A great deal has been written about Hitler in Vienna. How, scarred from his tussles with the unreasonable forces controlling the Viennese art world, he lived as a young man in a world where fantasy and reality were interlocked. Robustly anti-semitic, he acquired a foxy alertness, seeing Jewish grotesqueries through the outsider's viewfinder. His attitude to women being largely voyeuristic for, distanced from sexual entanglement, any sexual gratification must have been for the most part lonely and private. Somehow the black-garbed Jews were responsible for his lamentably low station in life — at a time when the young artist should have had the world at his feet.

One can naturally assume that his hatred of the Jews had a sexual basis. Describing the close connection between Judaism and prostitution in *Mein Kampf*, he saw the Jew as a 'cold and grasping organiser of a horrifying traffic in vice among the city's dregs'.

The Jews were 'parasites systematically violating our inexperienced young blonde girls; destroying something in the world that can't be replaced.' Full of hostility he foresaw the 'seduction of hundreds of thousands of girls by repulsive crooked-legged Jew bastards.'

Ill-fed, whatever sexual appetite the scruffily-dressed malcontent possessed could only be assuaged by channelling it into an elemental hatred. Allured in his teens by the glamour of danger, by the idea of flouting authority, Hitler overtly distrusted the system, inviting it in a superstitious way not to work.

Later a fellow soldier, Hans Mend, described him as 'a peculiar fellow. He behaved differently; he didn't care about leave; he wrote no letters; he never received a single parcel.' He was also, Mend believed, 'a woman-hater. He sat brooding in a corner, with his helmet on his head, buried deep in thought. None of the others were able to rouse him from his listlessness.'

If Hitler had contracted syphilis as a young man in Vienna — and Hanfstaengl, for example, reported this as a fact — then his somewhat detached posture in army barracks may have been due to guilt or self-disgust.

It is a fact that the chief propagandist for racial purity, however labelled with pathological and distressful disabilities, was not exactly eligible for the master race he attempted to create. The Fuhrer tended to be an alpine rather than a teutonic type, broad of bottom with squat, spindly legs and a distended belly.

Diana Mosley remembers him in the mid-thirties as being 'about 5ft 9ins, neither fat nor thin. 'His eyes were dark blue, his skin fair and his brown hair was exceptionally fine and neatly brushed. I never saw him with a lock of hair over his forehead . . . his hands were white and well shaped . . . his teeth had been mended with gold, as one saw when he laughed . . . he had a high forehead which almost jutted forward above the eyes.

'He was extremely polite to women; he bowed and kissed hands as is the custom in Germany and France, and he never sat down until they did. Such trivialities would not be worth mentioning were it not for the acres of print about Hitler in which his rudeness and bad manners to everyone are emphasised.'

Dorothy Thompson, the American writer, took a different view. She thought him 'formless, ill-poised and inconsequent. Only his eyes were noteworthy, dark and hyperthyroid . . .'

Elisabetta Cerruti, wife of the Italian ambassador to Germany (1932-1935), met Hitler several times. To her he was repellent, hideous, menacing and dangerous — although at times almost dignified. In his presence she felt disinclined to smile. Instead, he made her shiver — particularly at their first meeting.

'When Count von Bassewitz led him across the crowded room towards me, he followed without a sign of self-consciousness. As he bowed and kissed my hand we exchanged the usual banalities.

When dinner was announced he offered me his arm.

'As I touched his arm, curiously enough, I received a strong electric shock. I was already so keyed up with excitement it unnerved me a little and although I'm a sceptic and don't believe in the supernatural, I became convinced that he possessed some mystic, magnetic power that he could exercise at will. The shock was so strong I looked up in astonishment. He stood there as pale and calm as ever. Somewhat shaken, I walked in with him to the dining hall.'

It was a strange experience, she recalled, having the most controversial man in the world sitting beside her at dinner. Given an opportunity to observe him closely during the meal, she decided he wasn't coarse; he was common. 'He held his fork and knife in his clenched fists as simple people do, although he knew enough not to eat from his knife. The latter was of little use to him in any case since he never touched the meat. His eyes were large and fine, though the expression in them was always troubled; his skin was clear and of a healthy colour; his speaking voice was soft and warm. The worst feature of his face was his abominably shaped nose. His hands had no character, being white and lifeless. They did not seem to be natural attributes of his physical being but, rather, weapons necessary for the wild gestures that accompanied his conversation.'

Hanfstaengl's wife summed him up in an abrupt sentence. 'Putzi,' she told her husband, 'I can tell you he is a neuter.'

At best the Fuhrer was patently in poor condition, subject to suicidal depressions, plagued with stomach trouble and a progressively senescent sphincter. If he had applied to join his *Liebstandarte* he'd probably have failed the physical.

The first of an entire stable of medical advisers was Dr Conti. He advised a less rigorous diet. Hitler gorged himself for a few weeks on pasta, mayonnaise and hardboiled eggs. And put on twelve pounds. The pain in his gut persisted and the doctor was dismissed. Next came Surgeon Brandt, prepared to try anything from blood letting to enema purges. (An enthusiastic exponent of mass euthanasia, he was hanged by the allies in 1947 for flagrant butchery.)

In 1936, when Hitler's 'trouble' flared up again, Hoffman the fixer helpfully introduced the well-known VD Specialist Theo Morell into the Fuhrer's circle. The doctor, nicknamed by Goring 'the master of the imperial needle', suggested treatment for Hitler's intestinal disorder. He prescribed *Mutaflor* (emulsion of a strain of *Escherichia coli*) which neutralised the pains. And found himself appointed medical guru to the most powerful man in Germany. Hitler referred to him tenderly as the 'life-saver who relieved me of discomfort and wind'.

Morell, from then on, treated the Fuhrer with an entire pharmacopoeia of drugs which, during the next nine years, were to have a dangerously cumulative effect. There was *prostacrinum* (extract of seminal vesicles and prostate) to prevent depression; *sympatol* (p-hydroxyphenol methylamino ethanol tartrate) to quicken the heart; the doctor's own proprietary product, Vitamultin (containing *pervitin* and caffeine); and Dr Koster's antigas pills to prevent flatulence.

It became part of Linge's function to maintain the medicine chest and adminster treatment. Under Morell's tuition, he was soon adept at injecting various drugs into the hapless buttocks of his master.

Restricted as he was by a lack of medical knowledge, coupled with a vague suspicion that Morell seemed to be somewhat over-enthusiastic in prescribing his patent, life-enhancing elixirs, the valet confessed to having strong reservations about the vast amount of pills being poured down Hitler's throat and on the nature of the prophylactics jabbed into his backside. Lacking the authority to challenge the doctor pointblank, he nevertheless managed to express a certain amount of doubt.

The Kurfurstendamm VD specialist, displaying his usual air of confident reliability, met all doubts with a muted 'hurrumph'. He had no intention of abandoning his Fuhrer or curtailing his shockingly lucrative treatments merely on the representations of some fly-by-night member of the uniformed SS.

When the Fuhrer's pains recurred, Morell pointed an accusing finger at the luncheon menu — *nudelsuppe* with dumplings. Obviously impure, starchy food was doing the damage. Consequently a special vegetable garden was laid down, using carefully filtered water and the finest fertilisers. During World War II, as Hitler's health deteriorated and the pains persisted, Morell was able to attribute them to the tension arising from the stupidity of the leader's generals.

After the defeat at Stalingrad, the nervous tremors in Hitler's left hand increased. He was forced to disguise this by pressing the hand firmly to his chest, but the agitation gradually affected the entire side of his body, slowing his movements. He was also plagued by chronic itching. He was treated for dysentery in the summer of 1941 and Morell prescribed further addictive stimulants.

By 1944, he was in very bad shape indeed, his constitution shot to pieces. And the drug intake, turning in on itself like a scorpion, was slowly poisoning him. Added to which, his somewhat suspect hereditry: malnutrition and a touch of tuberculosis plus the possibility of tertiary syphilis, was of increasing influence.

A severe attack of jaundice struck Hitler in September, 1944 and it was sufficiently serious to justify calling in two Berlin consultants, Dr Giesing and Professor von Eicken.

During treatment they asked Linge to show them the medication Morell had been prescribing. Taking some 'harmless charcoal tablets' away for analysis, Giesing was alarmed to discover they contained both atropine and strychnine. Hitler was also taking two tablets a day of *Ultraseptyl*, a sulphonamide drug with questionable side effects which was not available from German pharmaceutical manufacturers. Morell, it was discovered, had a substantial holding in the Budapest firm which produced the pills.

After the assassination attempt in July, 1944, Hitler was troubled by severe sinusitis and for some time he was fearful he had sustained brain damage. 'It's vital,' he told Linge, 'that the old head stays in working order. That's more important than anything else.'

Giesing suggested eyedrops — containing a ten per cent solution of cocaine — for the sinus condition, to be administered by Linge once a day. In the last two weeks of his life the Fuhrer stepped up the dosage to ten times a day.

In the bunker, not only Hitler but practically all the other members of his entourage kept themselves going on drugs supplied by Morell.

*   *   *

Hitler, forty-four when he became leader, was remarkably durable and, for a number of years, lucky. Outwardly fatalistic, inwardly tormented, driven to make peace with himself at the price of declaring war on the world, he was to the party what the lion is to the jungle, the king of the beasts. He had an insatiable yearning for the unattainable and a nagging dissatisfaction with whatever was attained. Hyperactive when the gritty rhetoric of anger required it, he possessed a double-edged magnetism that could swing from a saving perspective of irony to peaks of pure venom.

As a skilled politician violently opposed to democracy, he accepted nothing less than total authority based on a Jesuitical concept — the blind obedience principle.

'You seem to have been extremely fortunate,' said Ambassadress Cerruti to her dinner partner, 'in everything you have undertaken.'

*   *   *

'I may have been lucky in my political life,' said Hitler, 'but in my private life I've been more unfortunate than anyone I've ever known.'

Jean-Marie Loret, who married a St Quentin girl, had nine children.

Just as their father before them, they would be forever haunted by a ghost from the past.

What is Pan-Germanism? Nationalism fell into the German soul like a match into a petrol tank. Pan-Germanism formed a block all over the world to destroy all the states which had German minorities.

Professor Friedrich Forster

When I hear the word 'culture', I undo the safety catch of my revolver.

Nazi poet Hans Johst

CHAPTER FIVE

Linge, in due time, grew familiar with Hitler's ways; understanding the explosive rages, the long spells of brooding silence, the occasional self-pity. As a result he found nothing at all alarming in the human being behind the perfectly-composed public facade.

He saw how ambition drove the Fuhrer on. And the manner in which he dealt with those who frustrated him. He saw him hard as stone in the face of betrayal, and saddened at the sight of a crippled child.

The stories — that the chief became *geisteskrank*, some kind of spooky cretin who spent his day taking bites out of the study carpet — were dismissed as feeble propaganda, betraying ignorance of the German mother tongue. *Teppichfresser*, literally 'carpet-chewer', implied that a chap was sufficiently incensed by circumstances to pace to and fro. Hitler was one of nature's born pacers. And he had a hungry eye for glaring examples of crass incompetence.

The practical, no-nonsense valet remembered that soon after they moved into the new Chancellery in January 1939, workmen were still drying the walls with blowlamps when an unexpected downpour disrupted the sewage system, leaving great patches of the walls moist and discoloured.

The plumbing in the ground floor cloakroom suffered a sudden seizure, causing the seepage to rise almost to ankle level, staining the carpet dirty brown, ruining works of art and necessitating the rapid removal of all the priceless bric-a-brac presented by various political minorities and envoys of eager-to-please Balkan nations.

With a noisome effluence spreading everywhere, Colonel Josef Beck, the Polish foreign minister, arrived early for an appointment with the Fuhrer. He was hurried upstairs to dry land and almost as speedily despatched from a rear exit.

In the interim the building supervisor had been summoned to Hitler's office to explain himself.

How had the calamity occurred?

The flinching architect stood at strained attention. It was the Berlin sewage system coupled with heavy rain, with floods rising to unprecedented levels and pumps unable to handle the pressure.

'Aha! So every building in Berlin is flooded?'

'— Er, not as far as I know, Herr Reichskanzler, only the Chancellery . . .'

'Fetch the detail drawings,' commanded Hitler.

The man scurried away.

Hitler, impatiently demanding reading glasses, bent over the plans. Structurally, the plumbing seemed on paper to be the best available. He turned back to the supervisor. At least he could get his teeth into these lackeys. And they could always be trusted never to return the compliment.

'I require an immediate undertaking from you that this kind of thing will never be repeated.'

The building supervisor spoke slowly, his voice as grey as his face.

'My entire staff are on their hands and knees cleaning the floor in the main corridor, my Fuhrer. I swear I will do everything in my power to ensure you will never be troubled by such unpleasantness again.'

Hitler turned from his desk. This was no time for the flaccid language of diplomacy. 'If you are unable to promise on oath that this abominable incident will never be repeated, I can tell you that you and your entire staff will be taken into protective custody and attached permanently to a concentration camp.'

'Heil Hitler.'

Linge recorded laconically that there were no further plumbing problems after that.

While the Fuhrer wore glasses for reading maps and documents, he took great pains to hide them in public. He considered that spectacles, like excess weight, ill became an all-powerful leader.

When the day went badly — and the days tended to get worse as World War II got into its stride — Hitler frequently found an outlet for his agitation by crushing the glasses in his clenched fists. Linge, detailed to carry spare sets, said the turnover of replacement pairs by 1945 was as many as three a week. At different Fuhrer headquarters during the war he was also in charge of writing materials and vital sets of coloured pencils — the valet had been colour blind from birth, which put him in a delicate position each time the chief demanded a particular colour.

Hitler explained their significance for marking maps. 'I use red to pinpoint the enemy; green denotes an Axis position; blue indicates an untrustworthy satellite state.' He used the blue most frequently, sometimes using whole bundles of pencils like darts, hurling them across the room in a blind fury.

Linge quickly developed the trick of handing over several at a time, hoping to hide his colour-blindness. His chief, if he ever noticed, never once complained.

Ever a man of routine, Hitler, before the outbreak of the war, took to organising his days with all the precision of a regimental orderly. At breakfast he went rapidly through the morning papers, marking items he wished to have filed for the records. One of his manias was clipping items from international magazines to have them translated and methodically stored, using them as an antidote to the boredom of sleepless nights.

Commenting on the Fuhrer's speeches, Linge stressed that the story that most of them were composed by Goebbels was a malicious lie. Foreigners, hearing Hitler on the radio or seeing him in newsreels, tended in their ignorance to sneer at his extravagant rantings, but the chief attached immense importance to every public utterance, toiling for hours over what would later emerge as spontaneous thoughts; carefully preparing each speech in his study while pacing up and down, hither and thither, occasionally clearing his throat and giving voice as if he were addressing thousands. No one was allowed to disturb him.

When Hitler worked on his dialogue, other matters took second place. It had been his great skill as an orator that had got him where he was; the same skill would keep him there — every phrase was calculated to whip up a violent reaction. With emotive words like 'brutality', 'recklessness', 'intolerance', the first casualty was the truth. The final draft of a speech was meticulously timed with a stop watch before being reproduced on a custom-built machine with large-size type.

Just before he appeared in public, the Fuhrer's mood tended to vacillate between extremes of euphoria and melancholia. Quantities of Morell's boosters were swallowed to help lift his lethargy, to keep him going beyond the limit of endurance. Once the speech was concluded, Linge was ready offstage with a glass of warm water mixed with glycerine and a heavy overcoat to wrap around the chief.

Hitler, bathed in perspiration, was immediately surrounded by burly, gun-carrying bodyguards, hurried to his armour-plated limousine and driven speedily back to the Chancellery to prevent him catching a chill or a conspirator's bullet.

Here we have a contrasting image of the leader: feeding the vapid springs of his own vitality by external stimuli; the spirit of an introvert forced to share corporeal quarters with an extrovert orator; retaining the strength derived from a mystic's inner life, and despising the slavish and easily misled mob, regarding them as a 'repulsive, effeminate and nauseating mass'.

Privately beset by quarrelsome factions, skilled in the ancient Austian art of playing enmities off one against the other, stoking fires of jealousy he intervened only when things got too hot. And the craven self-seekers who formed the inner circle were, with few exceptions, men of inferior quality. Any conflict of will would have been out of the question — although the chief was more indecisive in his ultimate aims than most of his deputies.

At Nuremberg, Schacht explained how Hitler, by probing every detail of their lives, by discovering something, a weakness, a misdemeanour, managed to attach his tribunes so closely to his cause. In the end they became bound to him by the threat of disclosure. 'A large number gradually became terrified of the results of the evil and atrocious crimes to which they were constantly incited by the system; attempting to still consciences by resorting to the most varied form of vice in order to dull their sensibilities. This factor was the main cause of their actions. Otherwise there could be no accounting for the numbers of suicides when the system collapsed.'

Hitler, the gangrene rather than the wound, dominated by fear. And in its emblematic role as his sword and shield, the SS guaranteed that domination.

It was Horace Greely Hjalmar Schacht (as a bright young man he'd brushed shoulders with Bismarck) who introduced order and system into the party's erratic financing of the Third Reich. As president of the Reichsbank from March 17, 1933, he was able to give the German economy a desperately needed kiss of life.

Notifying the international banks in 1934 that the Fatherland was unable to repay the huge interest on borrowings, he obtained more loans from British and American financial institutions. He then devoted his career to building up a *Wehrwirtschaft*, a military economy.

Under his guidance the Third Reich, largely lacking raw materials and natural resources, would concentrate on a work creation scheme financed by the Reichsbank to the tune of one thousand million marks.

Unemployment, over six million in January, 1933, gave way three years later to an extreme shortage of labour. Thousands of workers were taken on by Krupps and other armament plants. More were employed on public works throughout the country, formerly held up through lack of funds; on building the new autobahnen (for the use of motor vehicle traffic only) and erecting barracks for the armed forces.

An immediate consequence of Schacht's economic miracle was intensive investment in the steel, iron and chemical industries. Neglected copper and iron ore mines reopened; rubber was manufactured artificially (at enormous cost); oil was produced from coal (money didn't come into it); every scrap of scrap was recycled.

Millions of Reichsmarks were circulated without causing inflation — the cash going from the banks to employers to workers' wage packets to retail shops and back to the banks. Exchange controls ensured no marks left Germany to fall into the hands of speculators. An attempt to smuggle currency out was an act of disloyalty, punishable by an indefinite loss of freedom.

With capital restrictions imposed, money earned abroad went towards the repurchasing of greatly depreciated German bonds for a few cents on the dollar. As debtors paid in frozen marks, large amounts of cash went to the government. Creditor countries cooperated by devaluing their own currencies.

The government also collected forty per cent of the national income in taxes and levies, half of it going to support the economy — of which the government controlled two-thirds. In broad outline, what Roosevelt did with a full purse to finance his 'new deal' in America, Hitler, with the assistance of Schacht and an empty piggybank, achieved for Germany's 'new plan'.

And as Minister for Economic Affairs Schacht evidently reached an understanding with the German general staff; 'the most efficient collectivist organisation in the world' was finally able to emerge from its postwar chrysalis as the most powerful military machine in the world. Regular army officers held key posts in the Economic Ministry; their orders carried out by staff officers attached to various armament industries.

In terms of foreign trade Germany reaped the benefit of Schacht's expertise; her influence in central Europe increased; exports and imports being bilaterally balanced; non-essential imports were permitted only in exchange for German exports.

From 1938, currency circulation had tripled, there being ten billion marks' worth of printed money in addition to billions more in special 'credit bills', to be used by the army to pave the way in Austria and Czechoslovakia.

By 1939, the Third Reich could justifiably claim the privilege of doing as it pleased.

And two out of three workers and industrialists were dependent on the Third Reich for their livelihood; a livelihood that depended on their loyalty to the Fuhrer and his party.

Hitler, said Linge, knew little about economics which, in the valet's view, was a definite plus. Before Schacht, all the experts had failed to balance the books. And in terms of bettering people's lives there was no comparable period in Germany's history.

Admittedly the economy concentrated on maximum output rather than on raising living standards, but the Fuhrer had openly stressed the need for a belt-tightening package. 'At present,' he told the people, 'I am not in a position to promise you more meat or butter. To do so would put us at the mercy of foreign exporters. I can promise improved housing, greater opportunities and full employment.' And generous allowances were available to the sick and disabled, to newly-weds — even to mothers of illegitimate babies.

Understandably, Hitler's personal staff enjoyed a high standard of living. 'My servants see how well the leader lives, how it is necessary to keep up appearances. They also must keep up appearances, and enjoy life. I do not intend that any servant of mine should be tempted into dishonesty because of a shortage of money. At the same time I must emphasise that, if anyone is caught breaking my trust, the punishment will far outweigh the nature of the offence.'

There were only two transgressors in Linge's time. Two kitchen porters, dismissed for habitual drunkenness, illadvisedly removed a painting from the diplomats' hall in the Chancellery. They were arrested trying to dispose of it. The valet understood that after a trying five days spent at SS headquarters, 8 Prinz Albrecht Strasse, the pair were shipped off to enjoy 'protective custody' in a concentration camp. He never saw them again.

*Impressed by the great occasion when the leaders of the German
Evangelical Church met together in the company of the Chancellor
of the Third Reich, Herr Hitler, they unanimously reaffirm their
unconditional loyalty to the Third Reich and its Fuhrer. Church
leaders condemn in the strongest possible terms all machinations
on the part of critics of the State, the Nation and the National
Socialist Movement calculated to imperil the Third Reich.*

Meeting of Evangelical Bishops   1934

*In the long run we shall be able to bring full understanding to
this situation only when we appreciate the mysterious forces at
work in the universe of which Wallenstein says 'The earth belongs
to the spirit of evil not to the good'; and refers to the 'evil natured
powers of darkness who lurk beneath the light of day'. Adolf Hitler
was an outstanding instance of these powers of darkness whose
influence was the more baleful in that he was lacking in every form
of satanic greatness. He was and remained a half-educated,
completely unintellectual petit bourgeois who, furthermore, was
entirely without any sense of right or justice.*

Doctor Julius Dix   Nuremberg   1946

*Life must be lived forwards but it can only be understood
backwards.*

Kierkegaard

CHAPTER SIX

'Among Hitler's circle,' wrote Putzi Hanfstaengl from the safety of Canada, 'no one loves his neighbour. Envy, hate and personal advancement predominate. No one dares criticise the leader, not unless they want to be thrown out.'

While it couldn't have been all bad, there existed among the *unterfuhrers* no loyalty in the sense in which the concept is understood; as for instance, on the playing fields of Eton or Harrow.

The ties which bound the members of what Alan Bullock termed the 'gutter elite' must have been similar to those binding the Cosa Nostra, stiffened by a perverted idealism and the hypnotic power of Hitler.

As a tadpole in the swell of the leader's celebrity, Linge witnessed as did few others the deceits, evasions and insecurities of the supporting cast.

Sadly his thumbnail sketches shimmer with ambiguities and half-truths. He does, however, refresh a few details of familiar portraits; doing what he can to dispose of the myth that the blame for mass crimes can be assigned to one man.

There may have been many things he yearned to communicate but about the precise, day-to-day details of Chancellery life he seems to have been constrained by his position from speculating too much.

Two prime accomplices, as we know, were the fat man and the one with the deformed foot — neither of them exactly untrodden ground.

The valet clearly liked the wide-paunched, gregarious Goring, whose rounded personality typified a nostalgia for an imperial past, a richer National Socialist present and the promise of a militarised future. Devoted to the Fuhrer, he boasted to Linge: 'The one ruler in Europe who can sleep peacefully in his bed is Hitler, because I'm his guardian angel.' Skating over the predicaments of the Field

Marshal marinating in morphine during World War II, Linge says Goring disliked Goebbels intensely and looked on Ribbentrop as a political upstart. 'He's always ready to pull a sabre out of his pants,' protested Goring in one of the many heated bouts centring round the Foreign Minister during the Czech crisis. Temporarily stunned by the losses sustained by the Luftwaffe in 1940, the air force chief needed constant acclaim, admiration and reassurance.

If, as Goring stated, Hitler was able to sleep peacefully in his bed, that old charmer Goebbels rarely ever saw his. The joke downstairs in the Chancellery was that 'if ever the doctor wanted to hide effectively from everyone he had only to sleep in his own bed'. Goebbels had a rich and varied sex life. And the Fuhrer tended to cast an admiringly indulgent eye at his promiscuity, referring to him as his 'unterleibsminister', minister of the genitals. To the chief, the party's sexual antics were its own business. It was only when Frau Goebbels threatened to divorce her randy little husband that he intervened to steady the party boat.

That was in 1937, when Goebbels became involved with an actress, the Czech-born Leda Barrova.

As a result of a 'Pssst, have you heard?' campaign — craftily initiated by Goring — Berlin café society was buzzing with news of how Goebbels came a cropper one morning at the UFA film studios.

In a neat piece of timing, top German film actor Gustav Froehlich, uneasily married to Miss Barrova, had walked into her dressing room just as Goebbels was about to press bouncily on top of her — with Leda urgently vibrating on the corner couch. Barely giving the doctor time to adjust his braces, Froehlich shot out a fist like a Westphalian ham and sent Goebbels sprawling. He then made his excuses and left.

Magda Goebbels put her foot down. Hitler stepped in to soothe her febrile frenzy. He sent Leda into exile in Prague and allowed Froehlich to carry on making movies at UFA. Then he ordered Goebbels to forego such risky sorties, at least until the heat died down.

With his special brand of pleading Herr Propaganda Minister somewhat defiantly suggested that when a woman as compulsively attractive as Leda Barrova invited a chap to a tumble he could hardly tell her he had a headache. Hitler kept his thoughts to himself; the quieter glory of friendship was a longer lasting tie than sex.

So Goebbels continued in office, operating low to the ground, until Russia was invaded. Out of favour after that, he spent the time making excuses and rationalising appalling errors — such as the miscalculation of the strength of the Russian army. In an effort to restore credibility he was forced to play down the savage effects of food rationing. He was unpopular with the people who preferred food to propaganda; who, like the army, had him marked for the political opportunist he was. While preaching rigid austerity in 1940, he had over 30 million Reichsmarks in an account at the Berlin Handelsgesellschaft bank.

It was said that if Stalin took over the Third Reich Goebbels would manage to stay on as his propaganda chief.

Linge believed that Ribbentrop's rapid ascent went to his head. Although he never let sex interfere with work or with the pleasures of plotting against Goring and Co., he was frequently discourteous to the chief, keeping him waiting on the end of a telephone while he chatted to some foreign dignitary or other. Reprimanded several times he remained unrepentant. His peppery firebrand of a frau was worse, exercising so much influence on her unprincipled mate that the Chancellery staff referred to her as 'State Secret'. All Foreign office papers went through her hands first before Ribbentrop was allowed access to them.

The relationship that caused the greatest internal rift before the outbreak of war was the one between Ribbentrop and Goring. The Foreign Minister, all for giving war a chance, assured Hitler that the British were neither willing nor able to fight. In the end, Goring acrimoniously commented, he turned out to be 'Hitler's evil spirit'.

*   *   *

Ribbentrop's main ally was Himmler. Has Linge anything to say on the credit side for this owlish-looking hatchet man?

Hardly. His sensation on first meeting Himmler was a predictable chill down the spine. He disliked his peculiarly incisive manner of speaking, the way he moved with that odd mixture of confidence and stealth particular to a cat, the way he watched everyone, his eyes expressionless behind steel-rimmed glasses. Whatever prestige he enjoyed stemmed from the way in which he had moulded the Gestapo — with a maximum of secrecy and a minimum of accountability. No one outside the force understood how it functioned.

He believed Hitler was a mutation of Wotan, the god of war, inspired and all-powerful; a supreme lord who appeared once in a thousand years; the one to restore Germany to her rightful place in the world.

A dream dear to Himmler was the establishment of a pure race. By mating tall, athletic, blue-eyed SS men with handpicked blonde virgins, he hoped to breed strapping superbabies in an attempt to cleanse the compost heap of German geneaology.

Tolerant to the point of automatic consent most of the time, Hitler drew the line at some of Himmler's more bizarre proposals, such as the Gestapo chief's suggestion that in addition to bodily beauty, eligible frauleins should attain Reichsportsmedals for athletic prowess.

'My mother,' Hitler drily commented, 'never won a medal in her life. Yet she managed to produce a future world leader.'

All right, said Himmler, how do you feel about doing away with the Christian religion?

No, said the Fuhrer. But keep the SS away from church services. Once enough people were encouraged by their example, formal religion would simply fade away.

For some years Himmler was very much the man behind the scenes. Whenever discussions took place between the chief and himself it was just the two of them, manipulating the system: rigid ideas of loyalty and respect combining to justify extortion, corruption and murder.

In the event of war, said Hitler, with Himmler in charge of the Gestapo there'd be no possibility of sabotage, unlike World War I. He personally regretted the lack of such a body in 1914; there had been an urgent need for its services.

To Linge and to most of the Fuhrer's men, Himmler was an enigma. They preferred to see him drive off in his crimson Mercedes rather than arrive. The slightest breach of regulations observed by Herr Reichsfuhrer meant severe punishment.

While not denying (what can't be denied) the mass exterminations, Linge was more than reticent on the subject. Though he appears to deplore the excesses, he swears it was only after he had been captured by the Russians that he heard the truth about the deaths, the gas chambers, the charnel-house cruelty perpetrated by Himmler and his cohorts. Aware he would be disbelieved the valet emphasised his ignorance of the atrocities committed in the name of National Socialism.

Whatever conflict may have existed between his assertion and the truth, it was one he was unable to resolve. Like most Germans he found it cosier to believe that only common criminals or enemies of the state were sent to concentration camps. And if these people hadn't deserved it, they wouldn't have been arrested in the first place.

Agreeing it wasn't possible for Hitler to have stayed in the dark about Himmler's activities, Linge suggests that his chief was prepared to approve anything once he was satisfied it was for the betterment of the Reich. And the whole time he was in service he couldn't recall one occasion when Hitler personally visited a concentration camp.

*　　*　　*

Referring to Bormann, the valet summed him up as a mean, jealous personality, full of *bauernschlauheit*, peasant cunning; unscrupulously calculating in his campaign of self-aggrandisement which began when Hess absconded. Having furthered his cause by marrying the daughter of Buch, president of a party tribunal, Bormann constantly studied the Fuhrer's needs, feeding him titbits of malicious gossip concerning other officials. Finally, he carried so much weight he was able to vet every document intended for Hitler and — as the war progressed — he allowed him to see nothing unpalatable. He eventually built an impregnable wall around the chief so that no one could approach him without Bormann's say-so.

Ill-tempered most of the time he was away from Hitler's charismatic presence, the Reichsleiter, having taken over most of Hess's functions, became known in Berlin as 'God Almighty from Obersalzberg'.

One member of his staff was a well-built young man, Doctor Heim, who always stood his ground whenever a personality clash erupted between himself and the bullet-headed Bormann. One morning, referred to by his boss as a pettifogging penpusher, Heim merely nodded, then he turned and prepared to walk out of Bormann's office without saluting. The enraged Bormann rushed around his desk and threw a punch at him. Heim, an amateur boxer, parried the blow and smilingly apologised for his insolence.

When Linge discussed the incident with Heim afterwards, the

doctor shrugged. 'I have no desire to cross swords with the man,' he said. 'Like an animal, he is accustomed to react primitively. He is and always will be a brutal peasant at heart and when I look at him I pity his ignorance and lack of breeding.'

Hitler, when he heard about the matter from his valet, seemed more amused than angered. 'Take a note of the young man's name, Linge,' he said. 'He could be a useful addition to the Chancellery staff after the war.'

*   *   *

Professor Giesler, the architect in charge of town planning in Munich, was often consulted by Hitler. He had in mind a six-year project after the war involving the complete reconstruction of the city.

Giesler was always enthusiastic, complimenting the chief on his vision, praising his pencil sketches. Privately, Linge felt the architect tended to overdo it and he was most upset when Giesler drew him aside one afternoon to ask him to obtain copies of the chief's drawings — he needed to be thoroughly briefed for future discussions. Linge thought it more likely he had an eye for a future illustrated bestseller.

He remembered the professor more as a mimic than a town planner. Normally straitlaced party officials would laugh themselves to the brink of tears at his antics as an impressionist. His version of the triple-chinned Labour chief, Robert Ley, addressing a mass meeting was a Chancellery classic: 'I c-c-compare the German p-p-people with an e-e-eagle. The h-h-head is H-H-Hitler; the w-w-wings are the L-L-Luftwaffe; the body is the R-R-Reich and . . .' (a voice from the back of the hall) . . . 'A-a-and the a-a-arsehole is L-L-Ley!'

Ley, said Linge, was a bit of a bully with a weakness for drink. To the Fuhrer, though, he was 'the best National Socialist of them all' despite his shortcomings. A willing participant in the violence which characterised early Nazi gatherings, showing a chilling, almost lunatic savagery, Ley had been arrested and imprisoned many times. A few party members hoped he would be named in the June, 1934 purge, for he was suspected of embezzling large sums of money. Instead, he was allotted greater responsibility in the political machine. Another example of the wisdom of the chief.

77

Catch one of the boys out, threaten him, forgive him, make him sweat a little and he would willingly toe the line, repaying the chief with lifelong dedication.

Ley was a splendid example. He built up the labour front, coined the 'Mein Fuhrer' blandishment, claimed the 'Heil Hitler' slogan as his brainchild and — ranking as one of Hitler's first lieutenants — was able to dismantle the trade unions, drafting labour laws that appeared on the surface to be humane but whose operation prohibited freedom of thought or action.

'We begin with a child when he's three years old,' said Ley. 'As soon as he begins to think, we put a little flag in his hand; then comes school, the Hitler Youth, the SA and military training. We never let him go. After adolescence, there's the labour front which takes him up and doesn't drop him until he dies — whether he likes it or not.'

Linge recalled an incident involving Ley which gave the chief a certain amount of amusement. It was at the end of a Mayday rally when the Labour chief, sodden with schnapps and glowing with barbaric goodwill, insisted on speaking.

Addressing the crowd somewhat incoherently he assured everyone that *he* 'had become divinely fair and that *Germany* was tickled pink because of it.'

Everyone realised he had got it the wrong way around and applauded the error. Later, Hitler gave his impression of Ley, teetering unsteadily backwards and forwards, explaining in his throaty stutter how divinely fair he had become.

With the German labour front launched on a full-blooded policy of national self-sufficiency, Dr Ley was able to introduce his *Kraft durch Freude*, Strength through Joy, movement which offered workers vacations in luxurious cruise ships.

Hitler was invited to head the passenger list on the maiden voyage of the brand-new steamship *Robert Ley*. He gave specific instructions: no celebrities, no cheap publicity stunts. Only genuine German workers were allowed to accompany him and his staff. And they would all wear civilian clothes. 'No uniforms,' he told Linge, 'This is one time in my life I intend to live like a simple man and mix with ordinary people.'

This put the valet on something of a spot. He was forced to shop around in Hamburg, the port of embarkation, for something casual — having not been out of uniform since joining the SS in 1935.

Hitler was welcomed aboard wearing a comfortable blue suit and a yachting cap, symbolising national philanthropy in action — foreign travel within the reach of every worker. 'And if we haven't been able to give the people new-laid eggs, at least we have given them a brand new *Ley*,' The ship's crew cackled approvingly.

For months afterwards, until World War II occupied most of his thinking, he referred to the trip as 'the one real holiday of my entire life.'

In the dining room the chief usually invited several other ordinary passengers to share his table. Linge thought it a joy to watch them, ill at ease during the soup course, unbending over the entrée and entirely relaxed by the time the macaroni and herring salad was served. It was wonderful the way Hitler was able to talk to them in their own language, swapping army stories, keeping the conversation well away from politics. And, naturally, the holidaymakers loved his sense of humour, charmed by his no-nonsense approach and wide-open personality. Among themselves they may have referred to him familiarly as 'Adolf', but never in ridicule. There wasn't one of them who wouldn't trust him with their lives (and most of them did a couple of years later); or fail to go along with whatever measures he deemed necessary for the good of the nation.

When dancing followed dinner, Hitler stayed at his table on the edge of the floor, watching the couples moving in rhythm through half-closed eyes. Whenever he saw a girl sitting alone he detailed one of his boys to dance with her.

There were several little blonde beauties among the *liebchens* on board and Linge remembers, with a nudge to the ribs, how most of the SS personnel were able to give vent to their natural lusts, experiencing all manner of erotic activities below decks throughout the cruise.

Usually the chief seemed ready to retire to his stateroom just as most of the boys were beginning to get into their stride. Whoever drew the short straw would then sidle over to the bandstand and ask for a favourite number of the Fuhrer's, *The Donkey Serenade*. This could gain them respite for another dance and give them time to exchange cabin numbers. It seems the heavy sexual diet satisfied the most voracious of Schutzstaffelian appetites.

Back on dry land again Hitler's thoughts turned to something more lasting than wages, food or foreign travel. In an effort to divert attention from renewed fear of war in Europe, he devised a product that could give the people a better life: a cheap car produced so economically it would be within the range of every worker.

As he planned it in 1938, the 'Strength through Joy' Volkswagen would be produced under his patronage and in addition to normal output; enhancing the automobile industry domestically without affecting overall competition. That would help placate the car manufacturers, headed by Professor Porsche. Financed by the labour front, with hire purchase facilities available to everyone, the car would cost no more than 900 Reichsmarks (just over £80). If Henry Ford could do it in America, then Adolf Hitler would go one better in Germany — his own personal contribution to the nation's rebirth.

The Volkswagen was planned as a four-seater, grey-blue car driven by a four-cylinder, air-cooled engine located at the rear, capable of developing 24 horse-power, giving a speed of 62 mph on a fuel consumption of three gallons per hundred miles. By positioning the motor at the back, thus eliminating the need for a radiator and the transmission shaft, a saving in weight was achieved. The body would be all-steel and the latest German light metals such as magnesium alloy would also be used.

One of the earliest models completed was presented to Eva Braun and it was only the outbreak of war that prevented the car being manufactured in vast quantities in 1939.

At the end of World War II, Churchill offered the car as a prize of war to the British car industry — the blitzed site of the production plant was in the British zone of West Germany.

Lord Rootes went over to assess its possibilities and reported back that in his view the Volkswagen "Beetle" 'was out of date, noisy and would not sell'.

Some British army officers based in Germany were sufficiently farsighted to put the car back into production. By 1972, more than 16 million Beetles had been manufactured, overtaking the sales of Henry Ford's classic Model T. By May 1984, a world total of 21 million cars had been produced. VW still produce the Beetle in Mexico and Brazil.

In Vienna in March 1938 storm troopers, having deposited excrement on the pavements, supervised the cleaning of them by elderly male and female Jews on their knees — making obscene jokes at their expense. It was ended by the courage of a former general of the Imperial Army of half-Jewish descent and head of the Jewish ex-servicemen's association. In full dress uniform, wearing all his decorations, he reported for scrubbing duty. After a hasty consultation the operation was cancelled.

Wheeler-Bennett

The green barrack buildings could be distinguished through the barbed wire. Even at a distance you could see that all was meticulously clean; the merest fragment of litter was absent. An air of foreboding permeated the place, frightful, cold as death. Never before have I experienced an atmosphere so uncompromisingly dangerous or so fiendishly hostile.

Kupler-Koberwilz 1938

CHAPTER SEVEN

At dawn on the morning of Friday, March 11, 1938, Austrian Chancellor Schuschnigg was called from his bed to be told that the German frontier had been closed and all rail traffic halted.

In the Berlin Chancellery Goring, handling negotiations by phone, instructed their man in Vienna, one-legged Seyss-Inquart, to take over the leadership and prepare for the Fuhrer's arrival.

In his office, Hitler was wearing grooves in the floor fabric. On edge, finally unable to contain his anxiety, he scurried along the main corridor to the Cabinet Room ('Where the cabinet sleeps while I run the country'). Pushing Goring to one side, no mean achievement, he grabbed the phone.

'What's the present position?' Stuffed full of pervitin, his eyes were red, his face grey with fatigue.

The news was good; his tanks were on the move, meeting no resistance, their progress marked by cheering crowds.

Hitler had played his opening card, a major initiative shrewdly timed — as challenging as it was critical. 'Splendid. Check everything with Himmler and meet me in Linz tomorrow evening.'

He listened, muttered an impatient agreement and triumphantly slammed down the receiver.

The order for the troops to cross the frontier had been timed for 8.45 pm. Prince Philip of Hesse, the Fuhrer's special emissary in Rome, rang at 10.25 pm. Hitler, taking the call himself, was told the Duce had accepted the inevitable. 'Tell Mussolini,' Hitler said in a voice hoarse with gratitude, 'I will never ever forget him for this.' He added that as soon as Austria had been officially incorporated into the Reich, he'd be more than ready to go along with Mussolini, come hell or high water, no matter what.

Having settled Austria's fate — after twenty-seven separate phone calls to Vienna — Goring finally showed up at the lavish reception he had planned for the top diplomats and delegates from all the foreign embassies. A thousand invitations had been sent out to attend the *Haus de Flieger* (Aviation Club) and the state opera and ballet had been booked to appear. All the guests were forced to kick their heels in the foyer until the Field Marshal arrived. The first thing he did was shout jubilantly across the hall to Count Magistrati, Italian chargé d'affaires, that he 'had excellent news from Italy'. Everyone understood what he was getting at, but they were compelled to stay until the performance ended. By then the armoured divisions were well into Austria.

The British ambassador, Sir Nevile Henderson, later delivered a protest 'in the strongest terms' which produced no reaction whatsoever.

Hitler, after all, had built his career upon the belief that flagrant breaches of diplomatic practice usually elicited more alarm than retribution. And his experience in World War I had taught him that brute force and success alone counted, that abstracts like truth and justice were soon trampled into the dust by the marching boots of a determined army.

The following morning Linge, discreet and self-effacing as ever, flew with the Fuhrer and his men to Munich where Kempka was waiting to drive them down the autobahn to Braunau-on-the-Inn, Upper Austria, traditionally German territory and onetime jewel in the crown of the Holy Roman Empire. It was almost lunchtime as the Mercedes crossed the border and Kempka slowed as they approached Hitler's birthplace. The chief ordered him to keep going. Braunau meant nothing to him.

Linge, watching the view from a rear window, was reminded of the fairy tales of the Brothers' Grimm. He peered up at serene mountain slopes, snowcapped, rising from steep ravines on the edge of the river, covered in pine and fir forests. And every village had been decorated in honour of the Fuhrer, every villager out on the roads to cheer the cavalcade as it headed for Linz.

Hitler watched them with a clinical interest, blended with morbidity and distrust. He had grown up with these people, attended school with some of them. He knew what the majority of them, the underdogs, wanted: the same as the working class of Germany. Apathetic, selfish, all they wanted was to be left in peace with a decent job, a good, solid home and an opportunity for their offspring to aspire to bourgeois status.

Eighty per cent already favoured the extreme political views of national socialism. They realised there was little hope for Austria except in a union with the Third Reich, the natural ally.

He was anxious to reach Linz. In a way it was like going home. The ignoramus from out of town who had attended the *realschule*; treated with contempt by so many of his fellow students — the sons of doctors, lawyers, shopkeepers; the inadequate failure, subject of so many 'unsatisfactory' reports. The boy who rebelled against traditional authority in a bid to lead his own life was back.

Here he was, Chancellor of the Third Reich, dictator of a reborn Germany, overlord of its armed forces and future Protector of Austria. Having overcome hostility and antagonism, he had been able to exercise the ancient democratic right of rising higher than his origins.

The Mercedes drew up at the town hall in the Platz des Zwolften November (Platz Francis Josef until 1919) where Seyss-Inquart and a prudent Himmler waited, fresh from Vienna, having installed SS units for security purposes. The usual bodyguard was there to ensure the Fuhrer's safety, but few seriously expected the 'homecoming' to be violent.

As Hitler alighted he turned to face the crowd. Barely acknowledging the cheers, he stared across the square at a familiar landmark, the monument commemorating two events; the plague and the invasion by the Turks.

His valet, aware of the constant threat of assassination, studied the faces pressing close to the car. He was relieved to find the crowd apparently well-disposed. The young girls particularly — Linz had a reputation for attractive women — were rosy with goodwill; numbers of them, neat in white bodices and colourful dirndl pinafores, brandished portraits of Hitler, garlanded with leaves. There were party pennants everywhere.

It was almost dusk when Hitler, timing his appearance, stepped out on to the town hall balcony. The sun had set behind the Postlingberg mountain, plunging its blurred outline into sombre shadow. Lights sparkled above the Volksgarten, stretching away towards the Stadtwald.

There was a sudden thunder of 'Sieg heil, sieg heil, sieg heil!' By now accustomed to such displays, the chief merely responded with his own limp variation of the party salute. Then, with a gesture, he commanded attention.

84

This one time, no gush of words, no impassioned ranting, no script.

'Providence,' he said, 'called me away from this town many years ago to lead me step by step towards the fulfilment of a dream. That dream became a mission, the mission realised, the union of the country of my birth with the German Reich, the Fatherland.'

They spent the night in Linz. On Sunday morning, instead of travelling on to Vienna, Kempka was told to drive out to Leonding. Hitler wished to place a wreath on the grave of his parents.

Linge stood at the car door, watching the chief walk along a dusty path towards a simple stone. Once there he stood for a long time, head bowed low, peering at the inscription on the tombstone:

> *Hier ruhet in Gott Herr*
> *Alois Hitler*
> *K K Zollamts Oberoffizial IP*
> *und Hausbesitzer*
> *Gest. 3 Janner 1903 in 65*
> *Lebensjahre*
> *Dessin Gattin Frau*
> *Klara Hitler*
> *Gest. 21 Dez 1907 i Lebj*
> R I P

A small black and white photograph of Hitler's father was attached to a corner of the stone. It showed a heavy-featured man, bald, with sharp eyes and a thick moustache. In Braunau he had worn the 'Imperial beard' made popular by Francis Josef, but in Leonding only the moustache remained.

A free-thinking nationalist, loyal to the Emperor, his last words were characteristic. In his local tavern, having been served with his usual red wine he reached out for the journals hanging from the wall. Grabbing hold of the catholic paper by mistake he flung it on the floor, saying '*Pfui teufel*! The old black aunt.' He drained his glass and, catching his breath, asked the landlady to send for Klara — he was feeling unwell. As she called the pot boy, Alois keeled over. In a couple of minutes he was dead.

According to the death certificate he died as a result of a lung haemorrhage.

Over the door of the inn in which he died was a rough wood carving bearing the verse:

> *Whether christian, pagan, jew,*
> *We've a drink that waits for you.*

This was the father who had sneered at his young son as a weakling, a worthless idler and a dreamer. This thrice-married drunk he had detested.

He had loved his mother and still carried in his pocket the last picture taken of her. In it she was deathly pale, with large eyes over sunken cheekbones, and her hair was almost white.

Hitler, his mouth clamped shut, delicately nudged the wreath more towards the centre of the grave with the tip of his boot. Then he straightened up and walked briskly back to the car. He would be forty-nine in April.

He had less than eight years to live.

*   *   *

It has been recorded that the Fuhrer delayed his arrival in Vienna until the afternoon of Monday, March 14 because, as a result of the breakdown of so many of his armoured vehicles between Salzburg and the capital, the road was temporarily blocked.

Not so, says Linge; the army's *technisierung* was first-rate. The chief was simply waiting to hear the reaction of other European countries; whether any of them were prepared to align themselves with Austria and protect her independence.

Britain? Unlikely, as Chamberlain favoured conciliation.

France? Not a chance of a showdown there; the French were between prime ministers and had no government at all.

And Italy, thanks to the political sagacity of Mussolini, was no longer a threat. Although when Dollfuss was killed, the Duce's own newspaper had referred to the Third Reich leaders as 'a government of assassins and pederasts', since the signing of the Rome—Berlin Axis in the autumn of 1936, Mussolini had become a willing, if sometimes resentful ally.

As for the lesser states such as Poland, Hungary and Yugoslavia, they were forced to reassess the odds and sharpen their wits. Hitler had initiated a chain of events which again would jolt Europe to its foundations.

*   *   *

The cavalcade of cars arrived in Vienna, the spicy, worldly, frivolous, reflective city of love, laughter, Schoenberg, Lehar and Freud, in the afternoon of Monday, March 14.

Crowds of supporters had staked out spots along the route. Those who couldn't find room on the pavements herded at open windows and overflowed on to balconies. Several athletic young men had shinned up lamp standards, decked for the occasion in party red, white and black.

The leading limousine threaded its way through the streets to the centre of the city, skirting Die Forelle in the old town, where Schubert had created *Lilac Time*; through Praterstrasse — Strauss had written *The Blue Danube* when staying at number 54 (now a MacDonald's hamburger house) — and over the Sonnenfelgasse into Schonlaterngasse, the tiny street of the beautiful lamp; past Schonbrunn Palace, once the home of Maria Theresa and Napoleon (now a youth hostel) and the elegant building where the infant prodigy Mozart made his first public appearance (now the home of the Vienna Fire Brigade).

Hitler sat stiffly in the back seat, watching it all from behind the bulletproof glass. Passing the cathedral with its famous 'Christ with the toothache' statue, leaning forward slightly as the car proceeded around the cordoned approaches to the inner heart of Vienna, the Ringstrasse, spotting the landmarks of his youth: the Opera House, the cream-washed Bundeskanzleramt, one time palace of the Metternichs, the university and the Heeres Museum that held the bullet-pierced car and bloodstained tunic of Archduke Franz Ferdinand, and finally, the Imperial Hotel.

Outside the hotel, the Fuhrer paused long enough to acknowledge the enthusiastic crowd with his usual prim salute. It seemed that no one, apart from Hitler, could help cheering, applauding or waving flags.

As he walked slowly over the red carpet into the hotel, accompanied by his bodyguard and valet there was a half-smile on his lips. He was remembering the seedy youth with the threadbare suit and unwashed shirt who used to hang about outside the main entrance of the Imperial just to get in half-an-hour's hate, gazing at wealthy Jews and uniformed aristocrats parade along the same red carpet, escorting pampered, perfumed, bejewelled women on their arms. He knew he still hated them and that he would detest the city for the rest of his life. And there were several old scores to settle. (Within weeks of his visit Himmler had arrested 79,000 'political unreliables' in the city areas alone)

Linge went ahead to check up on the royal suite, three high-ceilinged state rooms furnished in white and gold and with heavy, red-plush curtains. The bathroom had been updated but the rest of the suite looked as though it hadn't been decorated since the Hapsburgs had slept in it.

The Fuhrer, with a couple of hours to spare before a reception in the Hofburg, relaxed on a sofa, allowing the valet to pull his boots off and serve him with a glass of warm milk. Like a lighthouse lamp, incandescent when switched on yet lacklustre when the circuit was broken, he was blazing with excitement during most of the brief stopover in Vienna.

He seemed anxious to relive his hard times.

'When I was here as a young man,' he told Linge, 'I used to hear people say that when they died they wanted to go to heaven and make an opening among the stars in order to see fair Vienna. I never felt that way about it. Oh yes, the highborn Hapsburgs and the army playboys looked on it as a place of untold pleasures, a kind of paradise. And of course, all the Jews were busy making money. The only way to make any kind of a decent living was to work for a Jew.

'Anyone with any principles practically starved for them. I even had to shovel snow outside the doors of this place to earn enough for a cup of coffee. That was the night I made a resolution that one day I'd come back here just to walk over that red carpet. I've waited a long time for that day and thanks to the workings of Providence I'm here at last.'

For the Imperial, it meant a return to better days. With the Fuhrer's seal of approval it would become an official party hotel, able to take its place alongside the White Elephant at Weimar, the Deutscherhof at Nuremberg, the Dreesen at Godesberg and the Berlin Kaiserhof.

For Schuschnigg it meant arrest as a political detainee destined to end up cleaning latrines in a concentration camp. Schacht, by then in disgrace himself, remembered seeing Schuschnigg with a wife and child among the 'prominten' at Dachau in 1945.

For the Third Reich it meant a free hand with the gold, foreign exchange and securities of the Austrian national bank amounting to 550 million Reichsmarks. The bank also controlled, through a majority shareholding in the Credit-Anstalt-Wiener Bankverein, ninety per cent of the chief Austrian industries. Control of armaments, chemicals and textiles passed into German hands and heavy industry was amalgamated into the vast Hermann Goring Works.

For Hitler it meant a successful quantum leap in his expansionist strategy. The Reich must soon include all German-speaking people.

But one thing at a time.

On the table in front of him was an invitation, signed by Victor Emmanuel, to visit Italy at the beginning of May.

As long as the Germans have need of us they will be courteous and even servile, but at the first opportunity they'll reveal themselves as the great rascals they really are.

King Victor Emmanuel III

The Germans are a military people but not a warrior people. Give them a great deal of sausage, butter, beer and a cheap car and they'll never want to risk their skins.

Mussolini

CHAPTER EIGHT

It can't have been easy, being the Fuhrer.

Just before his visit to Italy, Hitler was asked if he intended to seek an audience with the Pope. No, he replied, there were no plans to include the Vatican in his itinerary.

In fact, the Pope made a point of absenting himself from Rome, not wanting to be in the same city as the dictator. He thought it better to stay at Castelgandolfo, in the Alban Hills, south of the capital, spending the time in the shade of the cedars, meditating on the dangers of solipsism and the concomitant evils of totalitarianism.

The Vatican paper *L'Osservatore Romano* refrained from mentioning the Fuhrer's visit; the Vatican museums were closed for its duration.

A number of influential Italians hoped that Mussolini, his pride wounded at the way Hitler had annexed Austria, might have cancelled the visit. But it went ahead, with such a display of magnificence it cost the state well over five million lira.

The excitement started for Linge that morning in May, 1938, with the Fuhrer's team, hatted, gloved and bemedalled, assembled at Anhalt station. The minions left to mind the store were also there to wave them all away. The amount of luggage consigned to the valet's care, he felt, would have done justice to an army on the move. But then 'we always organised more thoroughly than anyone else; we were, after all, Germans.'

Hitler, in a freshly-tailored uniform, called his band of brothers together for a final briefing; stressing how important the visit to Italy was. They must think and act diplomatically; be on their best behaviour and avoid alcohol as much as possible; bearing in mind they represented the Third Reich twenty-four hours a day.

Just before the train pulled in, Linge was summoned to the number one coach — he was to warn the chief when they reached the station platform.

'When we arrive, I want you to keep an eye out for an elaborately dressed little man who'll appear to be covered in gold braid. For God's sake make sure none of the *Schwarze Korps* embarrass me by poking fun at him, for it'll be the King. Yes, I know what I've always said about European royalty, that they're kaput, finished. But Mussolini is my colleague. I support him and will defend him whenever necessary. If he wants me to pay homage to the little white-haired dwarf for the time being, then I'm prepared to forget my dislike and go along with him.

'I'm glad to say that nothing is as strong as the bond of understanding that exists between the Duce and myself.'

The hard-chinned Mussolini, still possessing some initiative of his own, hoping to strike a bargain or two, held to a different point of view.

As far as he was concerned the situation was one he accepted reluctantly, looking on it as God's will. He merely hoped to do whatever was best for Italy and in that way avoid 'displeasing God and also the enemies of God'. He had already put too many Italian noses out of joint in his struggle to get to the top.

As the Fuhrer's train slowed down, the SS contingent crowded the corridor, eager to see the kind of reception in store for them.

An *unterscharfuhrer* (sergeant) tactlessly leant out of the window and shouted 'Look! One little fellow's down on his knees before we've even got out of the train.' 'Shit scared,' said another NCO.

'Keep your mouths shut,' said Linge. 'You've had your orders. That one might look to you as if he's kneeling, but believe me he's the biggest man in Rome apart from the Duce.'

It was eight in the evening when Hitler warily boarded the royal coach outside Rome station to take his place next to the King. The bells of the Angelus tolling over the city added a touch of solemnity to the occasion.

Slowly the coach, with its six white horses and rubber-tyred wheels, moved through the streets of a Rome decorated in a spectacular fashion: searchlights played on the classical colonnades of historic buildings; and the flares burning in the gigantic urns all along the via del Impero seemed to give the remains of the old Forum and Palatine Hill a breathtaking beauty. The Colosseum, illuminated in the same way, was like an elaborate stage set, causing the Fuhrer to stare back in wonder before entering the Quirinal, in earlier days the summer palace of the popes.

Linge noted the king's residence as a fine-looking place but somewhat austere in comparison with the Berlin Chancellery, lacking comfortable furniture and efficient heating.

Next evening Linge was standing on the balcony of the chief's suite watching the sun setting. Hitler, until then somewhat quiet and withdrawn, walked through the open door to join him. He spoke about Rome, seeming in a more mellow mood, pointing out the palazzos, fountains and colonnades below them, explaining how the city was, more than any other on earth, steeped in history — with little to show for its former glories, apart from fine examples of elegant white elephants like the Forum and the Colosseum. He had been less than impressed, he said, by the formal reception and the lavish banquet but the beauty of the eternal city afforded him immense pleasure.

Linge nodded in agreement, adding that he hoped the mild climate might prove beneficial too.

More than anything, said Hitler, he wanted one day to come back as an unknown, ordinary citizen; he'd spend days simply sightseeing. The most tedious aspect of the visit was the boring manner in which he was paraded before the Roman nobility.

He was referring to the official welcome when, heralded by four cohorts in purple and gold blowing bugles, he was forced to escort Queen Elena, inches taller than he was, into the vast marble and gold reception hall. Victor Emmanuel was not the most gracious of hosts and although there were sufficient interpreters scattered about, there was little in the way of light conversation. The King made quite sure that everyone present realised he looked on the entire German contingent as a very dubious proposition indeed.

The valet was in a perpetual state of anxiety in case something went wrong during the visit. And had it not been for the intervention of Mussolini, it might have ended in disaster.

A march-past of the Italian armed forces was arranged before the Fuhrer, who took his place in the stand in the front row alongside members of the royal household, the King and Queen and the chamber of deputies. The Grand Fascist Council and their secretaries occupied the second row, leaving the topmost benches for Hitler's adjutants and staff.

The Fuhrer, seriously wondering whether a subtle Italian attempt was being made to outrage him, was forced to sound off, sotto voce, a few bars of black, apocalyptic rhetoric directed at the King. He intended, he told the Duce, to cut short his visit and return to Berlin that afternoon.

Mussolini, taken aback, attempted to soothe him by explaining that the seating plan had been left to some under-secretary who had no idea of protocol. Speaking all the while in the softest of undertones, he swore he would personally see that the incompetent idiot was clubbed into insensibility before being incarcerated in the local jail. He pleaded with the Fuhrer, in the meantime, to sit back and enjoy the spectacle of the splendid Italian army keeping perfectly in step with the recently introduced *paso romano* (a kind of operatic goosestep).

Hitler gradually calmed down, sitting back stiffly, moodily silent. There was nothing to be gained from pointing out that Titian, Michelangelo and Leonardo da Vinci meant far more to him than entire platoons of comic opera infantrymen. But, blaming Victor Emmanuel for the slight, he never forgave him.

At an informal lunch given to him by the Duce in the Palazzo Chigi — soft-boiled eggs and rice pudding on account of Mussolini's diseased stomach and the Fuhrer's vegetarianism — he questioned the way Mussolini tolerated the House of Savoy when what he ought to have done was to sweep the whole crowd into exile, ideally into the hinterland of Ethiopia. 'King Victor should go down on his knees in gratitude to you for allowing him to stay in the saddle all this time. Just remember this; neither he nor any member of his family will thank you for what you've done for Italy.'

He recounted his own hatred for the house of Hohenzollern: how when Prince August Wilhelm, the Kaiser's second son, applied to join the NSDAP he had strongly opposed allowing him in. To him the one worthwhile Hohenzollern had been Frederick the Great. And he had been dead for 152 years. The only reason he tolerated August Wilhelm in the party was that Goebbels had made such a strong case in his favour from a propaganda point of view.

Mussolini's reaction is unrecorded but one can imagine it may have grated on him a little to hear such criticism of the Italian royal family. Wasn't it a shade presumptuous of the German dictator to put him to rights?

Hitler, on the other hand, while he didn't doubt the Duce's political muscle as a leader, feared he was a bit past it. Nevertheless, the Italian head of state was the archetypal dictator, astute and very much a prima donna, while remaining ethically and philosophically a barbarian; the perfect partner. Because there were great disparities in military strength and wealth between Germany and Italy anyway, there couldn't possibly be consistent equality of respect. For a while longer the difference in power between the two of them could be masked under sentiment and esteem. But the state visit hadn't done much in the way of improving the quality of his own lifestyle.

There was that repulsive major-domo at the Quirinal who never left his side the whole time he was at the Palace; pushing Linge into the background, constantly interfering in the choice of suitable outfits, advising him, correcting him and pursing his lips at the comfortable uniform Hitler regarded as right for all occasions.

He had insisted on formal tails for a night at the San Carlo Opera and the Fuhrer, gritting his teeth, suffered the indignity of wearing striped trousers and starched shirt. At that point a royal equerry appeared.

Would the Herr Chancellor do the King the honour of appearing with him on the balcony — in uniform?

The chief looked over at Linge, who was sure there were sparks coming out of his eyes. He knew Hitler wouldn't have changed back into uniform if Victor Emmanuel had offered him Sicily as a summer retreat. Thinking quickly, the valet picked up the chief's military greatcoat and held it out. Hitler put it on over the dress suit and marched grimly out to stand beside the King. Saluting the rather unenthusiastic crowd gathered beneath the balcony, he managed to give the impression, if not of a man brimming over with benevolence, at least of an unbending dictator showing himself in all his military glory. Fortunately the balustrade concealed his striped trousers and thin patent pumps.

The evening, having got off to the worst of all possible starts, simply degenerated into disaster.

Detained in the foyer, the Fuhrer found himself surrounded by a number of raddled exiles from the German aristocracy, who milled around him in a kind of stumbling funeral march. He was forced to stand there, in a draught, stomach voicing its protest at the unwise amount of pasta he had consumed at dinner earlier, trying to locate the nearest lavatory while fending off vengeful small talk from relics of the House of Hapsburg.

And that wasn't all.

In the royal box, where four gilded chairs covered in the reddest of plush were placed, one of the King's daughters took it upon herself to sit in the Duce's chair. Mussolini was left standing, until a footman hurried in with an extra seat.

It was all too much for Hitler. Calling the Duce aside during the interval, he addressed him with his usual relentless, brass-edged, bluff approach.

'Why didn't you stamp your foot and tell that cow to get out of the box? You must not allow these people to intimidate you!

'Let me tell you that if anything like that had happened in Berlin, I'd have felt justified in calling one of my boys over to drop her into the orchestra stalls.'

The abashed Duce kept his head down. He knew a little German but not enough to be able to tell his chum to go *schrauben* himself. He nodded, smiling brightly and inviting Hitler to admire the superb floral displays garlanding the dress circle.

The Fuhrer was also extremely annoyed at the disdainful manner in which the royal family stared at him as if he were an unpredictable performing animal. It made him apprehensive as he waited for one of them to prod him with a finger, just to test the reaction.

He was more than relieved to see Berlin again. And the welcome home, arranged by Goring, went some way towards compensating him for the provocations he had endured in Italy. All along the avenue leading to the Chancellery (the East-West Axis) the trees were festooned with thousands of coloured lights, and Goring had seen to it that all available Berliners were on hand to cheer the party as they travelled from the station.

The chief, comfortable in his second-best uniform, stood in the back of his open Mercedes to salute the people, refreshed and gratified; it seemed as if the whole city had turned out to greet him. Then, following a late dinner, a dramatic firework display was staged in the Tiergarten in his honour.

Next morning the Fuhrer held a special meeting with Schacht, Goring and Goebbels to relay a specific instruction: the pensions of certain retired Weimar republicans were to be generously increased as a tribute from their leader for their good sense years earlier in dispensing with the house of Hohenzollern and making the Reich a republic.

He then entertained his inner circle by giving an impression of

King Victor Emmanuel, languorous to the point of torpor, attempting to sing the German national anthem.

According to Pope John XXIII — referring to the matter over twenty years later — the fact that Pius XI stayed away from Rome during the Fuhrer's visit didn't mean he would have refused to meet Hitler. He always acted on the principle that 'he'd have eaten with the devil if the good of souls required it'. Good and evil are interchangeable, after all, rather than unshakeable absolutes laid down by religious or political beliefs.

Shortly before his death in February, 1939, Pope Pius XI had been working on an encyclical intended for Italian bishops, denouncing the Duce's violations of the Lateran Treaties. After he died, copies of the speech were destroyed by Vatican officials.

Since he had been made the Holy Father in 1922 Pius XI, throughout the rise of fascism, had attempted to reconcile the brutal realities of Mussolini's regime with Catholic ideals; pragmatically accepting his reactionary doctrines, his fraudulent propaganda, while emphasising the need for Italians to keep within moral laws.

Fortunately, because Italy was, in the thirties, a backward country, the ranting of the Duce from a hundred balconies did little harm.

The greater menace to the Vatican was the brand of totalitarianism favoured by Stalin in his five-year plan and later by the Fuhrer in the national socialist 'paradise' of the Third Reich. National Socialism might have fallen on stonier ground had it not been for the overwhelming defeat of Germany in World War I and the increasing threat of communism. The same was true of Italy, where a loss of faith in democracy opened the way for fascism and the overthrow of the established order.

World War I brought about the sense of futility, the spiritual alienation prophesied by the various revolutionary movements of the nineteenth century, and ended hundreds of years of European predominance.

In Germany the failure to create an alternative to Prussian rule led to the rise of Hitler as Reichskanzler.

In Italy, Mussolini's 'corporate state' purportedly came into existence to solve the insoluble problem of capital versus labour. It also kept the Italian brand of communism at bay.

In America, where power was (as it still is) largely rooted in economic strength, capitalism was allowed to grow increasingly monopolistic.

In Russia, Stalin's mix of Marxism gradually headed towards totalitarianism.

*　　*　　*

In the 1980s, America and the Soviet Union represent the issues which will mark the most decisive struggle in world history, the East versus the West. With the overwhelming antagonism towards capitalistic America displayed not only by Europe but by world-wide revolutionary movements on both intellectual and social levels, it is beginning to look as though some form of revolutionary Marxism will eventually gain the upper hand and achieve world leadership.

Because the future is rooted in the present a third world war would, as Professor Carl Friedrich (of Harvard) puts it, 'be both the consequence and the cause of the spread of totalitarianism. War and totalitarianism are joint products of related forces rather than cause and effect.'

Which of the two super states, the United States or the Soviet Union — asks Major-General Fuller — is the more fitted to solve the crucial problem set to mankind by the industrial revolution: the status of man, his government and way of life in a fully mechanised world?

The German occupation of Czechoslovakia is in complete disregard of the principles laid down by the German government . . . Is this the end of an old adventure, or is it the beginning of a new? Is this the last attack upon a small state or is it to be followed by others?

Neville Chamberlain   March 1939

The action of the German government was a complete repudiation of the Munich agreement and a denial of the spirit in which the negotiators of that agreement bound themselves to cooperate for a peaceful settlement.

Viscount Halifax   March 1939

Can anything be more ridiculous than that a man should have the right to kill me because he lives on the other side of the water and because his ruler has a quarrel with mine?

Pascal

CHAPTER NINE

Two months after the notorious Munich settlement banker Schacht, in what was to be the last visit overseas in his capacity as Reichsbank president, arrived in London. He was there on Hitler's orders, to discuss proposals for the administration of Jewish property in Germany.

The Fuhrer, in the face of international condemnation after *Reichskristallnacht*, (the destruction of Jewish shops, businesses and private apartments organised by Heydrich on the night of November 9), thought it a sound move to send Schacht to talk to London financiers. The initiator of the 'controlled economy' was already under a cloud; arrangements were in hand for his removal from office.

Aware he had enemies, chief among them being Field Marshal Goring, Schacht was not a man to be intimidated by anyone he regarded as an inferior.

In London he contacted Lord Bearsted (of Samuel & Samuel) to discuss his proposals. All Jewish property in the Third Reich could be amalgamated under an umbrella trust company controlled by an international committee. The committee would be authorised to issue a loan on the world money market of 1500 million Reichsmarks, carrying an interest of five per cent repayable over twenty-five years — issued as a dollar loan.

While Bearsted expressed approval other financiers, English and American, rejected the proposal.

Schacht returned to Berlin with nothing more than a promise that an attempt would be made to hammer out a scheme favourable to Jewish interests.

With tension increasing in the Sudetenland and the Fuhrer's demand for some kind of military action growing shriller, Schacht gave warning that the *kriegswirtschaft* (war economy) still lacked sufficient resources for a major campaign. He compounded the felony by sending Hitler a memo signed by the bank's directors criticising the Government's extravagance.

Hitler, convinced of the necessity for war and determined to carry it through, if necessary against the wishes of the people, ordered Schacht to appear on January 20, 1939, at the Chancellery.

Linge showed the banker into the drawing room overlooking the garden and barely had time to wish him the compliments of the season before the chief came in with a piece of paper in his hand.

Brushing aside problems connected with Jewish property, he handed the paper to Schacht. 'I sent for you,' he said, 'to give you formal notice. You are dismissed from the office of president of the Reichsbank. It seems you no longer fit in with the national socialist scheme of things.'

There was a brief pause. When Hitler spoke again, there was a harder edge to his voice. 'You also openly criticised and condemned the events of November 9 to your employees.'

Schacht raised his eyebrows. 'If I'd known that you approved of that night's work, mein Fuhrer, I would have held my tongue.'

Hitler's eyes nearly popped out. The banker had always been outspoken, too ready to express his disapproval with party policy, but this kind of sarcasm was too much. The man had a genius for making enemies.

He restrained himself with a visible effort. 'I'm too upset to continue this conversation.'

Linge moved to open the door.

'And, Herr Schacht, whatever you might think, there'll be no inflation in Germany while I'm Chancellor.'

'I'm delighted to hear it, mein Fuhrer.'

Silently, Hitler escorted the banker through the rooms leading to the front entrance, where Schacht bowed and took his leave.

He was immediately replaced by the yes-man Funk.

Later the same day Hitler dispensed with the services of two directors of the Reichsbank, vice-president Dreyse and Herr Hulse. Three others, Vocke, Blessing and Ehrhardt handed in resignations. Messrs Puhl and Kretzschmann, party followers, stayed in office.

And Schacht who had brought order and system to the financing of the Third Reich, went into retirement. Along with General Halder, he was arrested following the July, 1944 bomb plot and escorted by the Gestapo to Ravensbruck.

That was his last involvement with the party until Nuremberg, when he was taken with Goring to a cell containing two bath tubs. The Lufwaffe chief in one and Schacht in the other, they proceeded in silence to soap themselves all over.

*   *   *

The dismemberment of Czechoslovakia was carried out in characteristic national socialist fashion. Not only was it the first of the series of major political errors executed by Hitler, but it served to emphasise the curious dualism that existed in him: a romantic idealism for the future of a greatly expanded Germany and a cynical indifference to the rights of man or the forces of morality. Regarding compromise as the lowest and most despicable means to which a leader could resort, he would contemptuously ignore existing universal laws.

By the late thirties the Czech nation had become, thanks to its tenacious, industrious people, one of the most significant industrial powers in Europe. As well as exporting arms, textiles and machinery, it was sending shoes, millions of pairs of them, all over the world — from factories in Zlin controlled by a self-made tycoon called Bata.

But it was not renowned for racial unity. Its Sudetenland Germans (20%), Hungarians and Ukrainians (10%), being minorities, suffered a degree of discrimination. The oppression of the Sudetens gave Hitler the excuse he needed to espouse their cause. Under his guidance, his man Henlein had risen from membership of the Bohemian NSFO (Foreign Organisation of the National Socialists) to command the largest political group in Czechoslovakia.

As far as the Fuhrer was concerned, following on from Munich, the rethinking of his attitude towards Bohemia—Moravia was perfectly proper, it being a natural field for the expansion of German trade. In his view the British would have been more usefully employed in getting to grips with the problem of Palestine. Prime Minister Chamberlain might be an accommodating old *scheisshund* but his aides were interfering arse-lickers. In regard to the French it was no contest: 'Every one of them had their price; they were Jew-ridden scum to a man'. Anyway, the British and the French trusted him more than they trusted each other. He believed both countries secretly hoped he'd attack Russia; which was why they did nothing to prevent Germany from rearming.

He maintained that if Britain and France had cast him in the role of the main bulwark against Bolshevism, then he was justified in continuing to prepare for an inevitable conflict. War, after all, was the essence of everything, and his sights were set on the Soviet Union. The Czech nation was nothing more than a troublesome bone in the throat of Germany, to be dislodged as soon as possible.

In the circumstances his philosophy of force was the only philosophy worthy of the name.

But this ingenuous philosophy — that any power daring to obstruct the realisation of his visions for the future of Germany was an enemy to be swiftly obliterated — again carried a fundamental contradiction. While rejecting previous philosophical thinking as an anachronism, he could only put forward a more primitive philosophy in place of it.

Where did justice figure in his scheme of things? No problem. He was the power absolute and justice was merely one of the functions of that power; the judicial function was subordinate to the political.

Hess had expressed it clearly at a law officers' convention in 1936 by quoting Treitschke: *'alle rechtspflege ist eine politische tatigkeit'*, all justice is political. It was this ascertained principle, this elevation of the national socialist party above the law, that advanced its cause and eventually sent it headlong to destruction.

Political observers in Europe in the autumn of 1938 listening to the Fuhrer's scathing denunciation of liberalism, humanitarianism and appeasement, reading Mussolini's propaganda offensive aimed at appropriating Nice, Corsica and Tunisia, might well have come to the conclusion that homo sapiens was about to become an endangered species.

And with the break-up of what was left of Czech independence in March, 1939, Hitler not only broke his word to Mr Chamberlain but he infringed the whole principle of self-determination on which the Munich agreement rested.

That was when Emil Hacha, the sixty-six-year-old successor to President Benes, put himself in the lion's den in an ineffective effort to ward off further disruption. The Fuhrer agreed to see him, together with his foreign minister Chvalkovski (later killed in an air raid on Berlin in 1944), so Hacha arrived at the Adlon hotel at 10.40 pm on March 14. He was gratified that the hotel staff treated him with great respect; flowers filled his suite; and there were lavish boxes of chocolates for his daughter, Madame Radl.

It was a different story at the Chancellery. Poor Hacha found himself sitting admiring fourteen Gobelin tapestries hung on the walls, until well after one o'clock in the morning. It was Chvalkovski who drew his attention to the horses depicted in the battle scenes. Every one of them was a stallion, apparently a fetish of the Fuhrer's.

He was finally escorted to Hitler's office by Linge to see that Ribbentrop and Keitel were present; Goring came in immediately, hurriedly recalled from a vacation at San Remo.

Hacha sat on the edge of his chair, wearing an expression of acute anxiety. The Fuhrer wore field grey. His valet, lurking in the background, wore sidearms. The Czech president was about to be given the treatment — the same type of tongue lashing administered to Chancellor Schuschnigg a year earlier.

Aware that Hacha suffered a heart condition, Hitler proceeded to bully him into submission; beginning in a cold, forceful manner, working his way up to a psychological penetration, and ending in a sustained monologue of orgiastic satisfaction.

He used the same kind of technique of misinformation, asserting assumptions authoritatively that had no foundation in fact, giving arbitrary judgements the standing of metaphysical truths, that has since become standard practice among cabinet ministers and the leaders of revolutionary terrorist organisations.

Citing the Czech brutalities against Sudeten Germans he justified his intervention in Bohemia—Moravia. He pointed out that all kinds of national, social and political reasons made the idea of Czech autonomy ludicrous. He thumped his desk several times before pushing some papers across it for Hacha to sign.

The Czech president, a decent conservative, a believer in moral standards, attempted a feeble protest.

Hitler outstared him. 'Behind me stands a nation of many millions. Who stands behind you?' He turned to Goring. 'How many aircraft have we capable of reducing Prague to dust?'

'As many as it takes,' replied Goring.

There was a prearranged tap on the door. Linge opened it and was handed the latest dispatch for Keitel. He told the Fuhrer that the Wehrmacht had occupied Witkowitz without meeting resistance.

Hitler nodded. 'How many divisions have we there?'

'Thirty, mein Fuhrer.'

Ribbentrop intervened to state that his bureau had information that Jewish dissidents in Czechoslovakia were still engaged in spreading anti-German propaganda. They had to be dealt with quickly, he said.

Hacha, sweating profusely, felt sharp pains radiating along his shoulder and down his left arm. A cramping sensation in the centre of his chest caused him suddenly to hunch over in his chair. Hitler clicked his fingers and Linge hurried from the room to summon medical help.

He came back with Morell who, after a rapid examination of the Czech president, diagnosed a mild heart attack. After a large dose of Sympatol Hacha breathed more easily and was allowed to contact Prague by phone before discussing the situation privately with Chvalkovski in an adjoining office.

It was nearly four o'clock in the morning when Hacha reached out a trembling hand for the papers to sign. There would be no further discussions.

Shortly after 8 am, as Hitler's train drew out of Anhalt station, German troops poured into Bohemia—Moravia. Hacha was still in his bed at the Adlon.

At the frontier, the Fuhrer spoke briefly to General Hoepner and Colonel Rommel before continuing towards Prague by car, together with Keitel, Ribbentrop and Himmler. Although it was well after midnight by the time he was installed in the presidential suite of Hradcany Castle (so much for the Hapsburgs), he immediately got down to work, mapping out the next moves.

Linge, hanging up the spare uniforms, checking the linen, once again had cause to marvel at the energy of the chief.

It would be the same following every new move. With Hitler high as a kite, unable to sleep, impatient for new triumphs and relishing the trappings of power. Then, a few hours later, came the inevitable down that left him physically washed out, at the mercy of all the old inner miseries.

His first act was to proclaim the Protectorate of Bohemia—Moravia with the two Sudeten leaders. Henlein and Frank were appointed head of civil administration and secretary of state respectively; Neurath was named Protector.

Henlein, arrested at the end of World War II by Czech resistance forces, committed suicide. Frank, sentenced to death by a Czech court, was publicly hanged near Prague on May 22, 1946. Neurath survived to appear at Nuremberg, and Hacha, arrested by the Czechs on May 14, 1945, died before being brought to trial.

*   *   *

Before returning to Germany, Hitler travelled in state through Prague, passing rows of sullen-faced Czechs stunned by the turn of events and angered at the sight of the Swastika flying over the Hradcany, the palace of the former Kings of Bohemia.

Linge, sitting alongside his chief, studied the faces with some cause for concern. Seeing the open hatred, aware of the anti-German feeling widespread in the city, he feared another assassination attempt, for the Fuhrer was a sitting target. But such was the nature of the man, he always left himself open to such a possibility.

Several attempts on his life had already been made. The previous summer an aide had been handed a nosegay of roses intended for the chief. He pricked his finger on one of the thorns and rapidly lost consciousness. The stems had been treated with a lethal poison. Following that incident, such gifts were only accepted by a member of the staff wearing thick leather gloves. Anyone caught throwing flowers at or into the Fuhrer's limousine was in danger of immediate arrest by the accompanying SS bodyguard.

A couple of years earlier a rare breed of dog was delivered to the staff entrance of the Berghof by an unknown donor. After the animal savagely went for one of the gardeners, it was found to be riddled with rabies. As the valet remembered, the gardener took a long time to die.

From then on, all unsolicited gifts were carefully examined by a special unit of the SS; none of the immediate household were allowed to handle them. Exotic fruit, jars of Beluga caviar, foreign delicacies had been sent to Hitler, all of them contaminated with a whole variety of quick-acting toxins. A rolled antique silken carpet had contained a cleverly fused timing device attached to an anti-personnel bomb. The Chancellery guard was continually on the alert for such suspicious packages, particularly if they had arrived from the Balkans.

The valet disobeyed his master's instructions just once. It very nearly cost him his life.

106

In the spring of 1944, a large hamper of fresh fruit arrived at the Berghof. Instead of sending it for analysis Linge ate some of the black grapes placed on top. He became seriously ill with dysentery and vomiting and was hospitalised for several days.

The chief, in his concern for the condition of his valet, ordered a daily bulletin on the state of his health. Happily the contrite valet suffered no lasting damage, apart from a future aversion to grapes.

After the Prague visit, Linge spoke to the chief, voicing his fears for his safety. It would only have taken one determined Czech sniper to aim a round at Hitler's exposed body and thus rewrite history.

The chief listened patiently before putting his own point of view.

'What you fail to take into account is the element of surprise. It never occurred to the Czechs that I'd appear in Prague so soon after the takeover. They were completely at a loss. The masses are predictable, Linge. And they'll always act in a predictable fashion.'

But what good came of it at length?
Quoth little Peterkin.
Why, that I cannot tell, said he
But 'twas a famous victory . . .

Southey

Nobody in England will blame Chamberlain for the disaster that befell our country. He meant well, he trusted too well, he will go down in history as a man of peace. His great mistake was that he decided to be a man of war as well.

George Sava

CHAPTER TEN

At first light on Friday, September 1, 1939 General Guderian led his 3rd Panzer Brigade across the frontier into Poland.

By 8.00 am he was on the outskirts of Gross Klavia, a town he knew well. The castle on the hill had been owned by his great-grandfather; his father was born there; and as a boy he had played in the castle gardens.

The forces defending the town, like the rest of the Polish army, fought valiantly, but the odds were overwhelming.

Hitler's Wehrmacht was superior in training, equipment and arms. Forty-four divisions were supported by 2,000 aircraft, including Stuka (Junkers 87) dive bombers which launched the attack. These highly effective, economically produced aircraft had been fitted with devices that produced a shrill, screaming noise, audible above the roar of engines and rattle of machine guns, which served to put the fear of god into hapless Polish civilians.

But the resistance offered Guderian and his army was more spirited than many a historian would have us believe. The insufficiently armed Polish cavalrymen had been trained for guerilla warfare, their strategy having been acquired against the Bolsheviks. But that was twenty years earlier. As they were in no way prepared to counter the German big battalions, the stand of the Polish forces at Warsaw was all the more heroic.

Poland, the tinder-box of Europe, was overrun in twenty-seven days. Hitler and Stalin divided the nation amicably — the Red army had crossed into Poland on September 17 — true to the spirit of the non-aggression pact signed five weeks earlier, and the Polish government, including foreign minister Beck (desperately ill with cancer) fled first to Rumania before finally taking refuge in Britain.

For years the surly, enigmatic Beck had clung on to Hitler's coat tails in a bid to distract his attention from the vexed problem of the Danzig corridor. Not until the dismemberment of Czechoslovakia did he realise that the Fuhrer, intent on altering the status of Danzig, had played him for a fool. By then it was too late. And a new word, Blitzkrieg, was added to the newspeak of war.

* * *

The curtain raisers to the final drama were the ending of the Spanish Civil War in Franco's favour and Mussolini's invasion of Albania on Good Friday, April 7. Hitler renewed activities on his eastern frontier and Chamberlain announced the assurance of British and French support for Poland 'in the event of any action that clearly threatened her independence'. The problem was that having betrayed Czechoslovakia, what guarantees could Britain and France offer Poland, a country in a far more vulnerable position? Intense diplomatic exchanges took place between London and Paris while ordinary people wondered aloud why it was so important to go to war over Poland. Years of successive appeasement had almost destroyed faith and hope in Europe: Britain was inadequately armed and the French lacked the will to fight.

The Fuhrer, off to a flying start, resolute, implacable, spoke at Wilhelmshaven on April 1.

'They can make agreements,' he told the citizens, 'make declarations — as many as they like. But I don't trust pieces of paper; I trust you, my *volksgenossen*.

'We Germans have been the victims of the greatest breach of promise of all time. Let us see to it that our people may never again become easy to break up, so that no one in the world will ever threaten us again. Peace will be maintained or if necessary enforced; the people must be allowed to flourish and prosper.

'Twenty years ago the national socialist party was founded, an exceedingly small structure at the beginning. I want you to recall the distance covered since that time; the extent of the miracle performed. Have faith that by the very nature of our miraculous progress we can take the road ahead towards a great future for the people of Germany.'

His final words, said Linge, scribbling furiously, were drowned in a crescendo chorus of '*Sieg heil! Sieg heil! Sieg heil!*'

Viscount Halifax, following traditional British policy of keeping Europe divided, 'desired greater cooperation with Germany . . . We are determined to resist force while recognising the world's

111

desire to get on with the constructive work of building peace.'

On June 3, the Danzig senate made accusations against Polish customs inspectors. These were denied on June 10. On Saturday, August 5, the Poles sent a note protesting at Danzig's threat to refuse permission for the customs officers to carry out their work. This note was immediately rejected by Danzig as being not only provocative but also based on false rumours.

On Monday, August 7, the Fuhrer's private aircraft arrived at Danzig. Albert Forster, the local gauleiter and his propaganda chief, Herr Zaske, were to be flown for urgent talks with Hitler at Berchtesgaden.

According to Linge's surreptitious notes, the main topic of conversation was the alleged prosecution of the German minority in Poland.

Indulging in his usual broad flourishes, the Fuhrer emphasised that such treatment 'sickened him to his stomach. I will not tolerate one German being humiliated by these Polish savages. I'll teach them a lesson they'll never forget. If they want war I'll fling down the gauntlet. And as to their ally, Britain, history will hold her responsible. For years I've sought their friendship only to see every offer treated with contempt. If direct action leads to war then Germany has nothing to lose and Britain everything. I have no wish to wage war but at the same time I won't shrink from it. I promise you that Germany will emerge victorious just as she did under Frederick the Great' (whose personality was later described as aggressive, a diseased pseudo-intellectual with homosexual tendencies).

Hitler's original plan had been a German—Polish alliance against Russia. Therefore he limited his early demands to a return of Danzig to the Third Reich and to a road/rail link across the Polish corridor to East Prussia; guaranteeing in return to safeguard Poland's frontiers.

Beck refused. Instead he sent a note to Germany warning Hitler that Poland would react to any attempt to compromise her rights and interests by using such measures as she thought fit to adopt. Any intervention by the German government would be considered an act of aggression.

That did it. It was the opening Hitler had hoped for.

While Herr Forster, in Danzig, was asserting that 'nothing will be done on the German side to provoke a conflict' all kinds of 'provocations' were stage-managed from Berlin. The Fuhrer had decided to Germanise Poland; to subject the primitive Slavs to a superior German culture. 'And one false move by the Poles and I'll fall on them like lightning — with all the arms at my disposal.'

'That could lead to war,' said Carl Burckhardt, High Commissioner at Danzig, discussing the situation with Hitler at Berchtesgaden on August 11.

'If I have to wage war,' said Hitler, 'I'd rather do it today than tomorrow. But it won't be the Kaiser's war all over again; it'll be a fight to the finish, without mercy, up to the extreme limit.'

The Reich chiefs of staff suggested a breathing space of a year or two before another move was made.

'No. Everything I undertake is directed against Bolshevism. If the governments of Britain and France are too stupid or too blind to understand that, then I will try to come to an understanding with Stalin in order to smash the western powers first. After they have been defeated, I can turn against Russia.'

Further action would be delayed but only until he determined Stalin's attitude. Accordingly, Ribbentrop was ordered to prepare the ground with the Russian foreign minister, Molotov. For the time being any question of Russian perfidy and aggressiveness was out. It must be dialogue, detente and promises, promises.

*　　*　　*

Stalin, more than any other Bolshevik, had grasped the essence of Leninism: anything for the sake of absolute power. He spat, as Lenin himself put it, on purely Russian interests because the Soviet Union was merely the base for the inevitable world revolution. In Stalin's view, the importance of war as midwife for that revolution could scarcely be exaggerated.

Under his leadership, Russia had achieved a rapid transformation. By 1939, it was a military nation, a security-obsessed, secrecy-shrouded super-power in a state of preparedness for war. A massive land force protected its frontiers — more was better, most was best.

Prior to Munich, Stalin had offered assistance to Czechoslovakia. Excluded from the four-power agreement, he took it as a serious rebuff. That he was suffering from paranoia was still a well-kept secret, only revealed much later in his daughter's memoirs.

Hitler mistakenly judged Russia in the same terms as he did

113

America, believing it to be feeble and unstable: disintegrating through Bolshevism just as capitalist corruption was corroding America.

With war looming, Chamberlain thought it expedient to welcome the Soviets into the fold while at the same time proclaiming his detestation of Bolshevism. In France, Daladier sided with Chamberlain, though in a halfhearted fashion.

Stalin, deeply suspicious of their motives, made his position clear. He required substantial guarantees for his plans to dominate Finland, eastern Poland and the Baltic. Britain and France were equally determined not to give him what he wanted.

The Russian leader, driven by self-interest, then allowed his attention to be distracted by proposals from his 'deadliest and most fanatical enemy, Hitler.' With eastern Poland as the bait he signed a pact with Hitler who, having outbid the West, walked away with the contract.

One observation provides the cornerstone of this chapter: *The outbreak of World War II stemmed from the failure of Britain and France to reach an agreement with Russia — a failure that had its roots in Stalin's conviction of his revolutionary mission.*

Stalin later confirmed that he signed the agreement with Hitler as a result of his exclusion from Munich. He was convinced that the pact signed then was a concerted attempt by Britain and France to force Hitler into a German—Soviet conflict. And for him to enjoy the benefits of the dowry, it was not necessary to embrace the bride.

But as Britain's influence over events in Europe waned, it seemed that Chamberlain's pretensions waxed to right the balance. Having won acclaim for Munich — he had been presented with a villa in France — he sternly reprimanded Hitler, pointing out that the West was fully prepared to go to war for the corner of a foreign field that was Poland. At the same time, in a letter to the Fuhrer, he repeated his conviction 'that war between our two peoples would be the greatest calamity that could occur.'

Ambassador Henderson saw the Fuhrer at the Berghof on August 23 and found him in an excitable and uncompromising mood. He attacked the Poles, spoke of 100,000 German refugees from Poland, of the systematic persecution of the German minority. Why, some Germans had even been castrated.

114

Henderson admitted he had heard of one case, but the German in question 'was a sex maniac who had been treated as he deserved'.

'There wasn't just one case,' shouted Hitler (who was obviously incensed at this kind of sperm warfare), 'there were six!' He followed this with a tirade against Britain.

Hitler returned to Berlin on August 24 and spoke to the British ambassador again in the next day. 'I'm now fifty years old,' he told him. 'I'd prefer to wage war now rather than when I'm fifty-five or sixty.' Things would have been different in 1914 if he had been Chancellor then. He no longer believed in Mr Chamberlain and that was why he had been forced into an agreement with Russia. Nothing short of a complete change of Britain's policy towards Germany would convince him of a British desire for good relations.

It wasn't long before he was back on his topic of the moment: the Polish 'persecutions'. 'Do you realise that when Herr Ribbentrop was returning from Moscow he had to fly over the sea via Konigsberg to avoid being shot down by the Poles? They fire at every German aircraft that crosses their frontier.' He paused for a moment. 'There has also been yet another case of castration reported.'

Henderson had nothing to say.

'The only winner,' the Fuhrer went on, 'of another European war would be Japan. Now I am by nature an artist, not a politician and once the Polish question is settled I intend to live as an artist, not as a warmonger. I have no wish to turn Germany into a military barracks. Once the Polish question is resolved, I'll settle down.

'All I require for an agreement with Poland is a gesture from Britain that she won't be unreasonable.'

He emphasised the irrevocable determination of Germany 'never again to enter into conflict with Russia. 'The agreement with the Soviet Union was unconditional and signified a change in foreign policy which would last a very long time. Russia and Germany would never again take up arms against each other. Therefore if it came to war with Britain and France, Germany would no longer have to fight on two fronts.

Hitler repeated that he was 'a man of ad infinitum decisions by which I myself am bound. Immediately after I have solved the

German-Polish question, I will approach the British government with an offer.'

*   *   *

Earlier, with Ribbentrop in Moscow conducting negotiations, Linge recalled going to the telephone exchange at the Berghof a dozen times the day the pact was due to be signed (August 23). In the morning, as he carefully placed the chief's uniform on the bed, he summoned up the nerve to inquire respectfully why the agreement with Russia was so important.

The chief told him. 'I'm prepared to come to terms with anyone,' he said blandly, 'if the outcome means greater living space for Germany. The birthrate is showing a steady increase and it is my responsibility to ensure future generations of Germans have room in which to live and breathe and work. I'm fully aware that Stalin thinks he has struck some kind of a clever bargain with me, but as a result Poland is in the position where the best solution will be by force. I'm only fearful that at the last moment some interfering power will try to submit a plan for mediation.'

Once the Nazi-Soviet pact was signed, Hitler ordered champagne to celebrate. The toast was 'Father Stalin'. (As a prisoner, when Linge told his Russian captors about this, they refused to believe him.)

Hitler and his aides flew back to Berlin in time to meet his foreign minister at Tempelhof airport. As Ribbentrop descended from his plane the Fuhrer hurried along the runway towards him. And although he didn't break into a dance, Linge felt he was near it; maybe in his elation he gave a little skip-and-a-jump without being aware of it. He certainly did something entirely out of character. As Ribbentrop bowed before him, the chief put both arms exuberantly around the man and hugged him close.

Naturally, the foreign minister was delighted. While his mission — to make any offer, accept every demand — had been successful, he had no idea such a reception awaited him.

At a celebration dinner that night, he found himself the star of a small circle of intimates surrounding the Fuhrer. Losing no opportunity to press home to Hitler how clever he had been, he described the way the Russians had pressed pots of caviar and lavished plates of lobster on his aides; and had insisted on pouring glass after glass of vodka down their throats. It was as well he had warned the Germans not to overdo the booze, at least until the final negotiations were well out of the way. But even then it took a great deal of effort to hold glasses steady for the toast; a tribute from Stalin to the Reich Chancellor.

The chief was cock-a-hoop. By then he was well into his own private world; grappling with a fantasy that fed on itself, leaving him in the grip of even more powerful compulsions — the supreme war lord with the smell of death. It would be that way until the end.

Then Ribbentrop uttered a warning note. Stalin had taken him aside to emphasise how seriously he took the pact with Germany. 'I guarantee on my word of honour that Russia will not betray Germany. But remind your Fuhrer that while I wish him the best of luck with his wall of concrete to the west, I want to remind him of my wall in the east: the flesh and blood of 180 million Russians.'

For Hitler, it was a personal matter. He was happy to sign an agreement splitting Poland with Stalin; to turn a blind eye (temporarily) to Soviet activity in Finland and to applaud (ironically) the setting up of Red Army bases in Estonia, Latvia and Lithuania. Just so long as he was able to score off Britain and France and show them he meant business. The Russo-German pact agreed 'that the two countries bound themselves to refrain from any act of force, any aggressive action and any attack on one another, both singly or jointly with other powers.'

Henderson was back at the Chancellery on August 28 with a note from Chamberlain pointing out that 'a failure to reach a settlement with Poland could ruin the hopes of a better understanding between Britain and Germany . . . and might well plunge the whole world into war'.

The British ambassador stressed that Britain would never break her word, once given. Hitler's eyebrows shot up. 'What about Czechoslovakia?'

'In the old days,' said Henderson, ignoring the interruption, 'Germany's word had the same value. You might remember Marshall Blucher's message to his men at Waterloo: "Forward, my children, I've given my word to my brother Wellington; you can't wish me to break it"'.

'That was 125 years ago,' said Hitler. 'Poland today will never see reason with Britain and France backing her; the Poles think that even if they're defeated they'll recover more than they might lose thanks to your help.' He had to satisfy the demands of the German people. His army was fully prepared and eager for battle, the people united behind them.

'Well, you must choose between England and Poland.'

'I'm not bluffing. You people will make a great mistake if you think I am,' retorted Hitler.

'We are fully aware of the fact.' (Pause) 'We're not bluffing either.' (Not much, thought the Fuhrer) 'I realise this is the case.'

Chamberlain told the House of Commons on August 29 that the British people were ready for any eventuality. He thought their calm remarkable but then 'none of us has any doubt where our duty lies; there's no difference of opinion among us, no weakness of determination.'

But his Chancellor of the Exchequer, Sir John Simon, was at the same time trying to stop over £1,000,000,000 in gold being sent from Britain to America. The wealthy were anxious about their money.

His Minister of Labour, Ernest Brown, was on a sailing vacation, promising to return to London 'if the call came'. His Minister of Supply, at least, was still at his desk, though he was looking forward to 'snatching a couple of weeks mountaineering in Switzerland'. Mr Burgin never made it, not that year.

In Britain as a whole, a surprising number of people preferred Hitler's brand of fascism to the possibility of communist domination. Sava defined them as the type who hated the prospect of socialism so much, they'd rather be under a foreign government; 'usually middle class people with little money but a great deal of snobbery, a slightly higher education making them intolerant towards the working class. They feared that the outcome of a second war might mean a social revaluation, if not revolution. And then where would they stand?'

In France, in 1939, most people were apathetic if not openly defeatist. For them, occupation by the Germans was preferable to war.

In Berlin, despite a gloomy atmosphere, most people believed the Fuhrer would win out once again. On the night of August 29, as anxious crowds gathered on Wilhelmplatz, hoping for Hitler to appear, he was otherwise engaged. He sat at a table with

118

Goebbels, in a small night-club next door to the Metropole Theatre, halfway along Behrenstrasse.

The club specialised in nude cabaret and was equipped with private booths overlooking the floor show. The star attraction that night was a trio of hula dancers; solidly-built German girls shaking their hips in the Hawaiian manner and shedding straw skirts as they twirled round the stage. Pierre Huss, sitting with an informant over a bottle of champagne, noticed the two men in a corner booth, both in light raincoats with the collars pulled over their ears, while the booths on either side overflowed with big men in plain black suits.

'It's Hitler and Goebbels,' the informant whispered. 'They came in half an hour ago.'

Good heavens, thought Huss. So that's what they get up to after a hard day's work gambling for high stakes in Poland against the bids of Britain and France.

'You see, there can't be any danger of war,' said his informant, a girl dancer, 'They must be here to celebrate the end of the crisis.'

In fact, Hitler had handed Henderson a memo that evening at 7.30 and regardless of the outcome, his tanks were set to roll into Poland. The campaign had to be concluded before the rainy season, which usually began on October 15 and turned the roads into a quagmire. He believed the British and the French would play war games for a few weeks, and then after he'd finished in Poland, they'd be more than ready to make a deal. He was celebrating that night, certainly, but he was toasting war, not peace.

Hitler addressed the Reichstag on Friday, September 1. 'Germany has no interest in the west; we have no aims of any kind there for the future. We have concluded a pact with Russia which rules out forever any use of violence between us. Russia and Germany fought against one another in World War I. That shall and will not happen a second time.'

He drew their attention to his new uniform of field grey, complete with Iron Cross and wound stripe.

'I swear I will not take it off again until victory is secured, or I'll not survive the outcome . . . Should anything happen to me, my first successor is Party Comrade Goring; should anything happen to Goring, my next successor is Party Comrade Hess. Should anything happen to Hess, you'll have to sort out a new leader among yourselves.'

119

Mussolini, the gauleiter of Italy, as he was called in Munich, proposed another 'mini-Munich' in a bid to avert war. He had the feeling he was becoming something of a laughing stock, 'Any time the Fuhrer wants to occupy another country in Europe, he just sends me a message he intends to do it.'

France was only too willing to talk. Halifax submitted the Duce's suggestion to the British prime minister, but there was no reply. That evening Mussolini was told that London had cut all communications with Italy.

On September 3, Britain and France, compromised by the alliance with Poland, honoured their pledge.

When Hitler was handed their ultimatums, he remained unmoved, ignoring them both. Nothing now would turn him away from his dream: his depersonalisation of modern Germany; with the barriers between factory and barrack eliminated, the people cogs in a military machine of warrior workers, with metallic backbones and working parts of steel, united, armed, ready to obey, to answer the call in a drive towards the millenium, towards world leadership.

A note was handed to Henderson at 11.20 am by Ribbentrop, with a refusal of acceptance of the ultimatum. It stated 'that Britain had encouraged Poland to continue her criminal attitude, thus threatening the peace of Europe. They had rejected Signor Mussolini's peace proposal in spite of the German government's willingness to agree to it. The British government, therefore, bear the responsibility for all the unhappiness and misery which have now overtaken or are about to overtake many peoples.'

On the Sunday war was declared, the Fuhrer's special train left Berlin for the eastern front.

It consisted of fifteen carriages with two steam engines to haul it. The specially armoured train had been constructed by the great locomotive and armament firms of Borsig and Henschell. Hitler's carriage was made up of a bedroom, bathroom, office and a combined dining-conference room large enough to accommodate twelve people. Linge and a staff of two hundred occupied other adjoining carriages, and heavily-armoured defence vans were attached to the front and rear of the train. A complete telephone switchboard had been installed, through which the Fuhrer could be connected with any part of the world with which he was not at war. It was also equipped with ten telex machines which spilled out an endless stream of military and political communiqués. One coach was custom-built, a press car presented to press chief, Otto ('little Sir Echo') Dietrich by the Fuhrer on his birthday in 1938. It had radio links with the propaganda ministry, the official news agency DNB and Transocean, which handled Nazi copy abroad. Otto was able to keep his fingers firmly attached to the nation's pulse on Hitler's behalf; foreign broadcasts could be received and translated. Dietrich also supplied him with a daily worldwide press digest.

Hitler's life aboard the train was a crowded one. Apart from endless discussions, he continued to attend to the smallest detail of a wide variety of problems in the course of each day. He did effect one significant promotion in Poland. Rommel was made commandant of FHQ. He later gained command of an entire armoured unit.

On October 5, a victory parade was staged in Warsaw with the Fuhrer, his personal magnetism greater than ever, taking the salute. He stood motionless for over an hour as tank after tank rumbled along the bomb-cratered streets, proof that his armour had scarcely been dented by its first blitz campaign.

The entire centre of the city had been devastated by a two-day fury of German air raids, illustrating the overwhelming superiority of the dive bomber as the air artillery of the future.

From the day they declared war on Germany, Beck had urged Britain and France to take some action of a military nature to relieve the pressure on Poland. Their aircraft, he said, could draw off a considerable number of German bombers by creating a diversion in the west.

Why didn't such a diversion occur?

Why didn't Britain and France declare war on Russia when Stalin's army, like a pack of hyenas scenting blood, fell upon the carcass of Poland two weeks after they had declared war on Germany? A guarantee had been given to fight on Poland's behalf. Hitler was convinced the two countries lacked the will. Which was why he left only twenty-three divisions (with no armour) and a handful of aircraft to guard the west.

Although the French army was superior in numbers to the Wehrmacht based in the west, augmented by a British token army, it was said that it was not possible to advance overland; that

Germany had closed the Baltic to their navies; and that they lacked aircraft. In September, 1939, the Royal Air Force had 1,982 operational aircraft (480 bombers) and the French 1,112 (186 bombers). The Lufwaffe had 4,162 aircraft including 308 troop transports.

Why didn't Britain and France attack from the west the day Hitler invaded Poland? Mr Chamberlain, in a broadcast on September 4 to the German people, said: 'We are not fighting against you, the people for whom we have no bitter feeling, but against a tyrannous and foresworn regime.'

Hitler hadn't bombed Britain, so Chamberlain refrained from bombing Germany. Having declared war, Chamberlain had no idea how he proposed to win it.

And the French had decided that defence was the best form of attack. They sheltered behind the Maginot Line, hoping for a stalemate.

But when Hitler made his peace offer on October 6, Chamberlain stated (on October 12) that he was not prepared to accept peace terms which began with the absolution of the aggressor. This supplied the Fuhrer with his alibi: having rejected the hand of peace, Chamberlain was deliberately choosing war.

For nine months, until Hitler invaded France, Chamberlain and his French counterparts did nothing to prepare for an attack they knew was imminent. More was done in a few weeks by Churchill than in almost a year of 'passive' war.

*   *   *

According to the *New York Times*, October 4, 1939, the only attack made by Germany was on the 'bad taste of Britain's first song of World War II,' *We're Going to Hang Out the Washing on the Siegfried Line*. In a Berlin newscast the announcer pointed out that it 'was not a soldier's song because soldier's don't brag. It wasn't written in a military camp but by Jewish scribes of the BBC. The Siegfried Line is still there and all the bragging of the BBC will not loosen one stone. The Englishmen's washing will be very dirty indeed before it can be hung out on the Line. A parcel-post package from mother might be more satisfactory.'

The lyric was in fact, written by songwriter Jimmy Kennedy,

an Irishman serving with the Royal Artillery and stationed at the time on an anti-aircraft gun battery.

*   *   *

On the evening of May 10, 1940, Chamberlain broadcast the news of his resignation. Next morning, it was not his successor, Churchill, who grabbed the headlines. Hitler was the main cause for comment. The Wehrmacht had invaded Belgium, Holland and France.

There is a growing belief that Hitler has one last political trick up his sleeve, namely, to let the Soviets advance so far in the west that the menace of Hitlerism will be overshadowed by the threat of Bolshevism. He can then promise the allies to repel the Russians, given peace and material support.

War correspondent. 1940

It was Hitler's desire to please, to create a sensation, to make himself the cynosure of all eyes that was strong enough to charm Unity Mitford, a naive member of the British nobility. This desire to please was hysterical in origin. It was a torment to him and made him a torment to others as he challenged them, fought for their favours or terrorised them.

Rudolf Olden

CHAPTER ELEVEN

It was in November, 1939 that Unity Mitford unwittingly saved Hitler's life.

After she had shot herself in the head the day war was declared, she was placed in a private room in Munich's Chirurgische Universitats Clinic. Surgeons located the bullet but because of its location near the brain were unable to remove it.

At the time, Hitler was fully occupied in Poland and had set up mobile headquarters at Gogolin. Told of the suicide bid, he telephoned Munich for news. As his train shunted from Polzin to Illnau to Goddentow-Lanz, he continued to phone the clinic to inquire about Unity.

Back in Berlin, on September 26, he ordered her flat in Munich to be sealed, and made arrangements for storage of her furniture. He also told Schaub, then in Munich, that he would be responsible for all medical bills for Miss Mitford.

On November 8, he travelled south to make his annual speech at the Burgerbraukeller, commemmorating his misadventures in the Munich putsch of 1923. Schaub was ordered to inform the clinic that the Fuhrer would be calling in on his way to the Beer Hall. It was his first and only visit.

Linge was with him, carrying a large bunch of chrysanthemums in one gloved hand.

The arrival of Hitler and his party caused something of a stir at the hospital, as the nursing staff, like blue and white beetles, scuttled for cover before the well-shod boots of Herr Reichskanzler's bodyguard.

He sat at the bedside for fifteen minutes. If there was any stirring of compassion he never showed it, sitting motionless, with hooded eyes and a grim smile, as reticent as a mole.

Lowering his mouth close to Unity's bandaged head he spoke softly. 'So, how do you feel?'

126

Schaub and Hauptsturmfuhrer Linge pretended to study the lime trees outside the window.

Unity stared at the chief for several minutes. He hemmed and cleared his throat.

'I'm a little better,' she whispered. 'Thank you.'

What did she wish to do? Stay in Germany or return to England? There was another long pause.

'England.'

Good, he said. When she felt strong enough to travel, he'd arrange for an ambulance train to take her to Switzerland. Abruptly, he rose to his feet and with an uncertain wave of his hand left the room.

It was the end of the relationship. He never saw her again.

He was at the Burgerbraukeller much earlier than expected. Somehow, his uncanny sense of self-preservation had prompted him to alter the schedule in order to catch the 9.30 pm train back to Berlin. After his speech, instead of chatting over mugs of beer as was customary, his group immediately left the hall.

If he had stayed at Unity's bedside a further ten minutes, the chances were he'd still have been in the Beer Hall when a bomb exploded, killing eight party comrades and seriously wounding another sixty. The explosion occurred twelve minutes after Hitler had driven away.

The brief life of the upper-class English girl 'who behaved in a rather foolish way', her rise and fall, has been viewed from all sides and many angles, her private problems exposed so often they have become public property. And with her well-documented inclination towards morbid adventure, her delicately balanced personality, she seems almost fated to have had a 'destiny'.

The only woman delegate — at nineteen — of Mosley's British Union of Fascists at Nuremberg in 1933, as soon as she clapped eyes on Hitler, all her inarticulate longings and flesh-tingling aspirations crystallised. Knowing nothing of his borderline existence between idealism and criminality, she 'knew from that moment there was no one in the world she would rather meet'.

Hitler, it appears, enjoyed her company. She was all of those things that fascinated him: a highly-sensitive female, an aristocrat and petulantly immature. She also closely resembled Geli Raubal. She spoke her mind, in market contrast to most German women. Hitler was intrigued by her robust and fluent vocabulary and she was able to satisfy his curiosity about the members of the British upper crust.

Highly opinionated, harbouring illusions of superiority, indifferent to the pain of others, constantly looking for strenuous ways of showing off, she was probably just another human being wanting to be loved. If she couldn't be loved, the next best thing was to be admired.

While most of the mellowed hooligans constituting the party elite fawned over her in front of the chief, privately they sniggered at her. The SS exploited her. There wasn't a girl in the *Bund Deutscher Madchen* who wouldn't have thrown acid in her face.

For reasons that are somewhat obscure and in a time when few women discussed their sexual exploits, Unity confessed that she had slept with Victor Lutze, the chief of the SA.

Perhaps it was Lutze's neat party trick that captivated her. Taking a glass of champagne, he would reach up to his left eye, neatly remove the artificial eyeball and drop it into the wine. He then stirred the drink and drained the glass, opening his mouth wide to show he had swallowed the eye. A moment later he made as though to belch and out it came.

Had she been Hitler's mistress?

No, says Linge unequivocally, 'She never went to bed with him.' The connection between them had been, for some time, strong but chaste, above sex.

The Fuhrer's desires didn't always find, or indeed attempt to find, straightforward sensual outlets. In the event it was unlikely that he'd have been able to satisfy her. He enjoyed having her sit at his feet so that he could caress her hair (while deftly probing the roots of her insecurity, no doubt).

Certainly, once the relationship was over, she was by then so bent out of shape there was no way anyone could bend her back again.

As the political situation with Britain deteriorated, Hitler's feelings for her tapered off. By the end of August he had begun to view the girl with disaffection and increasing indifference. It had been after all, from his point of view, a very minor conquest.

*   *   *

An interesting sidelight on the Mitfords concerns the youngest sister, Deborah, who married a son of the Duke of Devonshire

128

during World War II. When her husband's older brother, the Marquess of Hartington, was killed in Normandy, Deborah's husband was next in line to succeed the Duke. Hartington had married Kathleen Kennedy, the late John F. Kennedy's sister. She died in an aircraft accident in the South of France in 1948. If Hitler had married Unity Mitford, as many believed he might, he would have become, for a short time, a relative by marriage of the future President of the United States.

*   *   *

Linge describes how news of the bomb outrage reached them when the Fuhrer's train drew into Nuremberg station. Hitler seemed almost excited at the thought of his narrow escape. Providence had chipped in again in the nick of time.

Orders were given to the Nuremberg police chief to get on to Himmler right away. Whoever was responsible for planting the bomb in the Beer Hall had to be caught as soon as possible. And before the train was allowed to continue its journey the chief insisted on sending messages of condolence to the relatives of the victims.

In the forbiddingly grim building, 8 Prinz Albrechtstrasse, Berlin, that housed the headquarters of Heinrich Himmler, the Gestapo, the SS, Counter-espionage, Intelligence, all worked flat out on a twenty-four hour day. And they worked swiftly and efficiently.

Shortly after the Fuhrer was back in town, he was handed a full report. As a result of information received, a civilian had been intercepted at the Swiss border while attempting to leave the country. Two Britishers, Best and Stevens, had also been kidnapped by the Gestapo and taken to headquarters for questioning.

Originally, Himmler stated categorically that the bomb that had killed the *kameraden* in the Burgerbraukeller had been placed by the civilian, George Elser, but that the attempt had been organised by Best and Stevens. They had hired Elser to carry out the plan to kill Hitler.

Although the *Beobachter* published this version of events, Linge — who was present when Himmler made a further report — believed that Elser alone had been responsible for the explosion; no one else was involved. The man, a left-wing carpenter, saw it as a way in which he could make himself world-famous, as the communist who had killed the Fuhrer.

Elser confessed that a few days before the annual reunion he had sneaked into the Beer Hall with his homemade bomb and planted it behind the pillar. It had a timing device attached and could also be exploded by means of an electric switch.

The Fuhrer heard the evidence and studied the man's dossier at great length. Finding it hard to believe that the assassination attempt had been the work of one man alone, he favoured Himmler's suggestion that the two Englishmen had been involved. Finally, he gave orders for Elser to be supplied with the same components he had purportedly employed in manufacturing his bomb. The valet believed the idea was to test Elser; to find out if he was capable of making such a device. Under the bleak eyes of the Gestapo, he did. Elser was then taken to Sachsenhausen concentration camp where, says Linge, he was given workshop facilities. The chief apparently felt the man's expertise might as well be concentrated on experimenting with similar devices, such as anti-personnel bombs and booby traps useful for wartime sabotage. Elser cheerfully settled down to work, experimenting with even more 'hellish machines', until he was eventually transferred to Dachau. In the spring of 1945 it was said that Elser had been killed during an air raid. In fact, in April of that year, the Gestapo murdered him.

Best and Stevens were also imprisoned at Sachsenhausen until, on April 8, 1945 they were transferred to Dachau, together with such luminaries as General von Falkenhausen, Fritz Thyssen and his wife, Leon Blum and Hjalmar Schacht. The Britishers survived the war.

Deputy leader Hess stood in for the Fuhrer at the funeral of the dead *kameraden*, referring during the service to 'the miracle of the leader's deliverance. It has served to enhance our belief in him,' he told the weeping relatives. 'Providence spared him before and Providence will protect him in the future because of the need for the continuance of his great crusade. To our enemies we cry out, "You hoped to take the Fuhrer from us but you have only succeeded in drawing us even closer to him. You wanted to weaken us but you have only made us stronger"'.

His speech was like himself, painfully dull. He never was at ease in public, preferring to be on his own. He would sit motionless for hours at a time, lips clamped together, chin cupped in his hands, a faraway look in his eyes, dreaming his dreams of a national socialist Utopia.

Himmler was very much the man of the moment, the Fuhrer being full of gratitude at the way he had so promptly dealt with the bomb plot. The Reichsfuhrer was given greater powers in order to deal with Hitler's enemies.

Already the librettist of fear, anguish, torture and death, the flabby little crackpot set to work to eradicate dissidents, trouble-makers and 'internal enemies' in the newly acquired territories. He also put in motion his personal programme for organising and resettling aliens in Greater Germany. Or, as Ribbentrop put it — in a discussion with Ciano — 'there was a project under way to round up the Jews of Czechoslovakia and Poland and send them to Madagascar'.

In October 1939 the national socialist publication *Inner Front* carried an editorial extending the application of the racial doctrine from Jews to all subject races: 'We must guard the strict separation of blood from the start. We do not wish to become imperious because greater values live in our people than in others. We must never forget that a greater Reich can be led only by a master nation and that a master right is based at all times upon better blood.'

This article followed a series of convictions when sentences of between seven and fifteen years hard labour were imposed on German women for having had sexual intercourse with Polish prisoners of war.

'The Pole has no equal rights; he is a member of his people and that people are the enemy. The German judge who expresses this in his sentences obeys the law of his inner voice, which creation gave to our people as well.'

Like all levelling processes, the German process levelled down, not up.

The marked differentiation between the sexes was inherent in the Nazi *gleichschaltung* — ('co-ordination, equalisation, uniformity') — the application of the goosestep to politics, economics and realms of mind, spirit and soul.

And when news of a secret programme leaked out: planned euthanasia of the mentally sick, the only Germans to openly express disquiet were the clergy. Their protests went unheeded. Between January, 1940 and August, 1941 70,000 were put to death.

131

Shortly before 10 pm on May 28, 1948 Unity Mitford's brief, melancholy rite of passage towards maturity ended — in the West Highland Cottage Hospital at Oban.

Her health had deteriorated since her return from Germany in January 1940. The bullet lodged in her skull affected her sense of balance, she walked with a limp and was incontinent. The cause of death was described as 'purulent meningitis; cerebral abcess; old gunshot wound'.

The Fuhrer continued to pay for the storage of her furniture in Munich until he died in April 1945.

PART TWO

The political papers of Hore-Belisha (of 'beacon fame'), Secretary of State for War in 1939, were sold in March 1985 for £18,000.

They shed light on the bitter political controversy which raged after his dismissal by Chamberlain in 1940. Hore-Belisha had attempted to eliminate the '1914-18 mentality', the obsession with India and the army concept of "Buggins's turn" in preferment. He was finally sacked after expressing alarm over the defences of the British Expeditionary Forces under Lord Gort.

News Item. March, 1985

Goring was commanded to draw up plans for a mass attack on Britain. After careful consideration of all factors, the air chief told Hitler that such an attack would only be successful if Germany possessed air bases in Belgium. Hitler then ordered Halder to map out a plan of attack against Belgium. Halder returned to Hitler within a few days and declared he could not recommend such an operation and offered his resignation. The resignation was refused.

News Item. November, 1939

Hitler, talking to Brauschitsch, 'screamed that he knew very well the generals were planning something (a march on Berlin) other than the offensive he had ordered (an attack on France)'. Though he knew nothing of the kind, with so mediumistic a man as Hitler, this is to be doubted.

Walter Gorlitz, German historian

CHAPTER TWELVE

Early in the morning of Monday, June 24, 1940 four black Mercedes cars passed through the Porte de Clichy and headed for that notable landmark, the Eiffel Tower.

Paris at 6 am was a dead city of empty streets, closed shops and shuttered cafés. Only the newly risen sun showed signs of life, as it reflected in the windows of the ministries and mansions of the Quai d'Orsay, making it appear that the Left Bank was in flames.

The convoy travelled south-west, crossing the Seine on to the avenue Bosquet, skirting the Champ de Mars, before turning into the courtyard of the massive church of St Louis des Invalides. The first car held Hitler, Keitel, Dietrich, Amman and Linge; the others were occupied by members of the Elite Guard. They were out of their cars before the leading limousine stopped, ready to form a protective half-circle around it. Linge was the first to alight, having travelled beside the driver, Kempka. The Fuhrer, in a fawn raincoat, cap pulled down, placed his right leg gingerly on the cobblestones. It had been a long, hot drive; his body was stiff from inaction.

Two white-gloved Waffen NCOs, on sentry duty, slammed their rifles in salute. Hitler, lightheaded from exhaustion, nodded vacantly, peering over their shoulders at the Ecole Militaire, thinking of the man he had come to honour, he whose political ideas for Europe had inspired his own early flights of fancy into supernationalism.

For the Fuhrer this was more than a pilgrimage; it was a dream come true. The leader of the Third Reich, whose armies were sweeping through Europe, had come to visit Napoleon; after Frederick the Great, the soldier he most admired, but whose military mistakes he had sworn to avoid.

Dietrich, Baedeker to hand, was master-minding the visit. He led the way up the worn, stone steps into the vaulted antechamber,

136

followed by the bodyguard. To them it was just another boring monument, similar to others they'd seen in Rome, Vienna, Prague and Warsaw. Hands stayed close to sidearms as their eyes roved around, peering into dim corners, up into the arched roof — all of it was routine, for they had had constant practice. None of them spoke a word as they took up positions in the background and tried not to cough or sneeze or breathe too hard. Hitler stood by the marble balustrade, looking down at the tomb, cap still on his head, mouth clamped shut, face waxen and contracted by the effort of concealing his emotions.

It was Dietrich who broke the silence, reading from his guide book. He related how Napoleon's body, brought back from St Helena, had been dressed in the green uniform of the Chasseurs de la Garde and encased in six coffins, one inside the other. The first was iron, the second mahogany, two were made of lead, one of ebony and the outer case was of oak.

The sarcophagus (made of red granite) was presented by Czar Nicholas I; the pedestal (green granite from the Vosges) had been placed there in 1840. The twelve statues of Victories that framed the tomb were sculpted by Pradier.

Linge, the constant presence in the shadows, wondered whether Dietrich would ever stop speaking.

'They've made a mistake.' Hitler's voice sounded loud under the golden dome. 'The tomb should never have been put below eye-level. People should be able to look up, to be overwhelmed by the size of the memorial. This was a great man; he should have had a greater monument.'

He nodded impatiently down at the tomb. 'I'll not make such a mistake,' he said, speaking to no one in particular. 'I'll keep a hold on the people long after I've passed on. So great a monument will be built to my memory that people who see it will never forget. In a thousand years they'll remember and speak in awed tones of the Fuhrer who made all things possible.'

Dietrich led him around the balustrade to the open door of the church, where Napoleon's battle standards were displayed. Hitler folded his arms but didn't enter the church. He stood, staring disdainfully at the far altar for a moment before retracing his steps down into the courtyard. Before he re-entered his car, Dietrich drew his attention to the bronze cannon outside the Dome des Invalides, captured during the Napoleonic wars. (Five years later, two

137

German Panther tanks were added to the collection, captured by General Leclerc in the Vosges)

The Fuhrer would be back to make his formal visit to Paris a few days later, but this private pilgrimage was something set apart, ordained by Providence. 'It was,' he told Hoffman later, 'the greatest and finest moment of my life when I stood next to *mein lieber* Napoleon's tomb.'

*   *   *

Despite Ribbentrop's visit to Paris in December 1938 — made to sign an agreement binding France and Germany to keep the peace for ten years — Hitler's activities in Europe did little to encourage France in the belief that the two nations could live together as good neighbours.

When the German foreign minister returned to Berlin, he looked even more hollow-eyed that usual despite his exultant announcement. 'Mein-Fuhrer, you can march whenever you like. The British will reject conscription. The French will refuse to make sacrifices.'

He was right about the French.

He also had some firsthand tittle-tattle to impart on the Byzantine intrigues of French cabinet ministers.

How, for instance, prime minister Daladier, the provincial 'bull of Vaucluse', was reputed to take more notice of his mistress, the Marquise Marie Louise d'Uzes, than he did of his political advisers. A close friend since the death of the premier's wife, the Marquise (her own family was prominent in the sardine industry) was married to the grandson of the Duchess d'Uze. How Reynaud — who was to succeed Daladier — although ruthless in his economic strategy, seemed to be putty in the exquisitely manicured hands of the Countess Helene de Partes. They had been lovers for twenty years. (The Countess was killed in a car accident near St Maxime in 1940). He told how the leader of the opposition Socialist party, Leon Blum, would be no problem. He was well-disposed towards Germany; praised by Goebbels' *Angriff* paper, which cited his fine qualities 'as an inheritance from his mother'. But he did possess one or two flaws as far as the Fuhrer was concerned. He was a freemason. And Jewish. As for the French foreign minister, Bonnet, he was proud of his close friendship with Abetz, who organised the Franco-German Youth Alliance (as a front for fifth-column activities).

Abetz became German ambassador in Paris once the Vichy government was established.

When Hitler wanted to know how Ribbentrop came by his information, his deputy Hess's own private intelligence service, *Verbindungsstab*, supplied the answer.

Verbindungsstab acted both as a clearing house for controlling foreign collaborators and as a supply source for the Fuhrer concerning the private lives of his Reichministers. And it revealed that while Herr Ribbentrop had been lavishly entertained in Paris by Bonnet, his wife, the ravishing Odette — who made up in looks and personality for her grotesque husband — had been even more hospitable. For Joachim she had proved to be, in every way, a gift from heaven.

It was she who'd given him the confidential lowdown on the private lives of Bonnet's fellow ministers, together with other items of interest, such as her husband's financial trickery with the Lazard Bank.

After Munich, foreign minister Bonnet had been a staunch believer in continued appeasement. After the invasion of Czechoslovakia he did a quick about-turn, enthusiastically supporting Daladier's doctrine of foreign policy, announced on June 4, 1939 to the Radical Socialist Party's executive: 'If people (meaning Herr Hitler) think that they can menace the balance of power in Europe, we're justified in resolutely opposing such adventures. We say "no" to aggression, "no" to autarchic tyranny, "no" to ideological fanaticism, "no" to demands submitted on the pretext of supposed vital living spaces, and we say "no" to all that is violent and brutal. For the same reason, we say "yes" to all just and constructive proposals.'

But by then it was too late.

*   *   *

At Nuremberg, Ribbentrop denied he had said that Britain wouldn't fight. 'I said she would. Always there were violent arguments with the Fuhrer on this point.'

*   *   *

The story of the blitzkrieg from Belgium to Abbeville and the coast is now history; how the BEF, the Belgians and two French armies were cut off from the rest of the allied forces and trapped; how Belgium surrendered.

From 1920 until 1936 Belgium had been France's ally. But after Hitler occupied the Rhineland, Belgium decided to go back to her pre-World War I policy of neutrality, guaranteed by Germany. It proved to be a fatal decision. France failed to understand how it changed her own defensive position and had neglected to extend the Maginot Line along the Belgian frontier to the coast.

Linge recalled that after the German armies had walked around the Line at Sedan — where the French had also been defeated in 1870 — the Fuhrer forecast the end of the old static type of defence; trench warfare, he proclaimed, was a thing of the past. His swift-moving tanks then headed for Boulogne to prove the point.

One French officer had made much the same forecast five years earlier. The French army, he argued, should form an elite body of professionals capable of rapid mobility, operating in tanks and armoured cars, possessing superior fire power, and supported by aircraft. But chief of the general staff, Weygand, wrote: 'Nothing of that nature needs to be created. It already exists.'

The officer, Colonel de Gaulle, was a tank commander with the Fifth army in Alsace. On May 15, 1940, he was given command of the Fourth armoured division — the First, Second and Third had all been annihilated.

During the fighting at Abbeville he was promoted to temporary brigadier-general, at forty-nine, the youngest general in the French army. Appointed to a cabinet post under Reynaud on June 5, he soon realised that Petain intended to surrender and flew to London. He saw nothing of France for four years.

On August 3, the Petain government condemned him to death.

Reynaud, broadcasting on May 28 blamed the collapse of France on the lack of support from the Belgians, who surrendered suddenly and unconditionally in the middle of the battle, without warning either the French or the British.

In fact, Leopold (who died on September 25, 1983), *had* warned the allies and his army fought to the last possible moment to give the BEF 48 hours in which to reach Dunkirk. One factor of the King's decision not to flee to London was his hope that he would be regarded by the world as a prisoner of war, even though a palace was placed at his disposal by the Germans.

The Fuhrer, however, preferred to treat him as an ally and supplied a German aide, Colonel Kiewitz.

Hitler's policy of dividing the Flemish and French-speaking Belgians eventually led to violence which still persists — consequences of more importance to Belgian history than the sorry events of 1940. It was mainly the Flemish who collaborated with the German overlords. Leopold's wife was Flemish and was therefore looked upon as a collaborationist.

Enjoying a surprising degree of freedom, Leopold began openly criticising the Third Reich's political system, forcing the occupation commanders to treat him more as an adversary than an ally.

Hitler shrugged off the critical comments. 'The Belgian merely confirms something I've felt for many years. He runs true to type, a petty monarch by an accident of birth; another nonentity believing he can achieve a place in history by stirring up trouble; treating anyone who is genuinely prepared to befriend him like dirt. They're all the same, these people.'

Kiewitz, formerly a regular guest at the Berghof dinner table, occcasionally seated next to the chief, found himself persona non grata. The Fuhrer felt he had been brainwashed by the Belgian King.

Hitler's goal was Paris, not Brussels. Overruling his High Command, he ordered his armies to keep up the momentum for the drive south.

With the completion of the Dunkirk evacuation on June 4, the long occupation of France began.

On the subject of Dunkirk, Linge has a divergent point of view. It was the Fuhrer, not Runstedt, who gave the direct order to halt the advance, so as to prevent his armoured divisions from moving further forward. Hitler supplied an explanation at the end of the campaign.

'In Dunkirk was the remnants of a once great army, a handful of regiments without weapons, leadership and initiative. Utterly demoralised, they returned to Britain even less well organised than when they set out. To me, they were a terminally ill torso, lacking arms and legs, waiting to be lifted home. Soon, I know, there will be negotiations for peace.'

It was inaccurate, said the valet, for historians to write that 'the whole weight of the German army was flung against the retreating British . . .' It was the Fuhrer's foresight alone that saved their skins.

141

Just as it was his military genius and initiative that contributed to the Wehrmacht's success, so enabling his forces to achieve victory without heavy losses.

'Do whatever is necessary,' Hitler had urged his field commanders, 'to keep up the momentum by staying mobile, avoiding anything approaching trench warfare. In that way you will prevent our divisions being wasted unnecessarily.' As to Britain, even if she did refuse his peace diktat, 'We can go after them any time we like and make an end to it.'

Paris fell in mid-June, undefended, abandoned by the government. On June 16, Reynaud resigned as premier and the 84-year-old Petain took over.

Mussolini had declared war on France a week earlier on June 10, wanting to gain the spoils promised Italy in 1914: Nice, Tunis, Corsica and a substantial slice of the Croation/Dalmatian coast.

During Italy's nine month's neutrality in the first war, the Austro-German alliance sought her help by offering the same territories. The Croatian and Dalmatian coasts had harboured Italian communities since the days of the Venetian republic.

*   *   *

On June 20, the Duke of Windsor, a major-general with the British Military Mission at French GHQ, crossed into neutral Spain with his wife. She had a Jewish connection: her former husband, Ernest Simpson, was the son of a Dublin Jew, Leon Solomon. The Duke hoped to avoid capture by the Germans or internment by the defeated French.

In Spain, his main concern was for his property and he used influential Spanish diplomats to beg a favour of his former kingdom's enemies: would the German and Italian governments please ensure that a special guard was placed on both his houses — in Paris and on the French Riviera?

Linge says he never again saw Hitler as merry as he appeared to be when the French surrendered.

In the hut that served as his HQ at Bruly-de-Peche, the chief was on the top of his form, slapping himself delightedly on the knee, continually praising his invincible troops — it was indeed a formidable triumph for him.

The valet recalled the warm June afternoon when, accompanied by Hess and Ribbentrop, wearing his Iron Cross, Hitler was driven to Compiegne to witness the formal surrender in the same railway carriage in which Germany had struck her colours in 1918 and had accepted the armistice diktat.

They travelled along dusty roads, past miles of refugees heading back to Paris, past roadside graves surmounted by rifles, on top of them French helmets, past abandoned cannon and personal belongings. And once, in the Forest of Compiegne, Linge was keenly aware of the scent of rotting flesh.

The Fuhrer's standard flew from a flagpole, guarded by two sentries. Foch's dining car had been placed in the same spot as it stood in November 11, 1918.

It was 3.15 pm when Hitler, arms folded across his chest, marched over to examine the memorial stone beside the clearing: 'Here . . . was vanquished the criminal insolence of the German Empire by a free people whom it sought to victimise.'

At 3.20, the French delegation arrived, headed by General Huntziger. The Fuhrer entered the carriage with Goring, Keitel, Rader and Brauchitsch and listened as Keitel read out the preliminary terms of the agreement. Then he left the carriage.

As he stepped out into the sunshine, the German army band struck up the Deutschland *lieb* in his honour. Hitler led the way along the wooded avenue towards the waiting cars.

After the armistice, the dining car was shipped to Berlin — to be destroyed during an allied air raid in 1943. The monument, half a mile from the forest clearing, and commemorating the return of Alsace Lorraine to France was, on Hitler's orders, demolished.

The broadcast of the proceedings on German radio ended with Germany's answer to *We're Going to Hang Out Our Washing on the Siegfried Line: Wir Fahren Gegen Engelland* (We March Against England). The song, said the Reich Music Council, had to be taken seriously. They issued an order that it must not be played as a dance number.

In the evening, back at Bruly-de-Peche, Linge was told to break open the champagne so that the chief's glorious achievement could be suitably celebrated in the wine of the fallen country.

*   *   *

Three days after the armistice Hitler moved his headquarters to Tannenberg, on the Kniebis in the Black Forest. Perhaps feeling he was entitled to a small vacation, Hitler spent some time visiting the battlefields of World War I with his former sergeant, Max Amman. They set off in the Mercedes each morning, visiting Strasbourg, inspecting the damage done by shelling to the Maginot Line; returning each night, remembered Linge, 'to the damp and dreary bunkers at Tannenberg'.

For the generals, kicking their heels at FHQ, there was little to occupy their minds. Most of them spent the time sitting in one of the two village taverns in which they were billeted, knocking back quantities of *Erdbeerbowle*, a delicious iced punch garnished with wild strawberries.

On July 6, the Fuhrer returned to Berlin. He was by then less than euphoric — the British refusal to negotiate had disrupted the even tenor of his life, adding a dimension to the situation that threatened to put him in a most awkward position.

For once, the supreme war lord faltered.

With his sights set on Russia, he needed Churchill breathing down his neck about as much as Julius Caesar needed the lean and hungry Cassius.

The generals, when called upon, seemed even more reluctant to face facts than their commander-in-chief. Halder, for example, 'was greatly puzzled, like the Fuhrer, by Britain's unwillingness to make peace.'

Hitler, after all, had not intended to conquer Britain. To him it was nothing more than a small archipelago set in the German Ocean; all he asked was that it should keep its nose out of Europe. Otherwise, it faced elimination as a possible base from which war against Germany could be waged.

'I have no interest,' he told the Reichstag on July 19, 'in smashing whatever's left of the British Empire — that might prove too big a bite even for the Reich to swallow. And in that eventuality, Stalin would be banging on the door, demanding his share of the cake, and he could gulp India down in a single mouthful.'

He appealed once again 'to reason and common sense in England, speaking as the victor (in the name of reason). Why can't the British see they would have peace on such favourable terms they'd be staggered by the magnanimity I would display? I've no intention of laying a finger on their precious navy. No one knows better than your leader how sensitive an issue that is. They'd continue to wage war if I so much as asked for one small minesweeper. But I *would* seek the return of our colonies.' He was told the British government planned to fly to Canada to continue the war in the event of an invasion, while the people would have to stay in Britain. 'For those people, the suffering is just beginning.'

The Reichstag meeting was briefly interrupted to allow the Fuhrer to award field marshal's batons to Brauchitsch, Keitel, Runstedt, Bock, Leeb, List, Kluge, Witzleben and Reichenau; for the Lufwaffe: Milch, Sperlle and Kesselring. Goring was promoted to Reich Marshal of Greater Germany and awarded the Grand Cross (of the Iron Cross order); Halder was made a full general.

Linge understood the chief's point of view and felt there was a good deal to be said for it. If he was going to be stabbed in the back, Hitler wanted to keep his High Command sweet. That way he might sleep more soundly in his bed.

Victory in battle still left him haunted by the ghosts of self-doubt. Believing himself to be his own agent of retribution, he would continue secretly to imagine that for every triumph, fate would exact a massive penalty.

Goring was a help. Reading his leader better than anyone, the Reich Marshal was able tactfully to lead him along the path towards a solution of his private conflicts. He was still the Fuhrer, unchallenged, the centre of the universe, accepted by the Fatherland as an infallible divinity; able to mobilise the people's energies, ready to lead them on to more miraculous victories.

As to Britain, he could leave that to the Lufwaffe, Goring's air force. Within a short time the ports, military bases, industries, cities would all be destroyed — anything, in fact, that stood in the way of the Fuhrer's plans. And after all, much had already been accomplished; and in so short a space of time.

The chief listened attentively, poring over the latest intelligence reports with him. And was reassured.

All would be well as long as he was able to give full attention to the problem of Russia — and keep one eye on the Mediterranean. At all costs, he had to avoid a two-front war.

He was sufficiently optimistic to be able to tell a High Command conference on July 31 that 'Britain's only hope now lies with Russia and America. If the hope in Russia dies, then the hope in America will also die. The elimination of Russia as a threat will increase a hundredfold Japan's influence in the far east.'

Allowing himself, as always, to be led by intuition rather than reason, Hitler had overlooked a fundamental principle of war: when possible, an army on the run should be pursued.

On the surface, like Thomas More, he emerged (from 1940) with the stoic image he presented so doggedly to the world — the leader in control, master of himself and his followers. But it would eventually act like a boomerang. The weak link in the chain lay in the quality of the relationship between Hitler and his chiefs of staff. As a result of his arbitrary outlook, his undoubted ability in the art of war was hopelessly marred by an arrogant unwillingness to placate his generals. In this sense, he was unfit to fight a war. The wise leader is one who understands the need to compromise with his field commanders, particularly when so many of them regarded him as ignorant, superstitious and largely uneducated. Unquestionably, this lack of solidarity was responsible for the collapse of the regime at the time of its greatest strain. It also led, finally, to what is now regarded as a life-and-death campaign; a struggle between two opposing systems of government with vastly different social, political and economic outlooks. In the last analysis, the result will eventually spell the destruction of the present precarious balance of power, and will determine the future of the world, perhaps leading to a catastrophe of inconceivable dimensions.

'One would like to think,' wrote Barbara Tuchman, 'that historical factors were more rooted in natural law, less haphazard in scope, than the chance character of a minor individual who was neither heroic nor demonic. But history is not law-abiding or orderly and will often respond to a breeze as carelessly as a leaf upon a lake.'

When the Wehrmacht cracked open Holland, Belgium and France like ripe walnuts, the first obstacle to national socialist world revolution seemed to be removed, leading to the final goal, world rule by the German race.

Speer would have disagreed. Years later he expressed his doubts.

'The war,' wrote Hitler's onetime armaments chief, 'had in a sense been lost by the victories of 1940. It might have been better for Germany to have had a Dunkirk at the outset to spur her energies.'

*   *   *

Hitler enjoyed the support of Germany as long as the Fatherland, geared for war, stayed dominant. Once the dream of supremacy was shattered by the events of World War II, the fervour quickly waned. None of the theories of national socialism stood the acid test of time and the movement, not designed as an abiding form of government for a peaceful nation, ceased to exist.

Parallels were inevitably drawn between Britain's perilous position in June 1940 and her situation in 1802, when Napoleon's armies massed on the shores of Boulogne. But while Hitler's territorial conquests may have rivalled Napoleon's, in 19th century Europe far greater acreage was under cultivation. Wherever Bonaparte's armies moved, they were able to live on the land, their horses put out to grass close to the battlefields. Hitler's tanks and aircraft required vast quantities of fuel which had to be transported over great distances, from sources where the supply was by no means unlimited. And he required as much raw material to manufacture munitions for a week as Napoleon needed in a year.

Italy's so-called 'May King', Umberto II, died, aged 78, of bone cancer in Geneva in March 1983. He was commander in chief of the Italian army on the French front in 1940. King Victor Emmanuel abdicated in his favour on May 9, 1946, but on June 2, Italy became a republic and Umberto went into exile — he, his consort and male heirs forbidden to return to Italy. He was buried at Savoy, France, but it is possible that Italian officials may grant permission for his remains to be reinterred in his homeland.

News item, 1983

'The difference between Nazism and Fascism was that whereas Nazism absorbed every aspect of German life and thought, in Italy two other institutions went on existing side by side with the Fascist party: the church and the family. This was true to such an extent that the Germans used to say that Fascism in Italy was not a totalitarian regime at all. This was a matter of national temperament — which Mussolini himself understood.'

Ignazio Silone

Socialism used to say all equal and all rich. Experience has proved this to be impossible. We say all equal — and all sufficiently poor.

Mussolini

CHAPTER THIRTEEN

On July 29, 1983 thousands of Italians made a pilgrimage to Predappio, a village between Rimini and Bologna, to celebrate the centenary of the birth of Benito Mussolini.

Following a requiem mass, fifty were awarded certificates of lifetime fidelity to the *Movimento Sociale Italiano* by its neofascist co-founder, Giorgio Almirante.

Predappio's 6,000 villagers (traditionally part of Italy's 'red belt') welcomed the largest assembly of fascists since 1947 because the Duce's family mausoleum had been built there in the 1930s. And his remains, concealed by Dominican priests after World War II, were finally returned to his birthplace in the 1950s.

Apart from veteran fascists, many of the pilgrims were under thirty. 'People who,' according to Almirante, 'wanted order and justice, a clean sweep of public administration and a revision of our institutions — or what we call a new republic.'

Two days before the anniversary, the MSI announced that a mobile post office parked outside the mausoleum would frank letters and cards with a souvenir emblem encircled with the words 'Centenary of the birth of B. Mussolini, 1883-1983'.

By noon the same day, leftwing organisations persuaded the post office that it had gone too far.

The stamp cancelling machine was promptly cancelled.

It was, as Churchill put it, 'only common prudence' for Mussolini to await the result of the German offensive against France before committing Italy irrevocably to war — ideally at the most opportune moment.

Referring to the Duce's decision to fling Italy once more into the breach — on June 10 1940 — Ciano later pointed out that it was a chance which comes only once in five thousand years. Such chances, commented Churchill, though rare, are not necessarily good.

In 1943, shortly before his execution, Ciano wrote to Signor

Churchill from his Verona prison cell to emphasise how disgusted he had been 'by the cold, cruel and cynical preparation for the war by Hitler and the Germans . . . with whom later that tragic and vile puppet, Mussolini, associated himself through his vanity and disregard for moral values'.

For Mussolini, he of the piercing golden-brown eyes, victim of his own bombast, the stab in the back of France was a deplorable error of judgement. The absolute ruler of Italy, known as a man of passion and physical magnetism, was by 1940 also at his most aggressive. At the same time touchy and superstitious, he had little stomach for the Fuhrer's cat and mouse tactics.

And if his police chief, Arturo Bocchini, is to be believed, Mussolini's stomach was only part of his troubles. There was also a possibility of a blood clot on the brain, trachoma, a heart condition and recrudescent venereal disease. He had already lost his grip before he launched his army against the French. He was also morbidly infatuated with the girl less than half his age, the provocative Clara Petacci. If she failed to phone him at the appointed time he was unable to face the day. Important foreign emissaries were kept waiting in the Palazzo Venezia while he raced her around the Seven Hills in his powerful car.

Although scared of a long war, Mussolini was inclined to accept Hitler's view 'that by autumn, Britain would be out of it.'

Believing the Germans were home and dried, he had written to the Fuhrer in May 1940 suggesting it might be fortuitous for Italy to enter World War II. Hitler remained unenthusiastic. The last time the two dictators had met he had not informed the Duce of his military strategy. Hitler was never one to allow a relationship to obscure objectivity. 'Whenever I tell him something off the record,' he complained, 'Mussolini runs to tell Ciano. Ciano passes it on to the royal clique and they can't wait to tell the rest of the world.

'If Italy had joined us at the start, France would not have declared war. But Victor Emmanuel misinformed the British when he told them Italy had no intention of going to war. That's why Britain was so foolhardy over Poland.'

He found out — from the new Italian ambassador, Dino Alfieri — why the King agreed to a declaration of war on June 10, 1940. Victor Emmanuel was anxious to appoint Crown Prince Umberto commander-in-chief of the Italian forces in order to weaken further the influence Mussolini had with the army.

Linge remembered Hitler's reaction after Alfieri had left the Chancellery. He had never, he says, seen the chief in such a puffily ruffled state, padding backwards and forwards, hands shaking as he fought to regain control. Ignoring the valet's presence he began to talk out loud: 'What the hell do those easygoing, pleasure-loving Italians know about modern war? With their lack of raw materials, their fear of bombing, their long-winded declarations. The only way to wage war is my way, with a *kriegpermanenz* (undeclared but standing war): attack, attack, attack, at lightning speed.' He broke off suddenly, seeing Linge attempting to make himself invisible behind the open door.

Then he continued his train of thought, subsuming his outrage under a withering objectivity that would have convinced even the unconverted.

'D'you know what Marshal MacMahon said about the Italians? They somehow managed to lose every battle but ended up winning the war. For centuries they've been better negotiators than warriors, preferring to let other countries win their victories for them so they can flourish long after warlike strength is exhausted. I'm quite sure that if the French had the slightest suspicion that Italy was going to have a say in the armistice they'd have fought on until extinction.'

Linge nodded sagely. He'd never thought much of Italy anyway; still less of Italians.

But Mussolini had declared his hand and Hitler, critical though the issue was, conceded that there was precious little he could do about it.

The concept of unintended consequences is well-known in economics. If, for instance, the British navy had not sealed the Italian ports, Italy, from an economic point of view, producing little in the way of war materials, would not have become an immediate liability to Germany instead of an asset.

'There was something in Mussolini's corporative ideas,' wrote Arthur Salter in 1952, 'which might eventually find a framework of true parliamentary democracy in the form of functional representation. The Duce was like Napoleon, on whom he tried to model himself; he was a far better man before irresponsible power corrupted him.

'Personal excesses, frantic attempts to disguise the failure of his physical strength, led at last to the mental, moral and physical disintegration so vividly recorded in Ciano's diary. History records

152

no more tragic example of the inexorable logic of absolute personal power.'

Under his uniform, Mussolini was, like Hitler in many ways — not to mention Napoleon — a shrewd little man who discovered that the public image of the history-maker he intended to portray was really hollow; that his prosaic self was a sick, shallow being who, lacking the knowledge that every ambition is doomed to frustration, finally suffered the contempt of the world.

'The key to Mussolini's character,' said Ignazio Silone, 'is the inconsistency, both of character and ideas, combined with an extraordinary intuitive capacity for improvisation . . . the only constant was his desire for power.'

*   *   *

Linge was less concerned with the Fuhrer's satellite, Mussolini, in June, 1940 than with the goings-on at FHQ Tannenberg.

He noted that, despite the brooding gloom of the Black Forest, the chief's mood continued to be optimistic. Even Britain's refusal to break under the threat of invasion failed to shake his confidence. There was no foreboding about what lay ahead and the atmosphere at headquarters was lighthearted, free of tension.

It wasn't long before several young girls from nearby Freudenstadt were attracted to Tannenberg. One morning, the chief spotted them socialising with his bodyguard. Linge was told to invite them to take coffee with the Fuhrer in his bunker.

From then on it became a regular mid-morning ritual, with the girls bringing various homemade cakes to augment Hitler's meagre diet.

One particular girl, a tall, smiling blonde named Hildegard, attracted the valet's attention. Although apparently shy, she had given him several knowledgeable looks over the coffee — and it was real coffee.

Taking the initiative, Linge drew her apart from the others. After a certain amount of playful badinage he managed to make a date with her for later in the evening.

Diplomatically, he refrained from going into details about the physical aspects of the rendezvous, except to point out that he didn't get back to FHQ until dawn next day.

At lunch, the chief sat with his adjutants and, during a lull in the conversation, called Linge over to the table. 'I want you to discover who was supposed to be on watch during the early hours. Some fool with feet like an elephant was stumbling about, making enough noise to raise the dead. It ruined my sleep and I am very angry indeed.'

'If you ask me,' said Schmundt, ponderously, 'whoever it was should be severely punished.'

Linge, staring at the carpet, failed to notice the mockery in their eyes. Realising he had disturbed the Fuhrer when returning from his night out, going through the entire gamut of angst, his first thought was: 'I'm well and truly in the shit here.' His second: 'Oh Lord, supposing mein Fuhrer had wanted the *schatzi* for himself?' Only one thing for it, he decided, I must jump in with both boots and tell the whole story.

So, in front of his sniggering colleagues, he blurted out with flushed obsequiousness what had happened with Hildegard — only sparing her reputation by not revealing her name.

The chief, pointing a derisive finger, chortled like a gleeful schoolboy. 'Take a look at our disciplinarian, always devoted to duties. Now at last the animal in him has got the upper hand. So he acts like your typical, agitated Bavarian, creeping in after a night on the tiles. Well, he should have removed his shoes so that his wife wouldn't be disturbed.'

Linge smiled shamefacedly, begging to be excused. Leaving the bunker, he stumbled around in the damp and stifling forest for a couple of hours to work off his embarrassment and regain his dignity.

Imagine the chief knowing about it the whole time — and only laughing at the end. The mockery didn't matter, the valet was used to that. And at least there'd been no sting in the tail.

He knew that if Hitler had really been angry, Linge would even then have been packing his kit and making arrangements to present himself at the main gate of *Das Konzentrationslager Dachau*, with Herr Fuhrer's compliments.

* * *

Hitler spent most of July and August 1940 at the Berghof, keeping in touch with various commands through daily dispatches and taking a great interest in newsreels depicting world events.

He paid particular attention to those dealing with the Russian campaign in Finland, running the reels over and over in order that his field commanders might be able to comprehend the difficulties of waging an offensive in blizzard conditions.

Like a film fan he sat, day after day, eyes fixed on the screen, totally absorbed; correcting the commentary in a loud voice when German weapons were described inaccurately; careful to single out those newsreels that might unwittingly supply information to the enemy. These were immediately destroyed.

Linge recalled an incident one evening the chief was watching a Berlin-produced film comparing the Maginot Line with the formidable *Panzerwerke* fortresses of Hitler's Westwall.

One shot depicted the Fuhrer on one of the days he spent touring the former front line in the valley of the Meuse between Dinant and Sedan. As a contrast to the destruction wrought by the German spearhead in the lightning march from the Bulge to the coast at Abbeville, Hitler was seen standing at a farmyard gate feeding a pair of Belgian thoroughbred horses. Turning to his valet he motioned for more bread, one eye on the camera. Linge came into focus, reaching into his knapsack for the sandwiches prepared for lunch. Before handing them over to the chief, he surreptitiously removed the fillings from the bread.

The chief drew the attention of the rest of the staff to the shot. 'Look at that,' he cried out, 'a typical Linge trick; always palming the good stuff for himself, leaving his Fuhrer nothing but dry bread.'

Linge managed a sour smile as the audience hooted with laughter.

He accepted it, just as he had done at Tannenberg; putting it down to *schadenfreude*, jealousy. They were all so pleased when the Fuhrer's favourite got the rough end for a change. But no matter how loud the laughter it would certainly not diminish his standing with the chief. He was quite sure of that.

The Chief of the Sipo & the SD

Berlin SW Dec 31 1942
Prinz Albrechtstr 8

Subject: Assignment of prison labour to armament factories.

1. *'Anti-social' prisoners who are handed over by the judicial authorities are to be transferred to a concentration camp immediately.*

   So far the Minister of Justice has named approximately 12,000 such prisoners, a number of whom have already been transferred or are in the process of being transferred to a concentration camp.

2. *As has already been disclosed the sub-offices have been ordered to transfer approximately 35,000 prisoners immediately after arrest to the concentration camps using the simplified procedure.*

3. *All Polish prisoners at present in state prisons in the 'Generalgouvernement', who have to be kept in custody for a longer period of time, are also to be transferred immediately to the concentration camps.*

As soon as these procedures have been completed I shall issue further details. I should, however, like to point out that, as a result of the numerous deaths in the concentration camps, the total number of prisoners could not be raised in spite of the recent increase in the number of admittances; and that if deaths continue at the present rate, an improvement is not likely to be achieved even with increased admittances.

*Former Soviet Foreign Minister Vyacheslav Molotov has died,
aged 96, official Russian sources said last night.*

*Molotov, a veteran of the revolutionary movement that over-
threw the Tsar in 1917, had his name given to the Molotov Cocktail
petrol bomb.*

*In 1961, he was expelled from the Party's Central Committee
after being accused of drawing up Stalin's death lists.*

News Item: November 11, 1986

CHAPTER FOURTEEN

In the autumn of 1940, Linge found himself staring from a window of the Fuhrer's train *Atlas* at the lush green Basque countryside. Hitler was travelling across France in the slow-moving train for a meeting with the Spanish dictator, Franco. His destination was Hendaye on the Ile-des-Faisans, in the middle of the Bidassoa River separating France from Spain.

According to Linge, the engine drivers of *Atlas* were never allowed to exceed 35 mph. This followed an accident in 1936, when a special train travelling at 80 mph collided with a coachload of actors in a touring company — all of whom were killed. (This was also mentioned in Hoffman's story, *Hitler Was My Friend*, published in London in 1955).

The Fuhrer, his nose buried deep in dispatches, his mind on the importance of the impending talks, had little inclination to admire the view. With the Tripartite (Japan, Italy and Germany) Pact signed in September, the next step, because of the stubborn refusal of Britain to accept peace terms, had to be access to the Strait of Gibraltar, thus cutting off access to the Mediterranean and providing an alternate approach to North Africa and threatening the English Channel.

Franco arrived from Irun thirty minutes after *Atlas* had drawn into the station. With the Caudillo was the lanky, hard-eyed Ramon Serrano Suner, his foreign minister (and brother-in-law), a proud man and the power behind the chubby-cheeked dictator.

Suner was a kind of Himmler and Goebbels in one, having been appointed chief of police, propaganda minister and head of the fascist Falange since the mutiny against the Spanish monarchists in 1939. 'A man,' said Eugene Lennhoff, 'for whom obstacles didn't exist. An admirer of Hitler and Mussolini long before the civil war; a fanatical supporter of authoritarian leadership in politics and religion.' Even so, despite his energetic approval of totalitarianism, he had no intention of allowing Spain to bend under Axis pressure.

Because of Spain's strategic location in the Mediterranean, it was necessary, he had told France, to adopt a middle course of 'benevolent neutrality', at least as far as Germany was concerned.

Formal greetings concluded, guards of honour inspected, the bargaining began. Hitler, as always, was determined to do the imposing, to bear down heavily on any obstacles that threatened his militaristic aims.

The Caudillo, egged on by Suner, was equally determined to keep Spain out of the war. He opened the discussion by making impossible demands for shipments of German wheat and fuel supplies.

Suner chipped in, as he was to do throughout the nine-hour talks, to suggest that in his personal view the Reich was no longer in a position to supply anything, let alone petrol or grain. Happily, Spain, despite her economy being crippled by the civil war, had strong ties with America and Roosevelt had guaranteed them all the raw materials they required. Naturally, Roosevelt assumed that Spain would remain neutral.

By no stretch of the imagination could the meeting have been called an inspiring occasion. It seemed very warm in the railway compartment and Linge could feel the sweat on the back of his neck. And he wasn't a man who perspired easily. The chief was obviously getting nowhere in his demands against the obstinacy, the doggedness, traditionally a salient feature of the Latin temperament.

Finally, realising that there was no possibility of collaboration, Hitler curtly took his leave of the little general and his grey eminence, Suner.

Next morning, October 24, *Atlas* steamed out of Hendaye, heading north for the village of Montoire, in the occupied zone of France. Muffled in his winter greatcoat, despite the warmth of the coach, the Fuhrer was silent for a long time, turning over in his mind the conversation with Franco. The Caudillo had been polite but had produced all kinds of objections — eventually, aided by Suner, wearing him down.

'I would rather,' Hitler told his aides, 'have several teeth extracted without an anaesthetic than go through such a discussion again.' The Spaniards, having received every possible assistance from the Third Reich, refused to be subordinated to the needs of Axis strategy. Franco with his non-intervention bluff clearly lacked gratitude. Well, Hitler said, his dictatorship would not be of long duration. Franco's name was added to the black list.

*　　*　　*

At Montoire, on route N817 west of Vendome, Hitler nodded in brusque courtesy to Laval, the one time Radical communist, before shaking hands with Petain. The 'hero of Verdun', well into his eighties, wore his age well, holding himself erect, his ice-cold eyes clear blue and his hair and moustache as white as the snow on Mont Blanc.

Linge believed the chief had no wish to treat the Marshal as a vanquished enemy; at least, not if he hoped to persuade France to become a true ally. She still had a great deal to offer — her navy was intact and French North Africa was also another equally important strand in his overall Mediterranean structure.

Both Hitler and Ribbentrop urged the Frenchmen to see the advantages of a joint Franco-German collaboration. As far as the Reich was concerned, one country or the other, France or Britain would finally have to foot the bill for the war.

Wasn't it in France's best interests to make certain the Anglo-Saxons were made to pay the lion's share?

Laval, seizing the opportunity to distinguish himself, continually baring his yellow teeth and rubbing his hands together, airily promised all kinds of cooperation. While no one suggested an alliance was unreasonable, it was undeniable that France had suffered a savage defeat. And, a shrug of the shoulders, no one could argue that as the terms of the armistice had been so punitive, France was in no position to take up arms again, no matter how worthy the cause.

Hitler waved him aside impatiently, addressing his remarks to Petain. Pointing out that France and the West 'must be stone blind if they cannot see where the real threat lay,' he told them, 'We must all be prepared to take the fight to the true enemy, Russia.'

Usually when things failed to go his way in an argument, the chief resorted to splenetic ferocity, on the principle that most disputes were settled by superior ego, not logic. But surprisingly, considering the glacial atmosphere, he continued to treat the French chief of state with an almost gentle forbearance.

161

Possibly, thought Linge, he was remembering how, just before the outbreak of the war, Petain had been appointed ambassador to Spain; how Franco, making the most of his new found status, kept the Marshal, member of the French Academy and the defender of Verdun in 1916, cooling his heels for a week at Santander before rudely ordering him to Burgos for an interview that lasted less than twenty minutes.

Without making specific commitments, the Marshal agreed to recommend to the authoritarian regime at Vichy a policy of collaboration with the Reich.

The Fuhrer, wishing the Marshal well in his task of rebuilding a demoralised France, suggested a further meeting some time in the future.

Before the Germans left Montoire that evening Ribbentrop managed to get to a telephone. Contacting his friend Ciano in Rome, he gave his version of the talks.

As the Fuhrer had so far failed in his attempts to seal off the Mediterranean — by constructing a Latin fascist bloc, he proposed a meeting between Hitler and Mussolini. It was fixed for October 28, the venue Florence.

On the journey back to Berlin from Montoire, Linge overheard the chief's disparaging comments concerning Laval. Hitler believed the petty bourgeois had so many characteristics of a gipsy 'he might get a serious shock to his nervous system if I suggested he needed more than his head examining; or that Himmler should investigate his racial background together with those of the other Vichy jackals.'

A couple of days later Petain broadcast on French radio, to announce that 'it is with honour and in order to maintain French unity — ten centuries of unity within the framework of constructive activity of the new European order — that I embark today on a course of collaboration.' But his heart wasn't in it. He had already sent a secret emissary to London to make certain proposals to Churchill.

When Roosevelt was told of the Montoire meeting, he felt it might be necessary to find a worthy diplomat to represent America at Vichy, in order to persuade Petain to stand firm in the face of German pressure.

Henri Philippe Benoni Omer Petain, the marshal who surrendered the Third Republic to the Third Reich, was to face trial for treason in 1945 at the age of 89. He died in prison three months after his 95th birthday.

* * *

Hitler's own nervous system was severely put to the test shortly after his return to Berlin. A lengthy dispatch from Rome proved to be a fresh source of anxiety, for it announced that Mussolini was planning to send an army against Greece. Burning like a slow fuse, he confirmed the need for urgent discussions to take place at Florence and was inclined to lay the blame for what could turn out to be an act of supreme folly on the 'perfumed soaked Ciano.'

'That simpleton,' he ranted, 'has always been infatuated with himself! Lacking courage and the strength of character for his office he has surrounded himself with yes men who dare not tell him the truth.'

His mood of painful uncertainty stayed with him on the way to Florence, but it gave way to mounting anger when his train stopped briefly at Bologna. A dispatch was handed to him with confirmation that Italy had invaded Greece from bases in Albania early that morning.

By informing the Fuhrer at the last possible moment it almost seemed as if Mussolini was retaliating for the treatment he had so often received in the past.

To the chief, the move was an act of unprecedented lunacy. 'The Duce and his son-in-law are doing everything wrong and yet they can't see it. And their blindness could alter the whole conduct of the war. It's just the excuse the British are looking for to poke their snouts into the Balkans and cut off our oil supplies. And their army! Badly equipped and ill-disciplined, they're already experiencing great difficulty in supplying Graziani's front in North Africa. To embark on a campaign now, with winter a few weeks away, is absolute madness.'

Linge was sent to call the general staff to the Fuhrer's coach for an impromptu conference.

It was time for the technicians whose business it was to control Germany's fighting manpower to be told the truth — not facts, but Hitler truth.

So, deftly weaving together the main outlines of recent events, he professed he had few illusions about the problems facing the

163

Third Reich. He mentioned the negative aspects of Franco's lack of gratitude; the double-dealing displayed by Petain and his shifty sidekick, Laval; Mussolini's precipitate moves and the danger to Rumanian oil supplies, thus jeopardising the security of the small Balkan states.

Speaking in grim tones, he forecast that, instead of the war ending with the collapse of Britain, it now seemed likely that it was going to open up in the south-east, with a second or even a third front to contend with — precisely the kind of situation that had precipitated the destruction of Germany in 1918.

The most obvious source of danger — at this point Hitler swept his campaign maps off the table in order to bring a fist down forcefully on the polished surface — was Russia. No one was more familiar with Stalin's empty promises than the Fuhrer himself, than whom, as they well knew, no one more ardently desired peace. He was also well aware that the Russian war machine was preparing to rumble into action.

As *Oberfehlshaber der Wermacht* (Supreme commander of the defence forces) he reminded them of the astonishing courage and military skill his forces had shown in action against the west; pointing to the need for decisive action on their, the executives', part to prevent demoralisation spreading through the ranks. Consolidation was the keynote. He was able to promise that 'the immeasurable economic and military resources of Greater Germany would shortly be thrown into the balance in a quick campaign aimed at crushing, once and for all, Soviet Russia — even before the end of the war against Britain.'

Although the professional soldiers in the coach had questions to pose: 'Was the English coast so far away?' 'Why didn't the mass attack promised by Goring have the desired effect?' — they were not allowed the privilege of questioning the Fuhrer about the aspects of his views that appeared to them to be unsatisfactory.

They listened in silence, approving his suggested measures for the protection of Germany's right flank and for bringing together the Balkan states to safeguard the vital Rumanian oilfields.

Heil Hitler.

*   *   *

On the platform of Florence station, the dictators clasped hands as they stood beneath an obtrusively garlanded canopy, their words of greeting muffled by the noise of an army band. Mussolini, his brow furrowed with mock solicitude gazed at Hitler, who managed a wintry smile.

The Fuhrer's anger was mollified later by the special pleading of his old friend and the splendour of the magnificent apartment allocated to him in the Pitti Palace, which housed one of the world's finest collections of art.

A gilt-framed painting of vast size had been placed in his suite, a personal gift from the Duce. He studied it in silence for some time before turning to his valet. 'Mussolini,' he said, 'appears to know even less about fine art than he does about the art of war, otherwise he might not be so liberal with the priceless heritage of his people.'

Recalling his embarrassment of his last visit to Italy, he was nevertheless persuaded to appear before the crowd outside the Palace, standing patiently beside the Italian leader behind the balustrade. Finally, they began their discussions.

Later that evening, he attended a 'diversion' arranged by Edda Ciano, Mussolini's beloved daughter and the waspish wife of his foreign minister. This was a concert, featuring excerpts from the Fuhrer's favourite Wagnerian operas.

Hitler, arriving on time, was forced to wait for several minutes in the salon before Edda appeared, welcoming him enthusiastically and talking endlessly. The Fuhrer, although usually reserved on these occasions, seemed distracted, showing no irritation. He did turn to Ribbentrop, however, to whisper in a subdued aside, *'Sie ist ein Mordskerl!'* ('She's one hell of a woman!')

To Linge, she was very like her father, with the same steely gaze, the same harsh voice.

Edda, surprisingly to some, became an auxiliary nurse and worked diligently throughout the war, always ready to perform the most menial of hospital tasks. When the end finally came for her husband and her father, she was under no illusions. In the pre-war years of decadence she'd often been heard to say, 'I'm sure we'll all be lined up against a wall before we're finished.'

Perhaps, when the end came having put up a valiant fight for Ciano's life, she may have finally realised the folly of putting her faith in Hitler's Germany. At least, after Ciano was executed by the Gestapo in Verona, she managed to smuggle his famous diary out of Italy into Switzerland.

The talks in Florence ended with the Duce in very good humour; to his son-in-law 'the conference was of the greatest interest, proving that German support had not failed them'.

But Hitler left Italy in a mood of melancholy resignation. It was left to Ribbentrop to remind him how astute and farsighted a statesman he was, still the instrument of providence. According to the latest news from his Bureau, the reaction to Mussolini's move had been muted. No country had yet made an attempt to spring to the defence of Greece.

'Why not,' Ribbentrop asked, 'gain a little more time by inviting the Russian foreign minister, Molotov, to Berlin? After all, as far as the rest of the world is concerned, the Soviets are still our allies.'

*   *   *

Molotov arrived in Berlin on November 12 for a two-day visit. Those two days, according to Linge, were regarded as the longest, most burdensome of the chief's life. It was the first time the Russian had set foot in Germany and everything was done to ensure that he would take a favourable impression back to Moscow.

Hitler insisted on personally supervising the details, checking the accommodation prepared at the Bellevue Palace, inspecting the rooms, going over the proposed menus, even descending to the hotel basement to examine the air raid shelter, in case the unforeseen happened and the British air force managed to bomb the Bellevue.

The fifty-year-old Molotov (whose real name was Scriabin, and who was a nephew of the composer) had been a Bolshevik ever since he joined the underground movement at sixteen. Banished and imprisoned even more times than his close friend Stalin, once the party gained power, Molotov became the second secretary to the central committee.

As foreign secretary, Stalin knew he would never betray the trust which the Russian communist party had tacitly placed in him. Thickly-moustached, cool, impassive, eyes behind rimless spectacles and alert with candid suspicion, Molotov resembled a provincial banker. There was nothing of the fiery Bolshevik revolutionary, either in his demeanour or in his oratory and as a speaker, he had a dry, monotonous delivery.

Molotov, being Molotov, turned out to be the toughest adversary the Fuhrer had ever encountered. Prejudice and hatred of communism had already succeeded in blinding him to whatever virtues the envoy might have possessed. He simply despised him.

After a morning in his company, vainly trying to counter his arguments, the chief returned to his own quarters in a state of exhaustion. A blinding headache required him to lie down on his bed, the curtains tightly drawn, unable to stir until Linge called him later in the evening for his bath, an hour or so before the state banquet.

As the valet prepared warm towels, Hitler relaxed in soothing water, addressing members of his cabinet through the open bathroom door.

'That Russian *schweinehund*,' he shouted, 'reminds me of a dehydrated, unbending old teacher I once knew. I have never in all my life encountered such tedious guile.

'Did you notice how the cunning fox forced me to repeat every word I said, over and over again? You know why he did that? To stop me thinking ahead and anticipating his rebuffs. He did everything he could to outplay me verbally, to outlast me in debate.

'Well, although you might say the fortunes of war are still going well for us, Molotov didn't come all the way to Berlin to offer rosy promises or a glowing future. While the 1939 pact still holds and the subsequent trade deals are working in our favour, Stalin means to burrow into the bowels of Europe, beginning with Finland — and that will be the end of nickel and timber supplies from that quarter. You and I know that, whatever we tell the world about the strength of the Russian-German friendship, Stalin is merely marking time. Once he turns towards the Balkans, that'll cut off our Caucasian oil.

'We must consider the dangers that lie ahead. We must face them fearlessly, you and I and the German people, taking whatever steps may be necessary to protect the fatherland. Russia must never, ever, be allowed to establish a foothold near Germany.'

With Molotov back in Moscow, the Fuhrer knew he had reached a watershed. The time for a showdown with Stalin had come. The Soviets, he was convinced, were preparing to expand westwards, making a conflict inevitable — a prospect which, when emphasised to the general staff, evoked precious little enthusiasm. Seeing a 'no win' situation developing, they were all for standing back and taking a deep breath first.

But for Hitler, events appeared to bolster his waning self-confidence. Things were on the move again, cataclysmic, earth-shattering events — and that was the way he wanted it.

Every intelligence report that landed on his desk suggested that the Russian army would crack under the first blitzkrieg. Other dispatches stressed the campaign would last no longer than six weeks.

The Fuhrer sat back in his chair at the Chancellery, put on his reading glasses and pored over every document carefully. All the reports agreed with his own belief; that the Russian army lacked real striking power and military leadership. The road to Moscow looked reasonably clear. All it required was a little more time and patience on his part.

In December 1940, orders were sent out to those farmers of East Prussia who worked the land nearest to the Russian border, to dispense with their spring planting. Those living in the immediate vicinity of the frontier were later instructed to move their families and livestock to designated points further inland. Areas of what had been Poland, bordering that of the Soviets, were transformed into military zones.

If there was one fact Hitler's invasion of Russia was to display, it was the revelation of Russia's deception. Since 1930, Stalin had quietly built up a war machine and matching industrial complex the like of which had never before been seen.

* * *

The two momentous errors of judgement of World War II both concerned the Soviet Union. Hitler misjudged Russia's military capability. Roosevelt misunderstood Russia's political philosophy. These two blunders provided Stalin with an opportunity to establish Soviet Russia as the predominant power in Europe. To Russia, intent on world revolution, compromise signifies irresolution, not mutual understanding. Stemming from their wartime experiences, the Soviets only drive harder bargains and only respect strength — iron-heeled strength.

He is now 91 years old and has been a prisoner for forty-four of them. It was on May 10, 1941 that Rudolf Hess, deputy Fuhrer of the Third Reich, flew a Messerschmitt fighter from Augsburg in Germany to Scotland and parachuted into captivity.

Then he was a tall, commanding, bushy-browed figure, proudly wearing Luftwaffe uniform under his leather flying-coat. Now he is bowed and sunken-cheeked and shuffling — the last visible piece of the wreckage of the Nazi leadership, a relic pacing his cage in West Berlin long after the rest of the zoo has closed.

Hess did not see his wife, Ilse, for twenty-eight years because of the indignity of his imprisonment. Now he cannot see her because she is too ill to come. He usually sees his son, Wolf Rudiger Hess, who was only three when he flew to England, and his daughter-in-law Andrea.

Peter Lewis, Sunday Telegraph, May, 1985

The night of May 10, 1941 saw one of the heaviest attacks on London: the House of Commons chamber was wrecked, Westminster Abbey was damaged, 5,000 homes were destroyed, and 1,400 civilians killed.

News Item

At Nuremberg, Hess was confronted by his two secretaries — he didn't recognise them. He was also introduced to Goring, of whom he also showed no sign of recognition. His later counsel was Dr Alfred Seidl of Munich, who still represents the prisoner of Spandau.

News Item.

CHAPTER FIFTEEN

At 5.45 pm on Saturday, May 10, 1941 a Messerschmitt Bf 110 twin-engined 'Zerstorer' aircraft took off from Augsburg, north-west of Munich.

At 10.10 pm it was pinpointed on radar screens on Holy Island, off the coast of Northumberland.

The pilot said later that he had hoped to land his aircraft near Dungavel House, the home of the Duke of Hamilton. Hamilton, then a wing commander, was on duty that night in the operations room at RAF Turnhouse, Edinburgh.

Through an error of navigation, the pilot baled out over Eaglesham Moor, thirty miles west of his target. Arrested by the local home guard, he gave his name as Hauptmann Alfred Horn.

Later, he claimed to be Rudolf Hess 'on a special mission'. He informed the Duke of Hamilton that, as a result of meeting him at the Olympic games in Berlin in 1936, he had decided to seek his aid in helping to convince the British that the Fuhrer did not want to defeat England.

Treated as a prisoner of war, he was released on October 10, 1945 to stand trial at Nuremberg.

He escaped the death sentence because of his mental condition and was sentenced to life imprisonment in Spandau. On July 18, 1987, he will, if he is still alive, have spent a total of forty years there. For twenty-two of those years he refused to see any visitors apart from his lawyer, Dr Seidl. For twenty-eight years he would not allow his wife or son to visit Spandau.

When Frau Hess saw him in 1969 for the first time, delegates from the four powers, Britain, France, Russia and the United States, remained in hearing throughout the visit.

According to his son, Britain knew in advance of Hess's plan to fly to England in 1941.

Wolf Rudiger Hess held a press conference in April 1984

following his father's 90th birthday, revealing that he had proof that secret peace initiatives between Germany and Britain had been in process at that time. It was, he said, arranged that Rudolf Hess should fly to Britain to negotiate directly with the War Cabinet. Unfortunately, the plan came to the notice of the German underground movement and they notified British Intelligence.

Hess's mission, said his son, had been undertaken in an attempt to end the war and 'save 50 million lives'. If the British had wanted to they could have taken the initiative from Hess's mission to call a peace conference with Germany and Russia. 'Officially, it's always claimed that it is the Russians who refuse to release my father, but I have a small suspicion that the British are glad the Russians are so unyielding. There is a file about my father in the British war archives which has been declared classified until the year 2017.

'Anyway, if Britain really wanted to free my father what is to stop them, during their month of guard duty, simply unlocking the door? All they have to say is that they will not be so inhumane any longer.'

Does the closed file on Rudolf Hess justify his son's accusation that the British don't want to release the old man? A J P Taylor, the historian, believes so. 'I think there is a cover-up. Negotiations were proceeding before he flew over — but no one wants to be reminded of that,' he has claimed.

'It is a cover-up of the fact that top people in this country had been playing along with him for quite a time and wanted him shut up because he knew too much.'

The Duke of Hamilton's son, Lord James Douglas-Hamilton, doesn't agree. He believes it is merely a medical file in the war archives. It is standard practice to keep medical files confidential.

Is Hess the only man who can tell us what really happened?

*   *   *

Shortly before 7.00 am on May 11, 1941, Hess's adjutant, Karlheintz Pintsch, arrived at Berchtesgaden on the overnight train from Munich. From the station phone booth he immediately rang through to the Berghof asking for an appointment with the Fuhrer — he had 'an important message for Herr Hitler from his *stellvertreter* (deputy leader), Rudolf Hess'.

By 9.30 am, Pintsch was in the duty room at the Berghof arguing with Linge about the need to see the Fuhrer. Linge explained that no one was allowed to disturb the chief before lunchtime. The adjutant, by then extremely agitated, told him that Hess had taken off from the airfield of the Messerschmitt plant at Augsburg — without permission — and he had a personal letter from him.

Linge, sensing something odd, hurried along to knock loudly on the door of the master bedroom.

'What is it?' demanded Hitler.

An urgent message from Hess, delivered by his adjutant, Pintsch, who begged to see the Fuhrer personally.

Hitler emerged in a matter of seconds, fully dressed and as Pintsch handed him the letter he quickly made for the large window, tearing open the envelope. As his eyes scanned the page, his face changed and he drew in a sharp breath. 'Pintsch! Come over here!'

The adjutant went white. He began shaking and shifting from one foot to the other.

Hitler strode across the room.

'D'you know what this letter contains?' he demanded.

Pintsch slowly nodded his head. When he finally spoke, the words poured out of him, and he told how his boss had made several training flights from Augsburg; how he had tried several times to get to England, only to be turned back by bad weather; how he had been told by Hess to phone the Air ministry in Berlin at 9.00 pm the previous evening to ask for a radio signal to be beamed from Augsburg to Dungavel House; and how he, Pintsch, had been told to wait at Augsburg until 10.00 pm before returning to Munich.

The Fuhrer barked an order to Linge. 'Get Bormann and Hoegl in here right away.'

Hoegl, the duty Gestapo officer, was ordered to take Pintsch into custody — no one was to be allowed to talk to him. Bormann was to summon Goring, Himmler, Ribbentrop and Goebbels. He would also check with the Air ministry in Berlin: did Pintsch call them the previous evening? There was no record of the call.

Goring was on his estate near Nuremberg. He would have to send the Luftwaffe in pursuit of Hess. Ribbentrop was at Fuschl.

When the four party leaders arrived at the Berghof the first order Hitler gave them was that, in future, no leaders would be allowed to fly aircraft unattended or even drive a car without a suitable

SS escort. Pintsch had been arrested, he said, because of his duplicity. He had known something of Hess's plans, but he failed to take any action. Actually talking about his deputy's betrayal made Hitler roaring mad, and strident with fury, he insisted that he had no wish to make peace with Britain. He repeated this statement again and again, emphasising that he would not negotiate, not on any terms.

The inner circle made tactful, soothing noises, although Linge observed that the 'upstart' Bormann could scarcely conceal his delight at the bizarre flight of the chief's most trusted lieutenant. Pouring as much oil on the flames as possible, bursting with sham indignation, he was all for hanging Pintsch in the Berghof yard there and then. He also expressed his concern that Hess might have endangered the plans for the imminent attack on Russia.

Himmler suggested that Hess might have crashed into the North Sea — his aircraft might have had insufficient fuel — and as yet there had been no news from London. Pintsch, in his view, was blameless.

After a lengthy discussion it was decided to suppress any news of the defection until there was proof Hess had, in fact, landed in Britain.

An early dispatch indicated that the deputy leader *had* landed in Scotland; a second report referred to his injuries and that he had been placed in hospital.

Despite his acute embarrassment, Hitler decided to announce Hess's flight to the public. Investigations concluded that there had been no widespread conspiracy, no overt disloyalty. Hess's letter of explanation suggested some mental disturbance: he had decided, he wrote, to carry out his intention to negotiate with the British for peace 'even at the risk of the Fuhrer declaring him insane'. Hitler left the matter of publication of the announcement to Otto Dietrich. The press department would issue a release stating that pressure of work had resulted in the deputy leader undergoing a severe breakdown for which he had previously been admitted to a sanitarium for psychiatric treatment.

Thereafter, there would be no more mention of his name; every memory of him would be obliterated; any streets or public buildings named after him would be retitled. Most party members believed the Fuhrer would have had Hess shot at once, had he returned to Germany.

173

Linge told a different tale. He recalled the chief saying, 'If Hess were sent back during the war, naturally I would have him shot as a deserter. But personally I hope they keep him until it is all over. Then he is welcome to return; then who knows? Perhaps we can give him a small farm somewhere in the backwoods. After all, if he had managed to bring Britain in on our side, he would have become a national hero.'

Frau Hess was allowed to remain in the family home near Munich and a small pension was arranged for herself and her family.

One strange outcome of the incident was that after Hess flew to Britain, all fortune tellers and clairvoyants in Germany were arrested.

During the early years of the struggle for acceptance, many party leaders, including Hess, relied on clairvoyant insight and astrology for guidance.

'At Nuremberg,' wrote Shirer, 'Hess confided to the American prison psychiatrist, Dr Kelley, that late in 1940, one of his astrologers had read in the stars that he was ordained to bring about peace. He also related how his old mentor, Professor Haushofer, the Munich *Geopolitiker*, had seen him in a dream striding through the tapestried halls of English castles bringing peace between the two great "Nordic" nations.'

Karl Haushofer headed the *Deutsche Akademie* in Munich as well as lecturing on 'geopolitics' at the university. Hess, a student in the 1920s, later became Haushofer's assistant, and introduced him to the principles of National Socialism.

Haushofer was quickly able to demonstrate to Hitler that he believed there existed a sound scientific basis for both his political theories and territorial claims. As a result of his somewhat pedantic pseudo-science of geographical and economic abstracts, Hitler was able to rationalise his expansionist ambitions. Or, as Rauschning put it: 'they paved the way for Hitler's senseless ambition which plunged the world into misery'. Haushofer's schematics were the blue prints of Nazi policy.

After the failure of the 1923 putsch, Haushofer concealed Hess in his house for six weeks. To him, the two leading lights of the new movement were always thought of as 'the two lads'.

The redrawn scale maps of Czechoslovakia, submitted to Chamberlain in 1938, were Haushofer's work.

Later, he recoiled from the physical and moral chaos prevailing in Germany during the latter part of World War II. Shortly after his son, Albrecht — a close friend of Hess — was shot for his involvement in the 1944 bomb plot, Haushofer committed suicide.

Pintsch was imprisoned for three years. He was then released and posted to an infantry unit on the Eastern front. Captured by the Russians, his background was investigated and his former association with the deputy leader came to light. He was repeatedly tortured — during a final interrogation, all his fingers were broken — in an attempt to force him to reveal the truth, whatever that might have been, about Hess.

In 1955, together with Linge and other notable war prisoners, he was shipped back home to Germany. He died soon afterwards in Munich.

*   *   *

Although he was not subjected to physical maltreatment, Linge was grilled many times about Hess. It seemed that when the Russians tired of asking about Hitler's sex life, they turned to the private life of his deputy leader. Had Hess, for instance, shown any sign of mental aberration before he flew to Britain?

Linge knew he was on a tightrope. A couple of ill-judged answers and he'd suffer the same fate as former adjutant Pintsch. Having more respect for his fingers, he sought refuge and safety in vague generalities.

Was Hess raving mad?

Well no. In fact, he was the one man the staff turned to when they were in trouble. He was always helpful and sympathetic; softspoken, goodhearted and diplomatic.

Was he a capable pilot?

Oh yes. In 1934, he won the annual air race around the Zugspitze, Germany's highest mountain.

And whatever pressure he was under, Linge never saw him lose control. For years he had enjoyed Hitler's complete trust, even though he preferred at all times to stay in the background.

But hadn't he taken part in the beer cellar brawls in the early days?

Linge *had* noticed a scar on his head. A souvenir, he understood, of a well-aimed beer mug flung at him during a *hofbrau* punch up.

And his physical appearance?

Slim, athletic; grizzled black hair on a head usually uncovered; light blue eyes; prominent eyebrows that cut across his forehead like a smudge of charcoal.

When was the last time the valet saw Hess?

In April, 1941. At a *Kriegsrat* (war council) meeting in the Chancellery cabinet chamber.

He described the oblong-shaped room, which was dominated by a massive, highly polished table surrounded by red leather chairs engraved with black swastikas on white backgrounds, each place marked by an ornate leather folder stamped with a swastika. The Fuhrer's chair was situated midway along one side, dominating the others, with the initials AH inscribed below the eagle. Goring always took the seat on Hitler's left; Hess the one on his right.

When was the deputy leader last seen in public?

He delivered a patriotic war speech at a ceremony awarding the *Pionier der Arbeit* decoration — the highest distinction for civilians — to industrialists, among them Dr Ferdinand Porsche for his work on the Volkswagen and Hess's friend, Willy Messerschmitt, for aircraft achievements — that was on May 1, 1941 at Augsburg.

Linge thought it unwise to inform his captors that Hitler's second-in-command, admired and respected by most Germans, was a sworn hater of the communist gospel, bitter against all things Russian. He did wonder later why they were so insistent on pursuing such exhaustive inquiries about a man who had been a prisoner of the allies since his defection in 1941.

*   *   *

Prisoner No. 7 has been a subject of speculation ever since his incarceration in Spandau jail.

One doctor who examined him twice in 1973 claims he is an impostor, supplying medical evidence to support his assertion.

Hugh Thomas, a surgeon formerly attached to the British Military hospital in Berlin, also believes the Russians are aware of the truth; along with the British secret service, 'who may have known since 1941'.

Delving into Hess's background before medically examining him, Thomas discovered that Hitler's deputy was wounded twice in World War I when a gunshot wound in the chest injured his lung, leaving a scar on the chest. His examination of Hess revealed no trace of scarring.

'The real Hess was shot in the chest in 1917. Any experienced surgeon could see this at once; the torso cannot lie'.

The surgeon offers some photographic evidence in support of his theory. The aircraft in which Hess took off for Scotland had no fuel tanks under its wings; the Messerschmitt that landed in Scotland carried extra tanks.

According to Thomas the truth, shrouded in secrecy, contributed to one of the greatest deceptions of World War II.

If Prisoner No. 7 isn't Rudolf Hess, then who is he?

Thomas suggests Hess was shot down en route to Scotland on Himmler's orders between 19.28 and 19.58 hours the night he took off from Augsburg. A double, thinner in the face, then took off from Aalborg, Denmark, the operations centre for Messerschmitt night-fighter squadrons.

When the surgeon attempted to interview Galland, who had led the squadrons, it was made clear to him 'his inquiries were not welcome'.

Ilse Hess, while confessing herself astonished at Thomas's theory, confirmed that her husband had been shot through the lung in 1917, leaving a scar on the front and back of his torso.

Linge remembered one of the last conversations between Hitler and his deputy in the Spring of 1941. The Fuhrer, planning the Russian campaign, asked Hess what England's reaction would be.

Hess, believed to be on close terms with several influential Englishmen, felt that the English hatred of communism far outweighed their antagonism towards Hitler. He suggested, even at that late hour, that the Fuhrer might negotiate a sensible agreement with Churchill before turning towards Russia.

The Fuhrer dismissed the idea. 'I cannot waver now. We must unleash our attack first. It is imperative that I sweep Stalin from his war horse while he is still sitting loose in the stirrups. The argument has gone on too long and it is an argument that must be decided in my lifetime.

'Germany will never again be as united behind me as it is now. If the people need fire in their bellies, haven't France and our success in the Balkans supplied the fuel?

'It would be infinitely regrettable if we failed to seize this opportunity. The menace of Bolshevism exists; it will not go away. It is my destiny to destroy it.'

Hess suggested that the cooperation of Churchill might be a vital factor.

Hitler dismissed the suggestion. 'Once we have conquered Russia and are in a position to supply Europe with food and raw materials, we will be able to wage war on any front. Then the British will be only too anxious to negotiate peace.'

The Fuhrer, said Linge, decided to log his aims in a memo: Britain as the strongest sea power; Germany possessing the greatest land force; the two able to form a potent influence in the world. Britain allowed a free hand in maritime matters, with assistance from the Third Reich in the event of an attack. In return Hitler, free to attack to the East, would also request the eventual return of former German colonies.

This memo, its contents known only to the Fuhrer and his deputy Hess, formally witnessed by Linge, was locked in the Chancellery safe.

After Hess flew to England, it was never seen again.

Linge thought the conversation may have preyed on Hess's mind; and that he therefore decided, on his own initiative, to make a last-ditch effort to persuade Britain to negotiate peace terms. The deputy believed that Germany, without the help of Britain, might see its armies perish in the snows of Russia. He thought the risks were greater than Hitler had anticipated.

* * *

Why would Himmler have wished to have Hess killed? The SS chief knew that several peace offers had been made to Britain and he felt that 'nothing could be worse than war between Britain and Germany'.

For years, seeing himself as a replacement for Hitler, Himmler had played a double game. His name had been mentioned in connection with the shooting of Geli Raubal; her relationship with Hitler had, in his view, become an embarrassment to the party.

He was also primarily responsible for unmasking the so-called 'conspiracy' of his former friend Rohm.

And, to quote Dr Dix at Nuremberg: 'For Himmler, politics was a simile for murder, for the reason that, with his purely biological outlook, he saw human society only as a breeding ground, and never as a social and ethical community'.

*   *   *

There was more bad news for the Fuhrer. On May 27 he was told the battleship *Bismarck*, three days after sinking the *Hood*, had gone down before the guns of the British navy — with the loss of over two thousand of her crew.

The Fuhrer had regarded the launching of the *Bismarck* as symbolic of the Reich's rebirth as a world power.

Linge had been beside his chief on the morning that a grandchild of the Iron Chancellor had tried to break a bottle of champagne against the mighty bows. The bottle had failed to shatter on impact, leaving Hitler to ponder on the significance. Was it a bad omen?

An exhaustive tour of the battleship went some way towards alleviating his fears. To Linge, it was an example of the high standard of German naval engineering. He, like others, was convinced the *Bismarck* was unsinkable.

With the report of her loss confirmed, an air of dejection hung over the Berghof. The staff seemed to walk about on tiptoe, speaking in undertones. For days the entire household mourned the passing of the great ship and her gallant crew.

A belated signal was delivered from her commander, Admiral Gunther Lutjens. 'Mein Fuhrer: we will fight to the last shell, for our faith in eventual victory remains undiminished. Long live Germany.'

It was a chastened chief Linge saw that morning, as he stood forlornly at the window of his study, the Admiral's message in his hand. His face had clouded over and he looked isolated, exposed. He also complained of a recurrence of severe stomach cramps.

*   *   *

With the passage of time new skin grew over old wounds.

The news from Crete was heartening. With the success of the airborne forces in driving the enemy off the island, there was sufficient evidence that the German war machine was as unyielding as ever.

On June 18 a pact with Turkey signified the final link in the chain of preparations for the attack on Russia, and any suggestion of a negotiated peace with Britain was ruled out. Hitler's personal philosophy and programme of action presupposed a continuation of war.

He accused Stalin of plotting war. At the same time, tons of Russian wheat and fuel were delivered to Germany. He presented Russia with final demands and the Soviets had accepted them: German control of the Ukraine and the oil wells.

Conflict was inevitable and it was only natural that the Fuhrer, like Napoleon before the start of his 1812 campaign, should want to decide the date for himself.

The delay that ensued was significant in that it gave Hitler the opportunity to exert more influence on the strategy of the attack, for it was he who insisted, against the advice of his generals, on three offensive thrusts. Had he not interfered, it is now generally accepted that there would have been a German victory in the East.

Without doubt, at the beginning of the campaign, it appeared that Russia would be crushed under the might of that great German war-machine, as it moved with fearsome speed. In Moscow, the British Ambassador, Sir Stafford Cripps, had tried to warn Stalin. Other reports reaching the Soviet capital clearly indicated Hitler's intentions. They warned Stalin that there were over a hundred German divisions positioned along the frontier, but Stalin refused to believe any of them.

Three hours before the Wermacht invaded, the last shipment of grain left Russia for Germany. At 4 a.m. on the morning of June 22, 1941, the German armies took up their positions along a line that stretched from the Baltic to the Black Sea. Operation Barbarossa had begun.

Of the invasion of Russia, historian Friedrich Meinecke said, 'The enemy's real weapons were time, hunger and America.' It was, for Germany, the beginning of the end.

We are divided from England by a ditch 37 kilometres wide and we are not even able to get to know what is happening there.

Hitler. October, 1941

The ever present underestimation of enemy capabilities is becoming grotesque. One cannot any longer speak of serious work. Cranky reactions to the impression of the moment and complete lack of appreciation of the judgements of the command organisation and its capacities, give this 'leadership' its characteristic stamp.

Halder : Winter, 1941

Russia is our Africa; and the Russians are our negroes.

Hitler. 1942

If I don't get oil out of Maikop and Grozny, I must end this war.

Hitler. June, 1942

It is quite possible, of course, that there are madmen in Germany who dream of harnessing the elephant (of the Soviet Ukraine) to the gnat (of the Carpathian Ukraine). If there really are such lunatics in Germany, rest assured we shall find enough straitjackets for them in our country.

Stalin

CHAPTER SIXTEEN

Most of the German people received the news of the attack on Russia with relief, if not boundless enthusiasm. With the kind of luck their Fuhrer had enjoyed in the French campaign, it should all be over in six months at the most.

Civilians were more concerned with the shortages: shoe laces, wireless valves and electric plugs had vanished from retailers' shelves. Other commodities such as paint, knicker elastic, cotton wool, coffee and contraceptives were unobtainable, except on the flourishing black market.

However, they continued to have faith in their invincible leader, and with the first sweeping advances, there was little to shake their confidence.

Jodl was able to report on July 14 that the Wehrmacht was two-thirds of the way to Moscow; and that the roads to Leningrad and Kiev would present no problems to his panzers.

Much of the Press was less optimistic, particularly when the Russian army regrouped around Smolensk and mounted a counter-attack.

'The Russian soldier surpasses our adversary in the West in his contempt for death,' the *Volkischer Beobachter* reported somewhat huffily at the end of June. 'Endurance and fatalism make him hold out until he is blown up in his trench or falls in hand-to-hand fighting.'

'Our enemy in the East reacts in a completely different way from the French to German tactics of wedges and pincer movements,' said the *Frankfurter Zeitung* in early July. 'The mental paralysis which usually followed the breakthroughs in the West, do not occur to the same extent in the East. In most cases the enemy does not lose his capacity for action. He tries in his turn to break the arms of the German pincers.'

The uncouth Bolsheviks were not obeying the rules of the game.

In fact, they seemed to be completely lacking in fair play, believing it their duty to slaughter Germans regardless of circumstances. In addition, they went in for a barbarous policy of burning everything behind them thus preventing the Germans from capturing enemy supplies.

In 1941, Hitler came up against someone even more fanatical than himself, for Stalin's own tyrannical dogma had prepared Russia to mount total resistance to attack.

*   *   *

With the German armies moving forward along a line that began at the Baltic and finished at the Black Sea, Hitler set up headquarters at Rastenberg, East Prussia on June 24.

Linge gazed at the dank, gloomy forest. He saw the collection of huts above ground that had been set aside for the Fuhrer's aides, and promptly disappeared into Hitler's concrete bunker to work on his notebooks.

The Fuhrer spent most of his time in his quarters, working at his desk throughout the night, emerging like a fretful badger at around noon to sit in on the daily progress meetings.

Although Linge was excluded, his close contact with Hitler allowed him the rare privilege of listening to his nightly deliberations. Usually silent when deeply depressed, when in high spirits the chief talked incessantly to himself, which gave Linge the opportunity to make notes. And as the campaign progressed, Hitler became repetitious.

It was fortunate too that in the evenings, with little else to do in the 'wolf's lair' other than to watch newsreels in the large communal hut or to moan about the poor quality of the meals in the mess, the valet had time to fill in the details.

With his armies well on the road to Moscow, Hitler derived abundant satisfaction from enumerating his achievements since the beginning of the war.

Belgium, Holland and the northern industrial area of France were all under German administration. Norway had Vidkun Quisling as chief executive — but with extremely limited powers. In Spain, Franco feared the Russians more than he disliked the Third Reich. Hungary, Rumania, Bulgaria and Finland were all aligned with Germany, Finland being allowed to reduce her war effort so that she could begin domestic reconstruction. Bulgaria was the barrier against an allied move in Turkey. Antonescu of Rumania was an admired, trusted friend, supplying both oil stocks and troops.

And Italy? Fortunately there was no call for Italian divisions in Russia; not initially, anyway, as Mussolini's men were more urgently required in North Africa.

'The war potential of Europe is at the disposal of the Reich,' said Hitler, 'and our national pride has never been greater. No one can now point to a line on a map and say "Thus far and no further". We will have our "living space" even if it means we are forced to fight the bloodiest war in history to bring this about.'

'Our defensive base is established,' the Fuhrer went on. 'Our offensive is continuing along a thousand-mile front and it will accelerate as one Soviet division after another is defeated. Our first encirclement has resulted in the capture of hundreds of thousands of Russian soldiers. The German infantry is supported by the finest weapons in the world.

'Our armies have tasted victory in Poland, France, in North Africa. You may think things are different in Russia. They are. Our soldiers are already tempered by war. The Russians are novices.

'There is nothing to prevent us attaining our final objective: to secure both the Fatherland and Europe from Communism. We will destroy it beyond our frontier as we have put an end to it inside the Reich.

'We will populate these eastern territories; colonise them; construct roads, build towns; Germanise the country.

'Future colonies will be located on the same land mass as Germany, easily accessible by road. And, if we have to revolutionise the face of Europe to do this, it will be done.

'We won't always be regarded as a warrior nation. Once peace is restored, our farmers and technicians will restore the Russian desert; cultivating the soil; growing food in plenty to match all our needs. For the next thousand years German agricultural attainments will benefit humanity.

'And once Russia has ceased to be a threat we must come to an understanding with England.'

This was the kind of speech Hitler made to his chiefs-of-staff; and they were, in June, 1941, still prepared to listen to him. He was, after all, at the zenith of his success, militarily speaking. At the same time, they were beginning to realise that Guderian's estimate of three months to reach Moscow had been optimistic. And if, by some chance, the Russian powers of resistance *were* as fanatical as it was rumoured, then . . . But, of course, they reassured each other, Hitler's belief in Russia's vulnerability was surely correct.

Hitler frequently drew the attention of his generals to the Bolshevik philosophy of fermenting world unease in order to promote revolution. 'The suffering of the German people after 1918 and the initial opposition to National Socialism came about entirely as a result of a Communistic influence at work.'

Because of this, the Fuhrer inaugurated fundamental changes in the conduct of war.

Soviet soldiers would not be dealt with according to the 1907 Hague Convention's 'Rules of Land Warfare' nor according to the 1914 Geneva Convention on the treatment of prisoners-of-war.

The 'Commissar's Order' of June 6, 1941 decreed that all commissars and political functionaries captured in Russia were to be shot immediately.

The *Einsatzgruppen* (death squads) of the SS would follow their own judgement and decide who was to be executed.

In the autumn of 1941, separate prisoner-of-war camps were set up inside existing concentration camps. When the Russian prisoners arrived, tens of thousands of them were shot. As it happened, the physical condition of many of them was so poor, they didn't survive to experience execution. Very few of them had any involvement with Soviet politics.

In a letter dated November 9, 1941 SS General Heinrich Muller, chief of the Gestapo under Kaltenbrunner, wrote:

'The commanders of the camps are complaining that from five-to ten-per-cent of the Russians to be executed arrive in the camps dead or half dead. Thus the impression is created that this is how the prisoner-of-war camps dispose of such prisoners. In particular, it has been determined that in marching, for example, from the train station to the camp, a not insignificant number of prisoners collapse on the way, dead or half dead from exhaustion, and have to be picked up by a vehicle following behind. The German inhabitants cannot be prevented from taking notice of these events . . .' (Nuremberg Document No 3424).

At Dachau, mass shootings of Russian prisoners continued from

October 1941 to April 1942 on an SS shooting range located outside the camp perimeters. Then a change of policy incorporated the Soviet prisoners into the forced-labour system working for the armament industry, although individual executions continued to be carried out until the end of the war.

According to testimony supplied at Nuremberg, about 3,700,000 Soviet prisoners-of-war died in German occupied territory.

* * *

The much-discussed tension that existed between the Fuhrer and his field commanders and his distrust of so many of the generals is recorded by Linge.

Although there was no outright dissension at first, it was clear that Hitler found their attitude exasperating. He desperately needed their cooperation in what he knew was the most critical period in the history of the Third Reich, but the generals, most of them in their fifties and sixties, had experienced too many insults from a man who, to them, would always be little more than a wartime corporal.

They might obey the orders of their Fuhrer when he spoke as commander-in-chief, but among themselves they frequently criticised his strategy, his party hierarchy and his seeming lack of any moral code.

There were also too many unexplained deaths of military leaders in mysterious circumstances to allow the remaining high-ranking officers to place their 'unquestioning trust' in Hitler.

The murders of Generals von Schleicher and von Bredow; the frame-up of Fritsch and the easing out of Beck; the snubs to Halder, to Blaskowitz who had protested about SS activity in Poland; all these incidents were suspicious and dismaying. As regulars of the old Prussian school they also detested the Gestapo and had nothing but contempt for the ruthless methods used to intimidate anyone who did not follow the party line.

However, whatever private thoughts the Fuhrer entertained about the adult delinquents who were his personal policemen, he never voiced them to his military commanders.

* * *

As one triumph followed another, Hitler began to search for someone with whom to share his success. He chose General Antonescu, then commanding his Rumanian troops in the Ukrainian town of Berdichev. Impressed with the fighting spirit of his ally, he instructed Linge to pack a spare Iron Cross in his baggage and arrange transport to Berdichev.

The dapper little General with the compulsive, toothy smile would be the first foreign recipient of the decoration in World War II. Antonescu was also promised a slice of South Ukraine as a more substantial reward for his loyalty to the Fuhrer.

Elaborating on his future plans once the war had ended, Hitler gave Antonescu an opening to specify his own long term hopes.

High on the list of the former Bucharest lawyer's priorities was the handing back to Rumania of territory previously allocated to Hungary.

Smiling cheerfully, Antonescu delicately reminded the Fuhrer that Rumania came within the sphere of many other interests and influences, which was something for him to bear in mind when the time came to review the situation in south-eastern Europe.

Hitler listened closely, matching Antonescu smile for smile. Finally, he nodded. Anything was possible. Once Russia had been defeated and Communism crushed, his friends would not be forgotten.

Later, he recalled an earlier talk with Admiral Horthy, the Hungarian Regent, on the occasion of his asking the 73-year-old leader for military assistance.

The handsome Horthy, of the sharp features and hawklike eyes, was aware that Hungary's army could supply useful reinforcements in the Russian campaign; he also knew he was tied hand and foot to the Reich, both economically and militarily. While he believed the cards were stacked against the Soviets, he was at the same time reluctant to commit his army to the cause.

In recalling the occasion, Hitler gave one of his celebrated impressions. 'The Hungarian people,' he said in Horthy's clipped tones, 'naturally hate Communism. And we are certainly prepared spiritually to oppose the Russians. Unhappily, we are by no means ready materially.'

Horthy, the Admiral without a fleet, said Hitler with cynical frankness, would do anything to avoid being dragged into the war.

'If you want to eat the meal,' he had told him, 'you must help with the cooking.'

*   *   *

Towards the end of August, Mussolini visited Hitler at Rastenberg. By then, the headquarters had expanded considerably. An elaborate wireless station had been erected; it had its own telephone exchange; and central heating was installed in most of the chalets. Protected by a battery of anti-aircraft guns, the outer peripheries were patrolled night and day by a triple ring of specially selected SS guards.

The Duce, having sent some divisions to join the Wehrmacht in Russia, found Hitler in a confident, talkative mood. He was able to boast of his successes, rubbing his hands together briskly, slapping his thigh time after time. Yes, there had been some difficulties caused by inaccurate intelligence reports of the strength of resistance encountered, but his forces were penetrating deep into Russia.

Would the offer of more Italian divisions help? asked Mussolini.

Hitler looked almost embarrassed and rapidly changed the subject. There was no way the Duce was going to claim any of the glory. He invited Mussolini to fly with him to Field Marshal von Kluge's HQ at Brest Litovsk.

A four-engined Condor later took the party on to Uman for lunch with Runstedt, and while Hitler happily sat in the field kitchen among his soldiers, the Duce found himself set slightly apart, with only Runstedt for company. He was convinced his brother dictator was showing off, as he sat there reminiscing about the old days in the trenches of World War I.

Taking his leave, Hitler — with one eye on the Duce — called out in a loud voice: 'Did I exaggerate the situation in this so-called Soviet paradise?'

The men all shook their heads vigorously. 'You did not, Fuhrer,' they chorused. 'It is twenty times worse than any of us imagined.'

When an open car arrived to take the leaders closer to the front line, Linge found himself crammed between the driver and Schmundt, while Mussolini relaxed in the rear seat next to Hitler.

It so happened that, as the car was halted at an intersection, long lines of bedraggled Italian infantrymen were filing past. One young sergeant recognised the Duce and spread the word. The entire unit broke ranks and crowded around, cheering and chattering away in their own language. Mussolini — with a sidelong glance at the Fuhrer — rose to his feet, his vanity puffing him up like a toad on heat. His moment had come.

On the way back to the airfield, the Fuhrer talked volubly about his ideas for the future. Mussolini, head on one side, was given no opportunity to speak. He contented himself with an occasional murmur as if to signify complete agreement. Linge suspected that he was nodding off.

Hitler drew Mussolini's attention to the endless acres of ripe wheat and to the rich, black earth. 'Our people could do with this kind of land. The trouble with too much of our arable soil is that it is exhausted from over-production. Most of the peasant population nowadays are barely able to scratch a living. But I promise: once we have defeated Stalin, your people will share in the rich harvest.'

He drew the Duce's attention to the primitive huts that served as homes for the peasants. 'This is what Communism has given them; the worst kind of poverty. The sight gives me greater incentive to build a new future for these people. We can do so much more for workers everywhere, by spreading the word of National Socialism; and by improving living standards — our first priorities once the war is over. Our new order in Europe will ensure peace for a thousand years.'

Mussolini said nothing. Once the Fuhrer was off on that 'thousand year' soliloquy, he heard only what he wanted to hear.

Some months later an exhibition, 'Soviet Paradise', opened in the Lustgarten, Berlin. It mainly comprised a motley assembly of Russian homesteads, filthy shacks full of an appalling collection of rags, all transported from Minsk. Thousands of Berliners visited the exhibition, though none of them stayed longer than a few minutes — the offensive odours proved more powerful than the propaganda value.

*   *   *

Although Russian supplies were curtailed through the loss of the facilities of industrial Ukraine, the armament factories of the Urals and shipments from Britain and America partly made up for it.

The route through Persia became the important channel of allied supplies to the Russian armies. The German offensive was expected to concentrate on the oil wells of the Caucasus so that it was vital for the supplies to arrive in the right area for the defending forces.

By September, the Germans had reached the outer suburbs of Leningrad and their centre line held a hundred miles short of Moscow. To the south the Crimea had been overrun and the panzers were heading for Sebastapol. The Russians fought back with desperation.

It was deep in the Russians' nature to fight furiously for their country and their resilience and way of life were tremendous assets. The Soviet soldier's capacity for enduring hardship was to prove astonishing.

Linge heard rumours that millions of Russian soldiers had died, only to be replaced by hordes of Mongolian guerillas. Not so, said Hitler.

According to the Fuhrer, Russia was finished. 'It will never rise again.' His Wehrmacht was closer to Moscow by November. He urged them on from battle to battle, said his valet, ignoring those at headquarters who muttered about overstretched supply-lines or about insufficient war materials getting through.

The adviser who mentioned the oncoming winter and the imminent need for warmer clothing for the frontline troops was brushed aside. Hitler reminded his generals of an earlier campaign: Napoleon's Italian crusade; when the French, uniforms in tatters, desperately short of equipment, still emerged the winners. Then, every man had sublime faith in their leader; and he in turn gave them all the will to succeed.

Despite Hitler's confidence, two topics dominated every conference: lack of supplies and the need for winter clothing.

Hitler undeniably had military vision, but he tended to place too much emphasis on the power of the will to overcome strategic difficulties. He made no allowances for the Russians' strength and ability to impose *their* will. He was right, he maintained, and the General Staff were wrong.

Then the Russian winter, early that year, began to turn the ground to mud.

The Fuhrer spent hours on the phone, said Linge, growing more agitated as his military objective, the utter destruction of the Russian forces, receded further from his grasp.

Weather conditions deteriorated further and the generals' fears were rapidly confirmed by the turn of events. Savage frosts held up supplies and the troops frequently ran short of ammunition. It was only their fortitude and the granite will of their Fuhrer that prevented them from experiencing a complete reversal.

So the Russian army had survived; Leningrad had not been taken, nor Moscow nor Stalingrad, nor the oil wells in the south.

Fortunately, the lifelines in the north to Murmansk and the route through Persia remained open. But with Rumania asking for gold in exchange for oil, the situation for Germany at the end of 1941 was critical. Oil stocks were down from 380,000 to 150,000 tons.

Engineer Todt, who built the West Wall, ordered thousands of solid-fuel iron stoves to be sent up the line and began urgent research into the possibilities of producing a non-freeze oil. By then, the temperature along the front line had dropped to 31 degrees below zero.

Kleinman, Secretary of State for railways, was summoned to Rastenberg to be roundly abused by his Fuhrer for failing to keep supplies and reinforcements on the move. His only excuse was that similar problems existed during World War I.

Ignoring his valet's presence, Hitler began to shout at the man.

'A typical bourgeois reaction,' he fumed. 'Instead of trying to learn from past mistakes you simply hide them under the nearest carpet for someone else to clean up.' He started to splutter with rage. 'By God, I swear when this war is over, I will personally check up on every mistake made. Never, ever again will any of you miserable *schweinehunds* be able to commit stupid blunders.'

Kleinman was sacked on the spot and Ganzenmuller, younger, more alert, and as rigorous as the goosestep, replaced him.

His first assignment was to produce a railway engine able to withstand extremes of temperature. Next, over 1,000 miles of track was to be relaid to match the narrower German gauge — in Russia it was five feet.

As a result of the new man's efficiency, Hitler decided that seniority or long experience were not always rational reasons for promotion or potential leadership.

What had merit to do with length of service, he said, particularly in the army? Having discovered information which listed the ages of Napoleon's commanders, he was gratified to learn that most of them had been under forty.

The notion of replacing 'men of straw' with tough young officers appealed to him as a way of restoring morale to his frontline soldiers. Any general 'not wholehearted in his efforts to gain a decisive victory' would have to go. So many of them were like professional Jeremiahs, tending to reach for the sackcloth and ashes a little too readily.

He required, he said, energetic commanders who, showing some of his own iron will, were able to issue orders with rat-a-tat precision and stem the retreat. The army had to hold on, whatever the cost. Anything was preferable to retreat, the disaster that had destroyed Napoleon's forces.

It was at about this time that his valet noted changes taking place in the Fuhrer's personality. Constant frustration and imagined slights left him barely able to control his anger. He seemed unable to establish priorities and believed he could overcome reality by refusing to acknowledge its existence.

There were increasingly violent clashes with his generals, most of whom he considered to be intellectually sterile.

As Hitler began issuing peremptory orders, heads began to roll. Even Keitel, ever obsequious, was subjected to a constant stream of abuse.

Jodl discovered him sitting at his desk, writing a letter of resignation, a revolver to hand. He took the weapon away from Keitel and urged him to stay on and fight to the bitter end.

Field Marshal Brauchitsch, seeing no other way out and openly disapproving of the Fuhrer's tactics, offered his resignation on December 17.

The offer was accepted and Hitler, in an impressive display of authoritative zeal, announced that he would immediately take over as commander-in-chief. Not even in medieval times, said Shirer, nor even further back in barbarous tribal days, had any German assumed such tyrannical powers, nominal and legal as well as actual, to himself. The Reichstag agreed to the passing of a law giving the Fuhrer, head of state, minister of war, supreme commander of the armed forces and commander-in-chief of the army, absolute power of life and death over every German. Any previous laws that stood in the way of his overall power were immediately rescinded.

Brauchitsch's resignation was the first of many. It was followed by the departure of Runstedt, Bock and Guderian. Leeb was relieved of his post in January, 1942.

) 1922: 'The masses are so obtuse, they ... will remember the simplest idea
nly if it is repeated a thousand times.' *Hitler*

2) 1929: Eva Braun met Hitler for the first time at Hoffman's studio. He was forty; she was seventeen.
(Photo credit: Hoffman)

3) 1929: A rare photograph taken on Martin Bormann's wedding day, showing (l-r) Hess, Herbert Blank, von Pfeffer (head of Munich SA), Walter Busch (Bormann's father-in-law and Head Party Judge), Hitler, Albert Bormann (younger brother), Bormann and wife.
(Photo credit: Private source)

) 1932: The 'Bohemian Corporal' meets the Prussian Junker, Field Marshal
Hindenburg.
(Photo credit: Hoffman)

5) 1933: Hitler marching with the SA Chief of Staff, Ernst Rohm.
(Photo credit: Hoffman)

) 1934: Hitler, Goering and Rohm. After the purging of June 30, Hitler 'foamed
vith rage' at Rohm's homosexuality.
(Photo credit: Hoffman)

7) 1934: Unity Mitford (rt.) with her sister, Diana Lady Mosely, at a pre-war Nazi rally.
(Photo credit: Hoffman)

) *Top photo*
934: Hitler and Goebbels greeted outside the Prinz Albrecht Hotel, Berlin.
Photo Credit: Hoffman)

) *Lower photo*
940: Linge (extreme left) looks on as Hitler and Mussolini seal the Berlin-Rome
xis, a few days after Il Duce declared war.
Photo credit: Bild-Zeitung)

10) Linge checks the menu for dinner at the Fuhrer's wartime headquarters.
The stripe on the valet's sleeve indicates he joined the Nazi Party before 1933.
(Photo credit: Bild-Zeitung)

Udet of the Luftwaffe died in mysterious circumstances in November, 1941. At first it was claimed he had been killed testing a new weapon. Then he was said to have committed suicide. His death was followed by those of other senior officers in the Luftwaffe and several prominent executives in the civil service, and included the death of Udet's successor, Gablenz. Field Marshal Reichenau, who succeeded Runstedt, died from a cerebral haemorrhage on January 17. In all, thirty-five commanders were replaced during the winter retreat of 1941-42.

As Manstein told the Nuremberg tribunal:

'Of seventeen field-marshals, ten were sent home during the war; three lost their lives following the 1944 bomb plot. Only one fieldmarshal managed to emerge from the war retaining his rank.

'Out of thirty-six generals, eighteen were sent home, five died as a result of the bomb plot or were dishonourably discharged. Only three full generals survived the war without loss of rank.'

*   *   *

Hitler, as supreme commander, reviewed the situation on the Russian front and instructed his armies to stay where they were. Disregarding the cost in lives, he refused all requests to withdraw. Thousands of soldiers died of the cold and more manpower reserves were sent to the front.

And the Russians failed to break through.

*   *   *

Some historians have speculated as to whether Hitler's stubborn stand saved the German armies from disaster or cost him the campaign.

Linge considered that, despite the serious reverse, it was the Fuhrer's greatest achievement of the war. He believed that it was solely through his determination that the armies were saved from disintegration.

Those who heard the Fuhrer speak in the Sport Palace, Berlin that January thought differently. Many were able to trace the course of events in their leader's haggard features and hesitant attitude.

'Hitler lost his gift for working intuitively, which formerly had been his main asset,' said Speer. 'When he was forced to work rationally and logically, he was often incapable of coming to a decision.'

By then, according to Halder, 'he lived in a world of self-deception and over-confidence, which prevented him from distinguishing the possible from the impossible, and intuition prevailed over reason, improvisation over planning.'

After October, 1942 no long term planning studies were attempted. They would only have reached conclusions which Hitler could never have accepted.

'No one was told any more than the Fuhrer wanted him to know,' said Keitel.

Bormann and his cronies took care to prevent painful truths from reaching Hitler; nothing that might have undermined his belief in his ability or his mission was shown to him.

'Very little news from the outside penetrated the holy of holies,' said Jodl.

'The object was,' said Speer, 'to maintain his sleepwalker's sense of security.'

His sleepwalker's sense of security was almost shattered on December 6 when his forces, having suffered major losses, were finally driven back from Moscow.

The news next day went some way towards repairing the cracks — the Japanese attacked Pearl Harbour and the United States entered the war.

*   *   *

James Rusbridger, writing in *Encounter*, in May, 1985 suggested that the Japanese attack on Pearl Harbour in December, 1941 was precipitated by the incompetence of an unknown British official, who allowed secret papers to fall into enemy hands.

War Cabinet Minutes dated August 8, 1940, which gave a pessimistic assessment of Britain's ability to resist Japanese aggression in the Far East, were intercepted by the Germans. 'Incredibly,' said Rusbridger, an intelligence expert, 'this all-important document was sent to the Far East in the Blue Funnel steamer *Automedon*, instead of by flying boat service to Singapore.'

On November 11, 1940 the *Automedon* was attacked by the German raider *Atlantis* off the Nicobar Islands. A pouch marked 'Safe Hand — British master only' was seized and sent on to the

German naval attaché in Tokyo. The pouch contained the Cabinet document admitting that Hong Kong, Malaya, Singapore and the Dutch East Indies had no defences against a Japanese attack.

'It is fair to argue,' concluded Rusbridger, 'that the capture of this document was the catalyst that sent Japan on the path to Pearl Harbour.'

At the time, Britain had based a detachment of Naval Cyphers on Stonecutter's Island in order to monitor Japanese signals — they had details of the secret code. As a result, the United States knew well before December 7 of the Japanese plan to attack the naval base. The senior officer in charge of the Cyphers has confirmed that the information was passed to American Intelligence, together with details of when the assault would take place.

'Unfortunately,' wrote Cedric Brown (the senior officer) 'the United States appeared not to have taken the information seriously enough, and were therefore unprepared for the attack on Pearl Harbour.'

This little matter of operational command is something anyone can do. The task of the Commander-in-Chief is to train the army in a National Socialist way. I know of no general who could do that as I want it done. Consequently I've decided to take over command of the army myself.

Hitler, 1941.

Everything about the behaviour of American society reveals that one half is Judaised and the other half negrified. How can one expect a state like that to hold together — a country where everything is built on the dollar?

Hitler.

What became known in high Nazi circles as the 'Fuhrer's Order on the Final Solution' apparently was never committed to paper — at least, no copy of it has yet been unearthed in captured documents. All the evidence shows that it was most probably given verbally to Goring, Himmler and Heydrich, who passed it down during the summer . . . of 1941.

William L. Shirer

Military genius is not produced from a reading of Clausewitz and having been a lance-corporal in the last war.

Field Marshal von Leeb

CHAPTER SEVENTEEN

Hermann Goring, Heinrich Himmler, Rudolf Heydrich — these three men represented most effectively the malignancy of Nazism even more precisely than the Fuhrer himself.

'I can only regard Goring as immoral and criminal,' said Schacht at Nuremberg. 'Gifted from the start with a certain bonhomie, he was the most egocentric creature one could imagine. For him, the attainment of political power was only a means to personal enrichment and luxury.'

It was Goring who transmitted what became known among party leaders as 'The Fuhrer Order on the Final Solution' to Heydrich. The directive, dated July 31, 1941 (given in evidence at Nuremberg), stated:

'I herewith commission you to carry out all preparations with regard to a total solution of the Jewish question in those territories of Europe which are under German influence. I furthermore charge you to submit to me as soon as possible a draft showing the measures already taken for the execution of the intended final solution of the Jewish question.'

Heydrich, the laconic, detached bloodhound of the party, placed the memo on top of the pile in his pending tray. His first priority was a decree signed by Keitel, the *Nacht und Nebel* (Night and Fog) Order.

With unrest spreading throughout occupied Europe, anyone suspected of resistance was arrested under the order and sent to Germany without relatives being told of the prisoner's whereabouts. As this new breed of offenders were not dealt with in the special court established to handle political opponents, they were placed in concentration camps under a special category 'NN'.

In Czechoslovakia, because of the widespread revolt that had broken out against the occupying army, the Reich Protector von Neurath was recalled to Berlin. Heydrich was appointed in his place.

He acted swiftly. The Czech Prime Minister, Elias, was arrested in September and a wave of executions followed. By the end of the month, 123 Czechs had been put to death. As a result of a purge in the armed forces, a number of Czech officers were shot.

Heydrich was back in Berlin at the turn of the year, a blueprint for mass destruction in his brief case. Exuding, as usual, a lazy malevolence in the face of his own sublime evil, he summoned a meeting of the SS, ministry officials and civil occupation authorities on January 20, 1942. They met in the pleasant suburb of Wannsee — at the offices of Interpol, 16 am Kleinen.

*　　*　　*

The role played by Interpol during World War II has never been fully explained.

The International Criminal Police Commission, the organisation for cooperation between the CIDs of its member states, was established in Vienna in 1923. After the annexation of Austria, the headquarters were transferred to Berlin.

Heydrich, the head of the security service, became its president. He added a new crime to Interpol's list: being born a European Jew.

Because branch offices in France, Belgium and some of the neutral countries were controlled from Berlin, Heydrich was able to manipulate their police. Top international forgers were located and brought to Germany to counterfeit currency and manufacture various documents. Interpol files helped German agents contact people with dubious backgrounds, who were then pressurised into spying for the Reich.

For many years, Simon Wiesenthal has been investigating the wartime record of Interpol; trying to determine how much assistance it gave to the Nazis. He discovered that most of its files were destroyed, probably with good reason, during the final struggle for Berlin in 1945. However, he has reason to believe that the so-called 'S File', which contained Interpol warrants for Jews and political opponents of Hitler's regime who found refuge under assumed names in France, may still exist in the present Interpol headquarters in Paris.

He wrote to the French Justice Minister in 1983 suggesting that the world was entitled to know the truth. And if the file existed, it ought to be used to identify Heydrich's accomplices. If any of them were alive they could be tried as war criminals.

The matter was referred to Gaston Deferre, Minister of Interior.

*   *   *

At Wannsee, Heydrich discussed his plans, hoping 'to clear up the fundamental problems' involved in mass extermination — 'in the course of this Final Solution of the European Jewish problem, approximately eleven million Jews are involved'.

Speaking in terms of millions of people, he explained how they would be transported to Eastern occupied Europe; those suitable would be 'worked to death'. New camps would be opened at Sobibor, Majdanek and Treblinka. Mobile extermination units would be employed.

Transportation problems would be left in the dependable hands of the railway chief, Ganzenmuller. A comparatively low-ranking SS man named Adolf Eichmann would settle the details of deportation, forced labour and mass extermination. 'One hundred dead is a catastrophe,' he was to say later, 'five million dead is a statistic.'

Poland became the centre of operations. There, voluntary helpers brought up in the East European tradition of anti-Semitism, assisted the Gestapo and the SS. There was nothing secret about the operations. The trains carrying the victims to the camps appeared in the official timetables; the population knew about the concentration camps; they saw the prisoners on work details; some of them complained about the offensive smells emanating from the crematorium chimneys close to their villages.

In the first four months of its operations, the Einsatzgruppe A unit based in northern Russia, killed one hundred and thirty-five thousand Jews and communists.

Before the beginning of World War II, it is estimated that there were approximately ten million Jews living in territories later occupied by the Germans. Over half of them were exterminated on the orders of Hitler.

*   *   *

The situation was relatively calm in Berlin during the early months of 1942. Heydrich, although based in Czechoslovakia, made regular flights back to the capital to report on the activities of the so-called 'Jewish Office' of the Gestapo.

On May 13, with a twinge of self-satisfaction, he told Goring that 'in great columns — with the separation of the sexes — those Jews fit for work are being despatched to the eastern territories. In the process, a considerable reduction of numbers will undoubtedly take place by natural means.'

But back in Prague, Jan Kubis and Josef Gabchik were biding their time. For months they had been waiting for the right opportunity.

This finally came on the morning of May 27, some six miles from the centre of Prague. Heydrich was being driven to the airport by his personal minder, the 6ft. 7 ins. tall Klein, in his green open Mercedes.

Josef waited a few yards from a tram stop, a loaded Sten gun at the ready. Jan, some distance from him, acted as back-up, a grenade concealed in his overcoat.

As the Mercedes approached the tram stop, Josef took aim; and the gun jammed. Heydrich, quickly summing up the situation, rapped out an order in his staccato, high-pitched voice. As Klein braked, Jan pulled the pin from his grenade and flung it towards the car.

Heydrich flung himself to one side as the explosion devastated the rear body of his Mercedes, firing his revolver at the assailant, unaware that splinters from the grenade had penetrated his back, causing extensive damage to his spleen. Taken to hospital he lay in agony for ten days — vital cellular tissues had been poisoned by bacteria adhering to the grenade splinters.

The assassination attempt naturally caused a sensation in Berlin and after his death, a number of even more rigorous measures were imposed in Czechoslovakia. By June 6, the number of death sentences reached two hundred.

On June 10, German soldiers entered the village of Lidice a few miles from Prague. All the male inhabitants were shot and women and children were shipped to Ravensbruck concentration camp. The village was then razed to the ground. The official version of the atrocity stated that the two culprits, Kubis and Gabchik, had been discovered hiding in a church on June 18 and shot on the spot. They were described as two former Czech soldiers who had been trained in England, parachuted in, and had then been assisted by Czech resistance groups.

*   *   *

It was in January that Linge reached a decision. Dressed in his best black uniform, which by then fitted him like a second skin, he presented himself early one morning to his chief.

He told the Fuhrer that, after a sleepless night mulling over all the pros and cons, he had decided to seek the Fuhrer's consent to a posting on active service to the eastern front. So many of the friends he had grown up with in the Hitler Youth, comrades he had drilled with in the SS — they were all engaged in the life or death struggle. It was surely time for him to join them?

Hitler seemed surprised at his request. Russia was at its last gasp; the Japanese, having sunk half the US Navy, were about to administer a coup de grace to whatever was left of the British Empire east of Suez. And although he didn't suggest for a moment that his valet would in any way be a serious hindrance to imminent victory, he pointed out that the years Linge had spent cosseting the number one man in all Germany did not exactly fit his loyal servant for the more hazardous role of rifle bearer in the thick of the fighting.

'Why you?' he asked. 'A married man with children? If I thought it was necessary to send my personal staff to the front, it would be one of the bachelors, not a man with responsibilities.'

'That is not how I view things, my Fuhrer,' said Linge. 'Having done my duty by increasing the population, surely I should be the first to go?'

Hitler shook his head. 'No. You are necessary to me here because I can't think of anyone suitable to replace you. Remember your particular job is more important than killing Russians. So we'll say no more on the subject.'

Hitler was still confident. The news was good. His army was standing firm. His nerve had survived its most testing time to date. It was his body that was beginning to let him down.

Linge recalled a morning when an upsetting and acrimonious argument with his generals led to Hitler collapsing in his chair, gasping for breath. The valet helped to carry him back to his quarters, and summoned Dr Morell. He arrived within a few minutes and gave the Fuhrer a thorough going-over. Finding nothing physically wrong, he prescribed tablets, which he said would stimulate the appetite and combat exhaustion. Hitler should take them twice daily before meals and rest for at least a week.

The Fuhrer was on his feet, reaching for his riding boots within a couple of hours.

'I can assure you, Doctor,' he said, 'with time running out for the Russians, nothing can faze me at present. Whatever it was that affected me won't trouble me again; unless, of course, I get exceptionally bad news from the front.'

Morell said nothing. No doubt he was aware of the origins of Hitler's collapse, but by then he knew he was powerless to effect a permanent cure.

Some historians have suggested that Hitler no longer believed in victory after the savage winter of 1941; that his remaining energies were dedicated towards prolonging his own life. Linge dismisses such statements as nonsense.

He recalls certain generals arguing with the Fuhrer at the time. They thought the eastern front had too many loopholes and were all for pulling back as far as Poland. Hitler urged them forward towards Stalingrad.

To him, such a negative outlook as they displayed was pathetic: 'These fellows are too complicated; full of theories; with very little grasp of practical soldiering. I give them solutions to their problems and they fight shy of them; continually making excuses. They should remember what country people say: "What the farmer doesn't know he won't grow. What he won't grow he doesn't eat".'

Linge nodded sagely, although he was unable to grasp the connection.

Such incidents troubled him a great deal. Increasingly, from the summer of 1942, he found his chief's conversations becoming more disjointed, more rambling, more difficult to follow. At the same time, he stressed that Hitler didn't altogether disagree with his generals' tactics; nor did he totally ignore their suggestions. His duty lay in encouraging them but there were no lengths to which he wouldn't go in order to convince them that he was right. He was never insensitive to the dangers ahead for his men on the eastern front.

Whoever visited him at Rastenberg was under no illusions: the Fuhrer was firmly in control. Whether it was Horthy trying to wriggle out of a commitment, or King Boris pleading shortages of raw materials, his objective never wavered: these lesser mortals must do as they were told. If he required more manpower they must supply it. There was no argument; only forceful persuasion on his part.

In private, he referred to such encounters as 'the play' — mere diverting interludes which gave him an opportunity of playing with two minnows on one line.

*   *   *

In July, Hitler moved his headquarters to Vinnitsa in the Ukraine. Werewolf, located in lightly wooded country, consisted of chalets, blockhouses and a couple of concrete bunkers. Although partly concealed by trees, there was little protection from flies or the sun's glare, which prospect was not pleasing to the Fuhrer.

He loathed any form of bright light and was obliged to pull the visor of his cap low over his face whenever he left his bunker. He complained of severe headaches, blaming the intolerable climate. His temper grew increasingly short as the discord among his field commanders increased. This developed from his demands that they went all out for the Caucasus and Stalingrad.

'I would be a true *scheisskerl*,' he would say, 'if I can't convince them how important it is to gain the ground as far as the Caspian Sea. Why, for God's sake, can't they see the way is wide open; that the area is just begging to be subdued?

'Once we have it, we can take Stalingrad. But no, they prefer to take heed of the strategy of fear, and believe the stupid stories that there are hundreds of thousands of Soviet troops lurking on the other side of the Volga, waiting to swallow up the Wehrmacht. That kind of idle talk has no place at our discussions.

'Stalin would make short work of such idiots; those who can only put up obstacles to victory. I envy his foresight in getting rid of awkward commanders before the war started. My commanders are very similar to the old Czarists; vain, arrogant and incapable of understanding that today's battles are not decided with broadswords from the backs of cavalry chargers.'

No one had the courage to point out that his theories had already been disproved, and that if he insisted on remaining the chief architect of the situation, it could only lead to the downfall of his forces. With each desperate move his outlook deteriorated just a little more. It was also noticeable that, from 1942 on, Hitler seldom visited Berlin or the battle fronts.

In mid-August, the fighting slowed down in the Caucasus due to torrential rain, but the Germans made solid progress in their advance towards Stalingrad. When he was told the news that the 6th army had reached the city, the Fuhrer was delighted. But learning that a soldier had planted the Swastika flag on the summit of El'brus Mountain, 5,600 metres above Gora, he was furious; putting the blame on List for wasting time. List should have been well on the road to Tuapse. 'What was he trying to do? Impress the British with his mountaineering skill?' he raged.

Linge believed that this incident preyed on his mind. Seeing some kind of omen in the continuing stupidity of his commanders, he stopped taking his meals with them because he 'saw no point in debating the daily progress of the war with them any longer.'

The slightest setback made him resentful. Eventually, he refused to talk to anyone other than his close personal staff, lapsing into a mood of morose introspection, muttering constantly to himself about Frederick the Great; how 'he had exactly the same contempt for his officers — no wonder he came to despise every swaggering one of them.'

Military conferences in the future would be recorded, he decided, ordering a team of twelve stenographers, under the supervision of a Waffen SS officer, for this specific task. Quartered in a separate barrack block, no outsider could enter their block. Only Hitler, his closest adjutants and his valet were allowed access.

Before the writers put pen to paper, it was made obligatory for them to swear a solemn oath that they would transcribe every word as it was spoken. The Fuhrer was determined to ensure there would be no misunderstanding in regard to the orders he issued to his chiefs-of-staff from that time onwards.

Other incidents added to Hitler's unhappiness. A troublesome plague of mosquitoes and flies infuriated him, particularly when a fly alighted on a map as he was studying it. Linge was sharply reprimanded and was ordered to ensure that the conference room was insect-free at all times.

The order caused the valet a great deal of nail-biting stress. As soon as he had demolished a quantity of the pests, more came in the cracks of the doors and windows. He ferreted about, trying all kinds of gadgets and poisons and traps until by sheer, rugged, Teutonic persistence, he managed to get rid of every form of gnat, midge, mosquito and parasite in the place.

Unfortunately, Halder turned out to be the biggest pest in the Vinnitsa HQ. He seemed unable to grasp the fact that Soviet troops were capable of steering the Wehrmacht into a position that would allow them to stage a counter-attack. He apparently misunderstood the simplest orders and all his energies were spent in worrying over the apparently unlimited manpower of the Russians; or in trying to discover exactly how many troops the enemy held in reserve.

With Linge scurrying in and out of the room, the general and Hitler snapped at each other, the Fuhrer finally refusing to listen any more to meaningless, 'tawdry tittle-tattle', flinging both hands on the strategy map to indicate his armies were not only on the march but steadily advancing. Halder summoned up the nerve to contradict him.

Reasonably high in Hitler's estimation during the early part of the eastern front campaign, Halder's popularity had diminished to zero. He was tactless and he continually asked awkward questions. What was the supply situation? Why was there not sufficient fuel? Equipment? Men? Fuel to transport fuel to the army? Then, as a last insult, he brutally reminded his Fuhrer that another winter was looming ahead. Wasn't it time to hold back on the offensive? To learn the lesson of 1941?

Hitler deliberated, as Linge hovered outside the door, ready to record another pithy pronouncement in his notebook.

'If I had taken my generals' advice in 1941, we would have had what even you might recognise as a catastrophe on our hands. And yet, here you are again, mouthing the same worn-out refrain. Christ, it is so odiously repetitive. "Retreat, mein Fuhrer, we'd better retreat, mein Fuhrer." What the hell are you, Halder: a professional fighter or a broken-down ballet dancer?'

Linge assumed Halder's position as chief of general staff was about to be terminated.

Usually when one of Hitler's men fell out of favour, he was referred to as a contemptible, know-it-all schoolteacher. Whenever the Fuhrer recalled the schoolmasters he had known as a boy it was always with scorn: 'Their one object was to stuff our brains and turn us into erudite apes, as they were.'

Halder was an erudite ape in uniform, pedantic, predictable and dogmatic. He was a bore, especially when he quoted streams of statistics and random examples. 'Before Halder can finish a sentence, my front line has advanced another thirty kilometres,' Hitler said on one occasion.

The general took his dismissal well, admitting that he no longer felt up to the burden of responsibility. Erect, stern-faced, he marched out of Hitler's quarters — into oblivion.

When questioned at Nuremberg, he answered the question that many historians had posed: Why had the German officer corps, especially the generals, watched the development of affairs in Germany without interfering?

'When the army realised it was going to its doom,' said Halder, 'it was too late for collective measures, even if the military leaders could have overcome their aversion to such a step, which would have constituted mutiny. This explains the events of July 20, 1944, when personalities who were willing to sacrifice themselves in despair used means that were not approved. But (otherwise) the clear will and determined leaders were lacking, (so the generals) did their military duty silently to the bitter end.

'The prediction,' concluded Halder, 'made by General von Fritsch (who committed suicide at Warsaw in September, 1939) has been fulfilled. In 1937, Fritsch said resignedly, in reply to my impassioned demand for a fight against Hitler: "It is useless. This man is Germany's destiny and this destiny must run its course to the end".'

*   *   *

In Berlin, the capture of Stalingrad was generally thought to be only a question of time. 'The destruction of Stalingrad is imminent,' said the *Frankfurter Zeitung*.

Hitler was only too well aware how much the fall of the Russian city meant to the German people. He refused to listen to any talk of the possible dangers. He had appointed Zeitzler in place of Halder, whereas Keitel would have gone for Paulus or Manstein. Influenced by his adjutant, Schmundt, Hitler favoured the lively little Zeitzler, he with the moonshaped head — known at HQ as 'Globe lightning'. He was, said Hitler, readily able to adapt to the rapidly changing tactics of his Fuhrer. It says much for his personality that of all the staff officers, he was the only commander at the time to be greeted by his chief with a handshake.

One welcome visitor to HQ was Goring, who flew in to give such a glowing account of the Luftwaffe that Hitler was able to relax a little and almost believe he could still pull something out of the bag. And because of the sharp division between the Fuhrer and his commanders, Goring, formerly relegated to the peripheries of the party circle, suddenly found himself the man of the moment.

Clinging desperately to his faith in his 6th Army, irked by his self-imposed, hermit-like existence, Hitler seemed to draw immense comfort from the bulky if over-perfumed presence of the field-marshal.

Linge was instructed to scour the countryside for the kind of delicacies Goring preferred and was ordered to see nothing was lacking in the way of comfort for his quarters.

However, in the confused and bloody battle for Stalingrad that began on August 23, the Russians not only brought the German army to a standstill, they inflicted one of the greatest defeats in that sorry nation's history.

*   *   *

When Hitler invaded Russia, he made it possible for the West to think in terms of eventual victory. And when Germany declared war on the United States, this possibility grew to be regarded as certainty.

It was against the backcloth of the Russian campaign, in the summer and winter of 1942, that the sequel to Montgomery's victory at El Alamein took place. This was the march that swept the Eighth Army up to the mountainous region north of Tunisia, where they narrowed the circle around Bizerta and Tunis and where General von Arnim and the remnants of his axis divisions had taken refuge.

November, which saw the encirclement at Stalingrad and the allied landings in French North Africa, also added to the certainty of an allied victory. A Russian counter-offensive, a strategic surprise on the grand scale, was launched on November 19. From then on Russia was saved, its armies continuing the offensive that would take them eventually to Berlin. At the same time, the Eighth Army swept through to Benghazi.

Elsewhere too, the Soviets were on the move: in the Caucasus, below the Don, and on the threshold of the Donetz, closing in on Leningrad.

The plight of the 6th German Army under Paulus grew steadily worse. They had received no supplies and were half-starved. 'Frau Ju', the supply Junkers 52, was unable to get through, and by Christmas the men were down to a few ounces of black bread and a little rancid horse meat.

On January 27, American bombers made their first raid on

Germany, bombing Wilhelmshaven in daylight. On February 25, they began round-the-clock air raids.

Goring muttered his excuses and quickly left Vinnitsa to return to Berlin. In addition to material devastation, the bombing had profoundly adverse moral effects on the German people.

It was Linge's unpleasant task to wake the Fuhrer each day with the progress report from Stalingrad. More wakeful than ever, Hitler usually sprang up at once, dressing rapidly while glancing over the dispatches. On the morning of February 2, 1943 the valet, as always watching his chief's reactions, saw his face set like a death mask. It was a Russian communiqué that caused the change: 'In consequence of the complete extermination of the surrounded enemy forces, operations in the city of Stalingrad have ceased'.

For what seemed to Linge a very long time, Hitler said nothing. The valet busied himself collecting up discarded linen and straightening the rumpled bed. Then Hitler shook his head vigorously, visibly trying to get a grip on himself, before rapping out an order.

'Summon an immediate conference with the chiefs of staff.'

Only days earlier, he had announced he intended to make Paulus a Field-Marshal, hoping that the promotion would encourage him to hold out. 'Paulus is, from this moment, promoted,' he told his aides, 'because every hour, each day he holds on at Stalingrad is an hour, a day of victory somewhere else along the front.

'A soldier, an officer, can be taken prisoner without affecting the course of a campaign. But a German field-marshal is never captured. There is no precedent; it has never happened throughout the long history of Germany.' He had paused for several moments. 'It will not happen at Stalingrad.'

This particular morning, he ordered Linge to find out at once if the press release on Paulus' promotion had gone through to Berlin. If not, it had to be cancelled immediately. During the long night, Hitler had begun to doubt the ability of his 6th Army commander; instinct told him that Paulus was not going to hold his ground.

But it was too late. The release was already in the newspapers. Later, Goebbels' propaganda ministry was able to suggest that Paulus had died a hero's death. For some time his actual fate was uncertain, though he was know to have with him two revolvers and a cyanide capsule.

209

Hitler finally accepted that Paulus had been captured and that he appeared to be in much better shape than most of his men. This realisation nearly broke the Fuhrer. The loss of his army at Stalingrad was severe enough. His commander's treachery left him ravaged.

At the end of March, 1943 the war was beginning to show a contraction with every new phase of its expansion. What occurred in one part of the world had repercussions elsewhere in varying degrees. The allied air offensive in Europe disrupted the supply lines to the eastern front, while possibility of air attack from the west pinned down numbers of men who could otherwise have been posted to Russia. The only remaining question was the unity and strength of the allies. While there was any doubt, Germany could still hope to retrieve the initiative.

For the loss of Stalingrad — the official radio announcement had been followed by a performance of the 2nd movement of Beethoven's Fifth Symphony — there was four days of national mourning.

With Kursk retaken by the Soviets, the Wehrmacht continued to fall back.

And the SS — who always considered themselves above the ordinary army — continued in their efforts to preserve and strengthen Germanity through extermination. Those who refused to participate in the mass executions were either shot or sent home with dire threats of what would happen if they revealed anything. Some broke down and were committed to mental hospitals. Frequently, army doctors were called to treat SS men on leave for chronic insomnia, hysteria or the DTs — many members of the execution squads drank heavily before going on duty and most of them preferred to remain in an alcoholic haze during the killings. The use of drugs became prevalent among some of the officers, particularly methadrene. This stimulant, although addictive, was easily obtainable.

As for the German public, every effort was made to prevent them from finding out about the extermination camps. Most of the population had no knowledge at all of what was going on.

Himmler, in a speech to SS commanders in Poland in 1943 — and quoted at Nuremberg — posed the question as to whether it would ever be possible to tell the German people what was being done in their name. In his view, it would not be possible because they wouldn't understand. His own nephew was executed after an SS court martial found him guilty of discussing the exterminations while on leave in Germany.

Various rumours about the Fuhrer spread. It was said he was no longer capable of military leadership; that he had no idea of reality; that Bormann had finally isolated his Fuhrer from the rest of the world; that anyone who did manage to gain an audience with Hitler was briefed beforehand by the Reichsleiter not to reply if asked for information about the progress of the war. There was concern about Hitler's condition of health.

Linge's belief was that his chief, by the fourth year of the war, had aged twenty years. His hair was ash-grey, his eyes sunken, deep-set. When standing, he tended to adopt an awkward slouch and his left hand trembled continuously, no matter how hard he tried to control it, pressing it tightly against his body and grasping it rigidly in the other hand. When he walked, it was the walk of an old man. He continually complained to Morell about dizzy spells, severe stomach pains and blinding headaches.

All the doctor could do was pile on the doses of drugs. Some of the pills contained atropine, a poisonous alkaloid derived from deadly nightshade; others included a percentage of strychnine. Hitler was given ten drops of Sympatol daily to increase cardiac activity and injections of phosphorus to stimulate impaired muscles.

He barely touched solid food, only occasionally swallowing some mashed potatoes or pureed carrots or turnips.

He became suspicious of everyone, continuing to mutter to himself in a grumbling, querulous tone of voice. The theme was constant: the parallel misfortunes of Frederick the Great and himself.

'Now I understand why poor old Fritz failed. It didn't matter how miraculous was his intellectual ability or how gifted he was as a leader, because his officers let him down all the way. Even his own brother deserted him in the end.

'My grey hairs,' he told Linge, 'have not come from Russia but from having to wrangle with men I should have been able to trust with the welfare of my armies.'

His personal bodyguard remained as fervently faithful as ever, lynx-eyed shadows watching over their Fuhrer twenty-four hours a day. Always within call, only steps behind him whenever the weather was kind enough to allow him to exercise his dog Blondi

211

for fifteen minutes or so in the open woods surrounding head-quarters.

There were, on average, 200 sheets of dispatches awaiting him every morning and he had not lost the habit of running through them swiftly, allowing his eyes to glide along the pages, relying on his instinct to pick out vital information.

Another gift that had not yet deserted him was the ability to go through a report before him on the table, while at the same time listening to a detailed discussion on the disposition of German troops in Europe.

Back at Rastenberg in April, 1943 he rarely went to bed before 6 am. If the morning intelligence reports contained routine information he relaxed until noon, breakfasting on bread and milk or a cup of herbal tea and a little soft cheese. Morell would appear mid-morning with the daily dosage of drugs.

Early in the afternoon he would confer with the adjutants, occasionally fixing a time for a discussion with the chiefs-of-staff.

No longer able to stand for any length of time, he would sit at the map table, saying little, scarcely moving, even though the discussions sometimes dragged on for three or four hours, with as many as thirty staff officers crammed into the room.

Back in his quarters with only Linge for company, Hitler's thoughts turned frequently towards the Berghof and Eva Braun.

There was another change noted by the valet. Where formerly the Fuhrer was the least sentimental of anyone Linge had ever met, he found himself obliged to listen to long dissertations in praise of Eva — she was, it appeared, out of all the women Hitler had encountered since assuming office, the best, the most caring, the finest of them all. For the first time, he spoke openly about the relationship; of the way the bond between Eva and himself had developed because of her loyalty, generosity and the absolute trust and complete discretion she had shown.

On alternate mornings, Linge was instructed to phone the Berghof so that Hitler could talk to Eva. Although the valet indicated his willingness to leave the room during the call, Hitler told him to stay.

'I have nothing that needs to be said to Eva now that you or even the world can't hear.'

Usually Zeitzler dropped by late at night for a chat, being still on good terms with the Fuhrer. After he had left, Linge assembled a pile of gramophone records close to player and Hitler sat back in his easy chair, trying to ease his mind after the acute pressures of each day.

There were well over a thousand recordings, mostly Bruckner, Beethoven, and Wagner. If the mood required more lighthearted music, there was Strauss and Lehar.

Eventually as the Russians drew constantly nearer, Hitler found it impossible to listen to records. Then, close friends were called upon to sit with him throughout the night.

Hewel, Hoffman and Morell stayed until the early hours, talking; drinking tea; listening to reports of air raids on the radio. At the end of February, the British had increased the air war. Essen, as well as a number of other towns in west Germany, had been subjected to heavy bombing.

On March 1 it was Berlin's turn. Hundreds of high explosive bombs and incendiaries were dropped. It was the hardest blow the German capital had so far sustained. Deep depression reigned during the newscast and the company stayed with their Fuhrer until they were informed the RAF had turned for home.

Reports came in from abroad indicating that news of enemy air raids on Germany had left Hitler unmoved. Linge said this was nonsense. During the raids, he constantly heard him express sympathetic concern for the civilian families.

As to the gradual loss of his energies, it was more manifest to Linge than anyone else. He saw Hitler as he was not seen by his military staff, when the occasion demanded that he rouse himself to something of what he had once been. It was only when he was alone, when no special effort was required, that the defences crumbled. The progression was slow but inexorable, until he was no longer in a mental or physical condition as to be capable of handling the burdens of his office. By then many others saw clearly the end result of a decline that had in fact begun a long time before — as long ago, some suggested, as Hitler's teenage years in Vienna. The stresses which he had absorbed for many years like blotting paper began to seep to the surface, exposing raw nerve ends which had for a long time been hidden under layers of self-deception. The dead layers of his life were flaking away like old plaster, revealing the mental instability and confusion underneath.

SHE LOVES HITLER

A 35-year-old German woman, Cecilia Roesch, told a Great Yarmouth policeman that she came to town to meet Hitler. 'I love him,' she said. She was remanded yesterday on a charge of being in a defence area without permission.

News item : August 8, 1942

CHAPTER EIGHTEEN

'This war,' Hitler said in the autumn of 1943, 'will be won by technology.'

The question was: how long would it take?

The allies were preparing encircling operations that would inflict the first defeats on the Wehrmacht; the tide was turning against the Fuhrer. His V-1 and V-2s were not ready for mass production, but in Norway German scientists were experimenting with heavy water and particular metals. If they succeeded in splitting the atom they would be able to blow the part of the world inhabited by the allies to bits. They were almost at the point of solution. Six months, maybe a year — all they needed was a little more time.

In 1943, with the odds stacked against him, Hitler became increasingly remote from the realities. He spent most of his time at permanent headquarters at Rastenberg, occasionally visiting the Berghof but rarely returning to Berlin.

At HQ, the big event of the day was his situation conference, at which he listened to reports before studying the maps spread on the centre table. Each officer present would report on the latest situation — in Russia; North Africa; Italy, or in the war in the air. Then the Fuhrer would issue his orders.

'No one,' reported Jodl in 1943, 'would know more or be told more than he needed for his own immediate task.'

Jodl and Keitel were always present at the discussions together with the chiefs of staff of the army and Luftwaffe; a representative of the C-I-C, Navy; Himmler's man, SS Gruppenfuhrer Fegelein; Ribbentrop's representative, Ambassador Hewel, and the duty stenographers.

Later, Hitler held private meetings with Bormann, Himmler and Goebbels.

For Linge, the life at HQ was tedious for most of the time, the monotony only relieved by Hitler's choleric outbursts of rage or during the excitement of critical developments on one of the fighting fronts.

He recalled the time when news of the setback in North Africa reached Rastenberg — and the Fuhrer's reaction.

Because Rommel had been forced to carry the Italians with him, Hitler was inclined to blame them for the defeat. Once the facts filtered through, he cast a wintry, despairing eye on Mussolini, brooding over his failure to support him in Poland and the grisly record of his soldiers in combat. The Duce had been so determined to flex Italy's military muscles in the Middle East and 'in the one place he had a toehold, he has let me down again. If he had half the fighting force he claimed he had, he could have held the Mediterranean. Instead all he has are comic-opera soldiers who'd be better employed as waiters.

'They once put up statues in Rome to heroes who didn't deserve them. Now, they should dig holes in the ground in order to hide all the cowards.'

To show Rommel, the fallen hero, that his Fuhrer's finger was still on the military command button, the Desert Fox was ordered to present himself at HQ.

Rommel spoke his mind.

'With the supply lines stretched as thin as piano wires, there was nothing else we could do. The Afrika Korps drew back at Tripoli in a bid to make a stand at Tunis. My one hope was to hold back the enemy as long as possible. Anything else would have meant sacrificing our southern flank.'

'What are you talking about?' Hitler turned angrily on his onetime favourite field-marshal. 'My God, it wasn't all that long ago you were promising me Egypt on a silver plate. Now you're saying, "I'm terribly sorry, my Fuhrer, but I had to take your army all the way back to Tunis". What are you trying to do?'

His voice had risen to a scream — it was enough to send the rooks up out of the Rastenberg trees. 'Are you saying my soldiers in North Africa are nothing but a collection of craven milksops? I will never accept that from you.'

Rommel had seen Hitler indulge in tantrums before, but this near-hysterical harangue left him dumbfounded.

Trying to reason with the man, he spoke quietly and persuasively, pointing out the lack of support from the Italians, the desperate need for ammunition and the shortage of manpower — all factors that caused the eventual retreat.

The Fuhrer refused to be pacified. All he saw was the latest in a long line of betrayals. 'You are lying to me. Not long ago, when your panzers ran out of fuel, you were clever enough to take all you needed from enemy supplies. What has changed that policy?

'If you were capable of taking the Afrika Korps back over a thousand kilometres you must have been in possession of sufficient fuel. Why in the name of providence didn't you use it to attack?'

Rommel kept his temper, standing rigidly to attention — his features the colour of a wax candle. Hitler was so close to him when he spoke that his spittle flicked the Field-Marshal full in the face. Rommel waited without flinching until the harangue ran out of steam. Only his eyes betrayed his feelings. He was forced to control his breathing, hands clenched tightly by his sides.

The Fuhrer, moods and manners displacing each other, remembered the presence of his valet in the background and managed to gain a semblance of self-control. In a harshly menacing, though considerably quieter tone of voice, he said, 'When generals on the Eastern front disobey my orders I have them courtmartialled.'

A long silence followed his remark. Hitler paced up and down, left leg noticeably dragging behind. In a somewhat more conciliatory manner, he suggested that perhaps Rommel had lost his nerve. He should aim at regaining his health before resuming command. In the meantime, every effort would be made to supply reinforcements and ammunition in sufficient quantities for a successful operation against Casablanca.

Rommel nodded. He knew there would be no more reinforcements. All the reserve strength was being swallowed up in the black hole of Russia.

On May 12, the remnants of the Afrika Korps were trapped on Cape Bon. In less than six months, in Tunisia and at Stalingrad, Hitler lost well over half a million men.

*   *   *

When Hitler finally realised the Russians possessed vast reserves of manpower, he issued orders for a last round-up in Germany. In charge of the task was General von Unruh, who was given a free hand to ferret out as many fit men as he could find for the

218

front. It was up to him, Hitler said, to weed out the dodgers and surplus clerical workers and teenagers, and there was to be no appeal against his decision.

Not fooled for a moment by the long lists of essential war workers, von Unruh soon earned the nickname: 'Champion sneak'.

He travelled the length and breadth of Germany, frequently turning up in the middle of the night. To give warning of his arrival was a serious offence against military security, classified as high treason. The general was empowered to send entire garrisons to Russia, replacing them at home with elderly, time-served reservists. Women took over men's jobs in police stations and barracks.

Unfortunately the quality didn't match up to the quantity and the majority of Unruh's Army were below average. Those delegated to transform the feeble and unfit into fighting soldiers complained bitterly about the enormity of the task confronting them.

Considering the fifteen-year-olds from the Hitler Youth, both the Wehrmacht and the Waffen SS competed for their services. The Hitlerjugend opted for the fighting SS.

Hitler also decided it was time to straighten out his ordnance factories. By 1943, many tank designs had become obsolete and as a result several panzer chiefs were called to Rastenberg to discuss modifications and improvements.

When the Fuhrer addressed them it was obvious that, despite his physical condition, he still knew a hawk from a handsaw. And while what he said may have seemed like mere flakes of rust shed by a once powerful machine, he managed to make sense.

'We will produce greater quantities of more superior weapons,' he said. 'It is my intention that every soldier in the front line carries his own machine-gun.

'As to tanks, in my talks with Speer I have insisted on up-to-date models replacing the panzer IIIs and IVs. All unnecessary trimmings and fittings must be scrapped to facilitate mass production. You know that the Russians have more mobile, more robust tanks. There are far too many bits and pieces on ours, such as those ludicrous coat hangers, for instance. A tank driver is not an office clerk needing somewhere to hang his coat.'

He hinted at new weapons, superior to anything yet produced by Britain, Russia or America. Scientists were working on a revolutionary rocket system far in advance of enemy technology. 'A little more effort from everyone and we will increase our lead.

With these rockets installed in bases along the French coast, we can exact revenge for the destruction inflicted on Germany by enemy bombers.'

Dr Porsche had completed work on a new tank, the 180-ton *Jagdpanzer* with 100mm firepower. Quantities would soon be dispatched to the Eastern front.

And Guderian, back in favour, had been appointed inspector of the armoured formations. 'Since 1941,' the Fuhrer told him, 'I have come to regret any misunderstanding between us. You know about panzers and we need your knowledge.'

Hitler was persuaded by Speer to pay a rare visit to Insterburg, where Field Marshal Milch was turning out a thousand new aircraft a month. He was shown working drawings for a prototype diesel-powered plane, with an airspeed from take-off of over 1000 kilometres an hour. A promise was exacted from Milch to begin production before the end of the year.

Next, the Fuhrer turned his attention to the war at sea.

Admiral Rader was called to explain the increasing number of U-boats blown out of the waters of the Atlantic by British destroyers. It was impossible, said Rader, for them to stay submerged without being detected by the enemy. Rader's attitude triggered off another hysterical outburst from Hitler and in a stormy clearing of the air at Wolfsschanze, Rader was relieved of his command. Admiral 'The Lion' Donitz, appointed commander-in-chief, had been in charge of U-boats and his tactics proved more successful. Enemy tonnage losses rose considerably above the official figures for 1942.

With civilian morale at a low ebb, the Fuhrer — prompted by Goebbels — called a meeting of the party leadership in Berlin in May, 1943.

'The issue,' as Goebbels pointed out, 'is everything or nothing; with no question of trying to maintain peace-time conditions for the individual. The effort on the home front must be total; as the fighting at the front is total.'

Before the Fuhrer arrived arguments began among the deputies, who were unable to agree on the best arguments to put forward in order to find favour with the leader.

Hitler, arriving in the middle of the storm, quickly summed up the situation and made as if to leave the room.

'Gentlemen, my time is too precious to waste, and I am not prepared to waste it listening to people who spend their time trying to trip each other up. Do not invite me back into the room until you have reached agreement.'

Goebbels, trying to present a show of unity, however spurious, began honing his hyperbole. There was a mounting enemy effort to give 'the world conflagration another direction. Before we get burnt by it, we must throw comfort overboard and end all luxury.' Though, as it turned out, this did not necessarily apply to the leaders but more to the people.

In Berlin, a number of restaurants were closed, among them the Taverne, Horcher's and Zum Alten Schweden. Most jewellery, antique furniture and perfumery shops had to shut their doors; many papers and magazines ceased to appear.

As an example to his people, Hitler decided that cream should be banished from his table, together with eggs at breakfast. He explained to Linge that he was anxious to undergo the same hardships as his people.

One bright spot: the Food Minister, Backe, managed to increase the meat ration to 250 grammes, together with an additional 125 grammes of fat; 62 grammes of cheese and 50 grammes of coffee.

Of course, the black market was flourishing in Berlin and other cities — everything was available, but at extortionate prices. Linge recalls the frequent discussions on ways of stamping it out.

'Unless we can catch the brains behind it,' said Hitler, 'there is little we can do. If everyone who deals in the black market was arrested, it would involve most of the population, including the young.'

Occasionally an example was made and, if the offence merited it, the wrongdoer was executed. The Fuhrer liked to draw a comparison with 1918. 'He who tries to extract his sordid gains out of the distress of the Fatherland is a bloodsucker and a parasite who can expect no mercy.'

The worst examples, according to Linge, occurred in the Ukraine. There, soldiers of the Wehrmacht exchanged sheets of toilet paper for eggs: the rate of exchange being two eggs for one sheet. Apparently, the Russian civilians found the paper ideal for rolling cigarettes.

While some of the party leaders tended to look upon the occupied countries simply as centres for the collection of personal plunder, there were still thousands of party members who were not corrupt, despite serious abuses that were revealed from time to time, causing tremendous bitterness among the people. This put party representatives on the spot. They owed their positions to their criticism of political opponents on the grounds of corruption.

A story that dented the reputation of National Socialism had as its leading figure Viktor Lutze, the SA chief of staff. Early in May, 1943 he had gone on a black market expedition with his family. On their way back to Berlin, a pedestrian stepped out in front of the car on the autobahn. Lutze's son, driving at high speed, braked sharply, causing it to skid towards the shoulder and turn over. Lutze, seriously wounded, died the following night. Other drivers who stopped at the scene of the accident saw that the road was littered with hams, geese, eggs and butter.

Opportunity, sighed Goebbels, creates dishonesty. And the opportunities of the party hierarchy were plentiful and tempting.

The Fuhrer, hoping to help Goebbels in his fight against defeatism, announced that he had been using the same razor blade so often his face was lacerated with cuts — he had been told blades were scarce. And he also washed with the harsh army-issue soap which reeked of carbolic, made little lather and acted on the skin like coarse sandpaper.

One heartening aspect of the situation at the time, said Linge, was that most people accepted the hardships and their enthusiasm for the cause remained unimpaired.

Wives of prominent Berlin officials reported for menial work in factories and hospitals, and Eva Braun, in a touching gesture of loyalty to her Fuhrer's best interests, offered her services.

But Hitler refused to allow her to do war work.

'Your place is at the Berghof,' he said. 'I feel more at ease knowing you are reasonably safe there rather than risking your life in the constant air raids.'

And, apart from his dog, Blondi, who else could he trust?

He retired more and more into the background, deeply nostalgic for the sacred tribe of an earlier civilisation. 'The reason,' he said, 'why the ancient world was so pure, light and serene was that it knew nothing of the two great scourges: the pox and Christianity.'

ITALIAN WAR COMMUNIQUE 1942

On the Tobruk front, a large force of Italians attacked an enemy cyclist, causing him to dismount. After heavy and prolonged fighting they were able to puncture his tyres. The front wheel was destroyed and the loss of the rear wheel must also be considered a possibility. The handlebars are in our hands but possession of the frame is still being bitterly contested — HQ Royal Italian Army
German document captured in the Middle East

Within a few days, a sham tribunal will make public a sentence which has already been decided by Mussolini under the influence of that circle of prostitutes and white slavers which for years have plagued Italian political life and brought our country to the brink of the abyss. I accept calmly what is to be my infamous destiny.
Ciano December, 1943

To the Commandants of the Concentration Camps January, 1943
SECRET
In addition to the order (referred to previously) it is ordered that the smaller camps should also collect and keep the gold fillings for a longer period of time (one year) and not dispatch small amounts each month, as has occurred once again.
Chief of the Central Office
SS — Obersturmbann fuhrer

CHAPTER NINETEEN

The Americans began the final attack in Tunisia at the end of March, 1943, with the British moving towards them from the east. By May, enemy resistance had ended and 160,000 German and Italian prisoners were taken.

De Gaulle was in Algiers in June, eventually to head a new provisional French government, and the allied priority was to mop up the Mediterranean.

Churchill and Roosevelt, meeting at Casablanca, decided to land an Anglo-American force in Sicily. It would be the largest landing operation ever undertaken by the allies. It was the major offensive of 1943, leading to the postponement of a second front in France and to further operations on the Italian mainland.

In July, 1943, with the allies in Sicily, Hitler arranged an emergency meeting with Mussolini. Reports reaching FHQ suggested that Victor Emmanuel was planning to depose the Duce. Furthermore, with the economy on the point of collapse, the Italians, short of food, were growing increasingly resentful of the arrogance and appetites of the occupying German forces. Mussolini appeared to be losing his grip, which suggested that it might be time for the Fuhrer to seek an armistice in Russia in order to send in more troops for the protection of Italy.

The dictators met at Feltre, with Hitler doing most of the talking. In his view Mussolini would be better occupied in consolidating his position and regaining his former will of iron. There was treachery all around him; even his own fascists were not to be trusted.

Linge, told to watch out for double-dealing among the Italian detachment, sensed danger in the air. He had reason for caution if only on the grounds of superstition; it was the thirteenth time the two dictators had conferred.

The Duce was moodily silent for most of the time — except

when he was informed that Rome had been bombed by the allies. It was an act that infuriated Hitler.

'The hypocritical English and their backers, the Americans, have always claimed to be so cultured. They are barbarians who are, without the slightest justification, prepared to destroy the Eternal City and the treasure of centuries. If they were truly civilised, Rome should have been declared an open city.'

Later, he wondered whether the fine Italian hand of Victor Emmanuel might not have been behind the raid. Perhaps it had been an attempt to disrupt the Feltre conference.

A week later, on July 25, the Fascist Grand Council, meeting for the first time since 1939, decided enough was enough. Nineteen of them, including Ciano, requested the Duce to resign from office.

Mussolini called on the King the following afternoon, confident of his support. Victor Emmanuel, thanking him for all he had done for Italy, handed him over to the carabinieri.

After more than twenty years, the Duce's dream of a new Imperium Romanum was shattered. By then a physical wreck, variously reputed to be suffering from a blood clot on the brain, trachoma of the eye, heart trouble and, like his fellow dictator, the tertiary stage of syphilis, Mussolini was hurried to a door, bundled into an ambulance and driven to the nearest police barracks. Not a shot was fired in his defence, nor a voice raised in protest. The Italians had had enough of his foolhardiness, of his ungovernable rages, of his savage, deadly antagonism.

The reaction at Rastenberg was mixed. The Fuhrer, accepting the situation, immediately contacted Himmler to keep an eye on the situation on the home front. He felt that as long as the Reichsfuhrer and the Wehrmacht stuck together, history would not repeat itself. Any attempt at internal rebellion could be dealt with by the Gestapo.

He brushed aside the embarrassment voiced by other party leaders, the doubts expressed by some of the generals. His first impulse was to send in his 3rd panzergrenardier division, stationed outside Rome, to take King, crown prince, country and the Pope by force. And rescue his friend, Il Duce. In the end, he sent reinforcements to southern Italy and Rommel, plus eight divisions to seal off the Alpine passes.

Hewel asked what he intended to do about the Vatican.

'The Vatican doesn't bother me. I'll go right into it. We can take it over right away . . . then we can apologise if we have to.'

Later, under advice from Ribbentrop and Goebbels, he decided to steer clear of the Pope's domain. The first priority was to secure the release of Mussolini. He intended to keep his side of the bargain he had made.

Six officers, among them Waffen SS Hauptsturmfuhrer Otto Skorzeny, were summoned to FHQ.

Skorzeny, the big, broad-shouldered Viennese with a deeply scarred face and fists like sides of beef, recalls meeting his Fuhrer for the first time.

'All I heard was his curt voice, the sound of it well known to me through the wireless. There was no mistaking it. What struck me at the time was the unmistakable, soft Austrian accent even when he was emphatic. I thought it was extraordinary that this man who preached and embodied the old Prussian gospel could not conceal his origin, despite long absence from his homeland. I wondered whether he still retained something of the characteristic kindliness of the Austrian and whether he was a man of feeling . . .'

The Hauptsturmfuhrer gave a brief account of his career: service in France and Russia; holder of the Iron Cross, 2nd class, for fighting on the Eastern front; presently attached to the political intelligence wing of the army secret service. 'Adolf Hitler looked at me long and closely before he said, "The other gentlemen may go. I want you to stay, Hauptsturmfuhrer Skorzeny"'.

The Fuhrer gave him details of his mission, stressing the need for secrecy. Mussolini had to be rescued as soon as his whereabouts became known for the allies were anxious to get their hands on him. Skorzeny must do everything possible to carry out the rescue. If he was successful he would be rewarded with promotion.

'The longer Hitler spoke,' said Skorzeny, 'the more I could feel his influence upon me. His words seemed so convincing I had no doubt of the success of the project. There was such a warm, human inflection in his voice when he spoke of his loyalty to his Italian friend, that I was deeply moved. I could only reply: "I fully understand, my Fuhrer, and will do my best"'.

When Italy capitulated on September 8, Skorzeny was in Rome with a special commando force, completing preparations for his mission.

On Sunday September 12, Skorzeny and his commandoes crash-landed on the side of a hill high up in the Abruzzi mountains near Gran Sasso, and stormed the newly-built hotel. The Italian sentries barely had time to surrender before the Hauptsturmfuhrer had jumped them.

'We raced along the facade of the building and around the corner to find ourselves faced with a terrace three metres high. Corporal Himmel offered me his back and I was up and over in a trice. The others followed me in a bunch.

'My eyes swept the facade and spotted a well-known face at one of the windows of the first storey. It was the Duce. Now I knew that our effort had not been in vain.'

After noting a white bedspread hanging from another window, and deploying his men, Skorzeny was able to give Mussolini his undivided attention. 'Duce,' he said, 'the Fuhrer has sent me. You are free.'

Mussolini embraced him. 'I knew my friend Adolf Hitler would not leave me in the lurch,' he said.

In return for the full details of his imprisonment, Skorzeny was able to give the Duce some pleasant news. His wife, Donna Rachele, and his two youngest children, interned in the family villa at Rocca della Carminata, had been rescued by another commando unit.

The Duce shook him warmly by the hand. 'So, everything's all right. I'm very grateful to you.'

The party took off precariously in a Fieseler-Storch aircraft. 'The left landing wheel hit the ground, the machine tipped downwards and we made straight for the gulley. Veering left we shot over the edge. I closed my eyes, held my breath and waited for the inevitable end. The wind roared in our ears . . . but when I looked around again, Gerlach had got the machine out of its dive and we were almost on a level keel.'

Arriving in Rome, they took off again in a Heinkel III almost at once, bound for Vienna, where a suite awaited the Duce in the Hotel Imperial.

The Duce accepted the offer of a hot bath and a meal but declined the gift of a pair of new pyjamas. With something of his old ebullience he turned to his rescuer. 'It's unhealthy to wear clothes in bed,' he told Skorzeny. 'I have never worn them and, speaking from experience, I can advise you to follow my example.'

Just before midnight, there was a discreet tap on the door of Skorzeny's bedroom. A Wehrmacht officer had arrived to award him, on behalf of the Fuhrer, the Knight's Cross. Half-an-hour later the phone rang. It was Hitler, speaking from Rastenberg. 'You have performed an act of historical significance that will always be remembered. And in so doing you have restored my friend, Mussolini. You will by now be in possession of the Knight's Cross. From this moment, I promote you to Sturmbannfuhrer. Heartiest congratulations.' He asked to speak to Frau Skorzeny before handing the phone over to Goring, who wished to add his felicitations.

Next morning, at daylight, the rescue party, augmented by Kaltenbrunner and Ambassador Dornberg, took off for their final destination, the landing strip at Wolfsschanze. 'Brilliant sunshine greeted us at FHQ. When the Ju 52 touched down and we climbed out, the Duce was warmly welcomed by the Fuhrer in person and the two men stood together for a considerable time hand in hand. Then Hitler greeted me too, and in the afternoon I gave him a full description of our exploit. Our conference lasted nearly two hours. There seemed no limit to his gratitude. "I will not forget what I owe you," he said.'

Linge recalls the reunion of the two leaders. He was shocked at the alteration in Mussolini's appearance. It was an old man who stepped down from the aircraft, clad in a shabby overcoat, eyes downcast, chin slumped on his chest.

The valet watched his chief shuffle forward to grasp the Duce in an uncharacteristic gesture, speaking volubly, but out of earshot of the bystanders.

One incident stayed in Linge's mind. As he was about to take his customary place in the rear of Hitler's Mercedes, he was told to find a seat in one of the other cars. It was the first time since he had been appointed the Fuhrer's personal man that he was not able to accompany him in the same vehicle. It seemed that whatever the chief had to say to his Italian friend, it was meant for his ears alone.

To celebrate his deliverance, Hitler gave the Duce an ornate casket surmounted by a golden eagle, packed to the brim with precious stones. Skorzeny received a gold flying-badge-of-honour, the personal gift of Marshal Goring.

He was also invited to take midnight tea with Hitler, 'a great and rare honour'. The Fuhrer, sipping his tea out of a glass served on a silver saucer, did most of the talking. As well as the secretaries, Johanna Wolf and Traudl Jung, the company included Hewel and Kaltenbrunner, who spoke little, except when the subject of the future planning of his home town, Linz, came up.

* * *

Rather than having Mussolini brought to Germany to bury him, Hitler was bent on praising him, at the same time making it brutally clear that he intended to pursue his own interests, if necessary at Italy's expense.

The disposable, disconsolate Duce, always vulnerable to the little touch of steel beneath the third rib, had reason for a certain amount of scepticism about the future. On the understanding that he would be controlled by German advisers, he was appointed leader of a new social republic of Italy. In a state of melancholy acquiescence before the fates, Mussolini never returned to Rome. Instead, he preferred the seclusion of Rocca della Caminate, on the shore of Lake Garda, guarded by an SS detachment. From then on he was merely a catspaw, 'written off politically' as Goebbels put it, making few appearances in public, finding a greater comfort in a continuing libidinous dalliance with Clara Petacci than in the new fascist order. Under pressure from Hitler, he ordered the execution of Ciano, who was shot by a firing squad in Verona jail on January 11, 1944.

In Italy most of the people acted as though fascism had never existed. With no thought for politics, all they wanted was peace, enough food and their soldiers back from the war. Misery and discomfort were widespread, displacing pride, dignity and the corporate state. The country was economically and morally bankrupt.

General Marras, representing Badoglio's Italian government, arrived at FHQ for attestation as ambassador, but the Fuhrer, refusing to recognise his status, openly sneered at him. 'You are nothing but a wretched traitor,' he told him. 'How dare you come to me as an Italian envoy. You're nothing but a puppet from Badoglio. And that swine is, at the same time, seeking peace with the allies while feigning friendship with us. While I'm strongly tempted to have you arrested on the spot, I'd much prefer it if you got out of my sight immediately.'

The general was noticeably ill-at-ease when he arrived. He was ashen-faced and intimidated when he left.

*   *   *

The next vexed question for Hitler was the death in mysterious circumstances of his Bulgarian confrere, King Boris. Given its reputation for Balkan intrigue, he was certain the House of Savoy, the home of dirty tricks, was responsible — Boris's wife, Princess Giovanna, was the daughter of Victor Emmanuel.

The Fuhrer, determined to nail King Victor, sent a German 'medical' mission to Sofia, ostensibly to make inquiries into the cause of death. What he urgently required was more Bulgarian manpower, not a dead King.

When poison was discovered in the body, the searchlight of suspicion played on the staff, eventually coming to rest on the bony shoulders of an immigrant cook of Italian origin who worked in the royal kitchen.

One of King Victor's jackals, said Hitler, again doing his work for him. He summoned his special emissary to Rome, Prince Philip of Hesse, whose wife, Princess Mafalda was another of King Victor's daughters, to FHQ explain the circumstances of the assassination.

Before he arrived at Rastenberg, Linge was told to address the Prince with great courtesy. The Fuhrer wanted much bowing and scraping with His Royal Highness, at least in the initial stages of the visit. Later, when Linge learnt the phone had been tapped during a conversation between Hesse and his wife, he realised the formal approach had simply been a method of softening him up before the heavy questioning began.

The Fuhrer seated his guest, opening the discussion with a florid dissertation on European art — venturing the opinion that the picture galleries of Kassel, Prince Philip's domain, were among the finest he had ever seen. Linge, serving the drinks, watched as his chief lulled the Prince into a state of relaxation. Skilfully, inexorably, Hitler brought the conversation around to loyalty, reminding Hesse that as an Obergruppenfuhrer in the SS, a long-serving party member and holder of the coveted NSKK gold medal, he had every faith in the Prince's judgement.

Did he not agree that the House of Savoy had always shown

that aristocratic but regrettable tendency towards autocracy? Wasn't the idea that a monarch ruling a minuscule section of the world and having absolute control over his people, ludicrous? Hitler also voiced his belief that Victor had attempted to induce King Boris to work against Germany, and that he was killed simply because he remained loyal to the Reich.

After a frugal lunch that was to Linge a protracted war of nerves, with Hesse experiencing difficulty in preventing his knife and fork from clattering on the plate, Linge was sent to summon the SS detachment, who were cooling their heels outside the Fuhrer's bunker.

Whatever Hesse had said was sufficient to incriminate him. Hitler was convinced that Philip and 'that black carrion of a wife of his' were in the conspiracy up to their armpits.

Linge's last sight of Hesse was in the back of a black saloon car, surrounded by Gestapo, before he was driven to Koenigsberg prison. Later Mafalda joined him in a concentration camp. She died at Buchenwald.

* * *

The closing months of 1943 brought no glad tidings of comfort and joy to enliven the Christmas at Rastenberg. The news from Italy and the Mediterranean was bad; the counter-offensive in Russia had failed. Knowing his chief's credibility was on the line, Linge lent an ear to the whispering campaign being waged among high-ranking officers stationed at FHQ.

Words like 'defeat', 'failure', 'madness' figured prominently, with many of the opinion that events were threatening to spiral out of control.

With all disquiet on the Eastern front and the imminent possibility of an invasion to the West, the only solution seemed to be a final stand by a depleted Wehrmacht in fortress Germany, or a negotiation for peace with Russia; or the West.

Once the mutterings reached the Fuhrer's ears, relayed by his steadfast valet, he grew so angry, his voice almost failed him. Where formerly he was able to call on ceaseless flows of deep-throated invective, this time he could barely manage short, cryptic barks.

From then on, he would become immersed in a deep melancholy, shutting himself away from reality. Nothing really mattered and he was long past the stage at which drugs were any use. They just made matters more bearable. Sections of the High Command said, 'We told you so.' But they said it to each other.

The Fuhrer, suffering deeply, needed time, faith, something to restore his illusions; miracle weapons, the hope of a split between the allied powers, anything. Yes, he'd order a retreat. But only when he believed it was necessary. And the blame for the shocking deterioration of discipline and the blunders lay with the field commanders who had failed to carry out his orders. And their failure could only have been contrived by a providence who had given them up in despair.

With a waspish repugnance, which by then may also have embraced himself, he roundly condemned them. 'They have lost the ability to look forward. Our armament factories have been turning out vast quantities of arms and ammunition; we have been sending them more and more men and they don't know what to do with them. Their one thought is for personal survival. My God, they must have very precious skins, these generals, when all they can think of is retreat, retreat, retreat.'

Unable to transmute words into deeds, he was like a eunuch bemoaning his own impotence; suffering the self-destructive rage of a lonely man who realises in his heart that his dream of *drang nach osten* — the eastward expansion — will never be realised.

To round off the year, news reached him that General von Seydlitz, captured at Stalingrad, had gone over to the Soviets to start a new 'Free Germany' movement. The permanent staff men at FHQ were naturally quite disgusted, voicing their utter amazement at an officer bearing such a fine old Prussian name stooping to such caddish behaviour.

Hitler, thick beads of sweat on his brow, shouted them down. 'You gentlemen make me sick,' he said. 'Your self-important little souls are so puffed up with pride in your own superiority, you've no room for reality in you. A man isn't Prussian simply through an accident of birth. A man is Prussian through deeds. No matter what his name, the swine Seydlitz has gone beyond treachery. He has besmirched for all time the name of Germany.'

In one of his increasingly rare spells of reality, the Fuhrer knew that, somehow, since his future and that of his staff officers was bound inextricably together, he would have to attempt a compromise with them. Trying to do something to counter and at the same time placate the commanders, he called for a top-level conference at FHQ, to be held early in 1944. Almost 200 of them assembled in the canteen to hear Hitler assess the situation. Everything, he said, was still in his control. He read a couple of dispatches dealing with the unrest in Italy. He touched on earlier triumphs, of battles fought and won. He suggested there was frequently an impasse at the penultimate stage before a supreme commander found the way to victory. Small defeats were merely the incidental expenses of war.

The case he put forward was long on speculation but short on evidence.

'The English have little interest in opening a second front. Churchill looks to Italy, anxious for a firmer footing in the Balkans. He shares a mutual interest with Stalin there, a greed for more territory.

'Although the Russians are noisily demanding an allied landing in Europe, I don't think the English are ready to risk it. Neither they nor the Americans wish to place even more power in the hands of the Soviets. Obviously it would be in their interests to see the Reich defeat Russia. The time has come for us to take full advantage of this fact.

'But . . .' The Fuhrer paused, gazing around the crowded room. Those in the front row noted his sagging features, circled blue eyes, still knowing yet strangely beseeching. '. . . but if the worst happens, if Germany is forced to face its final hour as a great nation, I pray you will stand alongside me on the barricade. How proud I would be to have my marshals gathered around me, swords drawn, ready to fight to the very last breath.'

He had barely concluded when Manstein, prodded into positive action, jumped to his feet. 'My beloved Fuhrer,' he cried, 'you can always count on us to stand by you.'

Hitler stared blankly at him.

Keitel stood up, waving both arms in the air. 'Of course! And if you require a military success, we will provide it. All for the Fuhrer. *Sig heil! Sig heil! Sig heil!*'

By then, the whole sycophantic bunch had surged forward, easily browbeaten into agreement, demonstrating their faith in their cause and in their leader, all of them sharing an ancient nostalgia, those descendants of many generals, scions of elite Junker families, men who still regarded it as an honour to die fighting for the Fatherland. As one, they joined hands and sang the national anthem and *Deutschland uber Alles*.

Linge, standing exultantly at the back, was sure that whatever tension there had been between Hitler and his commanders was, for the time being, completely dissolved.

Back in his quarters, Hitler seemed to have regained some of his old confidence. He sat sipping tea with Schmundt and Bormann, his interest in the progress of the war temporarily revived. It was Bormann, always the stirrer up of strife, who spoilt the mood of the evening.

'I thought it rather pathetic,' he said, 'the way Manstein, by no means one of the party faithful, made such an exhibition of himself. We all know he didn't mean a word of what he said. And after all, it was supposed to be a serious discussion on strategy, not a concert at the Sports Palace.

'Manstein may be a good soldier. He is certainly adept at diverting everyone's attention away from the stench of the countless corpses of our soldiers; men he has sacrificed too readily wherever he has held command.'

Linge, clearing the table, was aghast at such a character assassination of someone he had always regarded as an outstanding general. He glanced at the Fuhrer, but his eyes were on Bormann and he was paying close attention to everything he said. When Schmundt stood up, asking permission to return to his quarters, Hitler told him to bring Manstein back with him after dinner.

Whether it was as a result of Bormann's vitriolic outburst, as the valet believed, or that the Fuhrer had other grounds — Schmundt's theory — the end result was the same. Manstein was out of favour.

There would be no logical development in Hitler's outlook from then on, only fitful spells of fiery but inconsistent impulse as he reached out to clutch at the straws dangled in front of him by his few remaining lickspittles.

*   *   *

It comes as something of a surprise to find that Linge, who saw the physical and mental decline of Hitler from its outset, still retained a doglike devotion to his chief throughout the remaining months of his troubled life.

It appears that, despite Hitler's outward churlishness and the terrible strain imposed upon him, he was for most of the time unfailingly goodnatured and civil to his valet; finding time to take an interest in his private life; treating him on equal terms; trusting him implicitly.

At the beginning of the sojourn at Wolfsschanze, Linge had pictured his own role as a kind of personal lightning conductor. Being in such close contact with the chief, he was sure that in the traumatic, critical moments he would be subjected to the storms and flashes of ill-temper. This was not the case, however, not even when the Fuhrer had every reason to show displeasure at his servant's occasional lapses. And whenever he received — in his own phrase — 'the hot cigar up his arse', he felt he thoroughly deserved it.

But being an easygoing, adaptable person, the big valet found himself, most of the time, on excellent terms with his chief. If he had an opinion of his own and he wanted to express it, he did. There were never unpleasant repercussions, and Hitler was always receptive to constructive ideas about domestic matters.

Linge soon learned when to be talkative and when to stay silent. He realised early on in his career that the Fuhrer hated yes-men. Nor would he accept white lies or lame excuses, for he loathed any sign of weakness in a man.

One night, early in the new year, the valet was offered a seat in a transport aircraft due to fly to Berlin to collect fresh supplies for FHQ. Briefing a junior orderly, Linge took advantage of the opportunity to spend a few hours in the capital.

Unfortunately, Hitler rang for him later in the evening. Discovering he had left for Berlin without permission, he angrily left word for the valet to see him as soon as he got back.

Next morning the shamefaced Linge sat at breakfast with the rest of the staff, most of them chuckling with delight at his discomfiture. Would he be only reprimanded? Courtmartialled? Or simply taken out and shot? He drank his coffee absentmindedly, ignoring the weak jokes about all the action he must have seen in Mme Rosa's or the Pompadour and speculating about the hell that was due to break loose once the Fuhrer knew he was back.

By the time he was knocking on Hitler's door, his knees had turned to jelly. He entered the room stolidly, prepared at least for a knuckle rapping. 'My Fuhrer,' he said, 'I report my return, having absented in Berlin myself without permission.'

Seemingly occupied with map-reading Hitler took an inordinately long time to remove his glasses and peer up at Linge. His voice was harsh. 'Did you inform me you were going to Berlin last night?'

Linge stared straight ahead. 'No, my Fuhrer.'

Hitler frowned, his good hand rubbing his face. He looked up at his valet expectantly. Was he waiting for the lame excuse? Linge held his tongue.

His chief sat back, the lines on his face relaxed. 'Before you take it upon yourself to go gadding off on another excursion, all I ask is that you let me know beforehand. Then there'll be no misunderstanding. You look as though you could do with a few hours sleep, so you'd better go to your quarters for the rest of the day.'

Linge left the room, hungover but immensely relieved, thanking Providence he hadn't tried to bluff his way out of trouble.

How could anyone hope to fathom the inscrutable nature of the chief? The rantings and ravings for little apparent reason — apart from the terrible burdens of his office; the manner in which he so quickly regained control of himself; the strange humanity when it was least expected. Was it that his capacity for biting anger might have been more sharply exercised had he been in better physical condition? Or that, on the threshold of total collapse, he was finally able to achieve — if only in brief intervals — a measure of serenity?

*   *   *

It was at this time that everyone at FHQ realised that the long-awaited invasion of the European mainland was imminent.

Rommel, a short stocky figure in a heavy greatcoat, with an old muffler round his throat, stalked up and down waving his 'informal' marshal's baton, a two-foot, silver-topped black stick with a red, black and white tassel. He pointed to the sands and said, 'The war will be won or lost on the beaches. We'll have only one chance to stop the enemy and that's while he's in the water struggling to get ashore . . . the Hauptkampflinie (main line of resistance) will be here . . . Everything we have must be on the coast. Believe me, Lang, the first twenty-four hours of the invasion will be decisive . . . for the allies, as well as Germany, it will be the longest day.'

Cornelius Ryan

Today this whole area of Normandy, green and sweet in the early summer sunshine, is dotted with museums and monuments to the events of June 6, 1944. French schoolchildren swarm around Sherman tanks, German 88 mm guns and models of the amazing Mulberry harbour, of which half-submerged chunks can still be seen at Arromanches.

Peter Chambers 1984

CHAPTER TWENTY

It was the beginning of June, 1944 and the stretch of country between Munich and Berchtesgaden was looking at its best.

To Linge, there was something reassuring and solid about the strings of whitewashed farmhouses scattered among the rich pasture lands of the lower Alps; something orderly about the modest chalets with their decorative eaves and flower-filled window boxes, perched above smooth green fields and blossoming apple orchards; something charming about the sturdy children in woollen stockings and leather shorts, who put down their milk cans to watch the big Mercedes climb the steep, narrow road leading to the Berghof. One little girl puckered her lips as if about to blow a kiss.

The Fuhrer too was aware of his surroundings. Outwardly, at least, here were peace and contentment. The weather had something to do with it. That and the familiar landmarks and the fact that he was going back to his own place, the solid, middle-class basis of Bavarian living.

But as much as he looked forward to being with Eva again there was a darker side to his thoughts. Perhaps it was a premonition of the horrors ahead. Frequently, the burden of responsibility he carried almost made him groan aloud. He was fifty-five but looked years older. With so little exposure to fresh air, he required the constant use of an oxygen mask; a habit he had started at Rastenberg. Increasingly, he felt his life was running down like an unwinding clock.

Had he finally failed? Reneged on his promises? His decimated armies were falling back in the east and now, with the allies preparing to invade Europe, it looked as if there would be new agonies to endure.

The Wehrmacht was pulling back in Italy; the Russians were sweeping westwards; the allies had taken to sending out heavy bombers, determined to root out his headquarters at Rastenberg and wipe it from the face of the earth. The situation in Germany itself was critical, with most people aware of the dangers facing them.

Had he been guilty of folly on a monumental scale? No, despite everything it was a just crusade. And when eventually the long-awaited assault was launched to the west, in the days and weeks ahead he must do everything to ensure a strong defence. It would take new formations, emergency measures, massive artillery replacements, clear-headed field commanders and the need to urge every soldier to fight to his last breath. Thanks to his leadership and with the guiding spirit of providence, he was convinced that any invasion would ultimately fail. And thanks to the steadfast courage of his troops on the Eastern front, the Red Army would finally drown in its own savage blood-bath.

Any treacherous commander who ordered retreat would be placed under immediate arrest and shot on the spot, never mind what rank he held.

Any unit that abandoned its position was a disgrace to the name of Germany, to the thousands of women and children who had been subjected to terrorist bombing tactics, to all those dedicated to the defence of the fatherland.

The one deeply disturbing factor that troubled his thoughts was the instability of so many of his military chiefs. Against the Soviets, who were ferociously reckless, they had been so often outfought, outgeneralled and overwhelmed.

God knows how many hours he had wasted arguing with them; about strategy, tactics and leadership.

Runstedt, the 68-year-old C-in-C, West, a command which included France, Belgium and Holland — with two army groups and a panzer formation at his disposal.

Rommel, appointed to oppose his old enemy, Montgomery, but as always headstrong and erratic. He thought the focus of enemy landing operations would probably be directed between Boulogne and the Somme estuary. Runstedt agreed with him. As a result the coastal defences were strengthened. Because Hitler believed the landing would be attempted along the Normandy coast, Rommel set out an arrangement of strong points manned by infantry with gun positions and protected by heavy concrete pillboxes from naval gunfire or air attack. Minefields, barbed wire entanglements and sinister prongs tipped with high explosives extended into the sea. On beaches below the high-water mark, these underwater obstacles — known as 'Rommel's asparagus' — would destroy landing craft upon impact.

In the event, neither the Fuhrer nor Rommel had grasped the need for a fluid defence — a lesson Runstedt had learnt in Russia. Rommel was determined to hold the impregnable Atlantic Wall, so he asked for the reserves to be stationed close to the beaches. Runstedt, supported by Guderian, argued that until it was known where the enemy intended to land, the reserves should be left further back.

The different theories led to a compromise, with the infantry committed to the coast line and the armoured reserves held well back. Hitler took it upon himself to issue direct orders to those commanders who should have been Runstedt's subordinates.

There would be little unity of command during the campaign.

*   *   *

By the time the Fuhrer reached the Berghof, he felt considerably better. He was relaxed and, installed in his private suite, ready to forget the war and its preoccupations and commitments for a while. Eva too seemed more amenable than usual. She did all she could to lighten the load for him. Small entertainments had been planned; several guests — robust party leaders and one or two industrialists and their wives from the Ruhr — had been invited, people noted for their intelligent conversation and sense of humour.

The Fuhrer didn't appear the following morning, June 5, until shortly before the midday conference. He had breakfasted well on porridge, fruit and wheat germ soaked in milk, and seemed to his valet to be in a benign mood.

During the conference, he rapidly scanned the dispatches, picking out scraps of information. The French Resistance had stepped up sabotage activities. Fortunately, members of the SD in France had infiltrated units of the maquis. They would alert headquarters in the event of a seaborne invasion. Once he knew the exact extent of the operation he would order his armoured divisions in to oppose it and push the enemy back into the sea.

Bormann wanted to discuss other eventualities privately with him. He mentioned the aircraft which had appeared out of the morning sky from the direction of Trieste. Circling at a considerable height, they had frightened several of the guests, causing them to gather up clothes and valuables and scurry off to the safety of the Obersalzberg bunkers. And there was one more item: the possibility existed of a group of officers in Germany whose objective was to destroy the regime and dispose of the Fuhrer.

Unabashed, Hitler jovially appointed Bormann his bulldog of the Berghof terraces, charged with the job of sniffing cautiously at every change of wind direction; every sound of enemy aircraft, and to growl at the approach of hostile strangers.

Lunch was delayed until four in the afternoon. At the table, Hitler joined Eva and the remaining guests, where he ate a little of the vegetable casserole followed by a salad and a baked potato. From a large bowl of fruit he carefully selected an apple, peeling and slicing it with the small knife Linge had placed at the side of his plate. He slowly cut the fruit into sections, eating them one by one, leaning forward, looking around at his friends, speaking between mouthfuls. Blondi, his alsatian dog, lay quietly at his feet.

At the end of the meal, the party walked over to the tea-house, Blondi running ahead but stopping frequently to check that his master was following. Everyone there knew that the dog would have torn to pieces any stranger who tried to get too close to the Fuhrer.

After a cup or two of lime-blossom tea, and some idle conversation, Hitler sank back into his armchair and fell fast asleep. Awake an hour later, he ordered Linge to call a car to take him back to the house.

His mood had changed, and in his suite he ordered further medication from Morell, complaining that some internal disorder was plaguing him.

*   *   *

Dinner was later than usual and after a second conference, Hitler kept his guests up long after midnight, listening to records; mostly Wagner, Strauss and some Lehar. It was almost 4 am before the Fuhrer retired to his room. He told Linge he was only to be disturbed in the direst of emergencies, as Morell had given him a more powerful sleeping pill.

At the OKW headquarters in Berchtesgaden, Jodl and Keitel had gone to their beds, having placed the army groups in France on the alert. A wireless message had been intercepted and decoded earlier that night, calling on the French resistance to prepare pre-invasion sabotage attacks.

Rommel was on a visit to his wife at Heerlingen, near Ulm. Tuesday, June 6 was Lucie-Maria's birthday.

Runstedt was at his headquarters, St Germain, outside Paris, studying weather reports. Off the coast of France, conditions were bad, with gale force winds and stormy seas. There seemed to be little chance of an invasion at present.

Dietrich (1st Panzer Korps) was in Brussels — his troops were based at Beverloo in Belgium. Dollman (Commander of the 7th army) was on manoeuvres at Rennes.

At 7.25 am on the Tuesday morning, the allied sea armada had reached the coast. Earlier, airborne forces had captured the bridges over the River Orne and the Canal de Caen, while naval bombardment squadrons had opened fire on German shore defences. When the first reports reached Runstedt, he thought the Normandy landings were simply a diversionary attack. Even so, he sent a dispatch to OKW asking permission to commit two panzer reserve divisions to counter the seaborne landing.

Jodl's staff, not wishing to disturb the chief of operations' sleep, held the message until morning.

At the Berghof, news came through of 'some sort of landings in France'. The duty officer, thinking the report too vague, took no action and Hitler slept on undisturbed.

With the allies inching up the Normandy beaches Speidel, Rommel's chief of staff, managed to get a message through to Jodl. Jodl waited over an hour before discussing the matter with Keitel. Both felt bound by the strict order not to disturb the Fuhrer until he emerged from his room. It wasn't until the midday conference that the Fuhrer heard the news.

Linge, in common with the generals and staff officers, had anticipated a tempestuous reaction from the chief. But Hitler appeared to accept the situation with unruffled calm, asking Jodl to indicate on the map precisely where the landings had taken place. He noted with a wry smile that the invasion had not taken place where Runstedt had expected. 'The news could not be better as far as I'm concerned. While the enemy stayed in England there was little we could do to defeat them. Now at last we have them where we want them. Whatever allied bridgeheads have been established, we should be able to dispose of them by midnight tonight.'

By the time he had agreed to send the panzer reserves forward — at four o'clock that afternoon — it was too late to bring them into action that day.

Just before the conference ended, Linge announced the arrival of Goring. Hitler grabbed a large-scale map and hurried out to the ante-room with it. 'Goring,' he exclaimed, 'they have landed exactly where I forecast they would. It's up to us to fling them back into the English channel.'

Linge was astounded at the transformation in him. For the first time in over three years he was his old self: bright-eyed, fizzing with optimism, rising yet again to the challenge. The dominating forcefulness, the compelling leadership quality, the magnetism, all restored to life. He spoke rapidly, confidently, outlining his plans, slapping his thigh enthusiastically in the old way, grasping Goring by the arm. It would be the two old comrades again, the Fuhrer and his second-in-command on the move again, old errors forgotten, past differences dead and buried. This time, it was the nothing-to-lose, all the way from the beerhalls to final victory outlook that would prevail — at least for a few days.

Hitler had no intention of giving up an inch of the territory he had fought so hard to gain, especially with his star on the ascent. The invasion forces had to be stopped where they had landed and driven back. They must never be allowed to obtain a foothold in France.

Every hour, as reports poured in, he examined them carefully. But, as the facts came to light, so his attitude changed.

Why were the invasion forces not meeting the kind of resistance he had planned? What the hell was Runstedt playing at? What had Rommel done about bringing in the heavy artillery? In every area he could only discover inertia, apathy and all-round slackness. What did Jodl and Keitel intend to do? Throw the war into the enemy's lap? None of the seaborne landings had been repulsed. All, in varying stages, had been successful. The counter-offensive had been feeble and the Luftwaffe had not shot down a single enemy aircraft.

'From June 9 onwards,' wrote Speidel, 'the initiative lay with the allies, who fought the battle entirely as it suited them.' It was Speidel who later refused to obey Hitler's orders to destroy Paris. A born survivor, by 1961 he was the commander of the Nato land forces in Europe.

Skorzeny saw the invasion as a brilliant military feat on the part of the enemy. 'No clearsighted man could doubt that, from a purely military point of view, we had lost the war.'

On June 12, Hitler launched the first of his flying bombs — pilotless, jet-propelled rockets with 1,000 kg warheads. 8,000 of the missiles were dispatched from bases north of the Seine towards London. Only 2,400 got through, killing 6,000 people and injuring another 18,000. On September 8, V2 rockets began to fall on London. With a 200-mile range, the V2's had tremendous speed but were lacking in accuracy. With good reason, the Fuhrer had placed all his hopes on the flying bombs. Underground factories had been established and by October 1944, he expected to increase the output by five times. Werner von Braun, in charge of the project, had explained the use of the V1 and its application to the Luftwaffe. 'The weapon will be used in concentrated batches, so that anything from fifty to a hundred can be released simultaneously. Aimed at the heart of troop movements, the effects would be devastating.'

It was Rommel's task to protect the launching sites, which produced a dilemma. What if the allies landed near Calais, with the intention of destroying the V1 stations and he had not been able to deploy a large enough garrison for their protection? He desperately needed the Fifteenth Army, then at Calais, to reinforce his divisions in Normandy. As a compromise, therefore, he took divisions away piecemeal, only to find them worn down one by one.

Matters had deteriorated so quickly by June 15 that Rommel was openly expressing the opinion that Normandy would have to be given up.

On June 17 the Fuhrer flew to Metz for an on-the-spot assessment of the situation with his commanders. He conferred with them in a concrete bunker at Margival, 60 miles from Paris, the spot from which in 1940 he had hoped to launch an invasion against England.

'He looked worn and sleepless,' remembers Speidel, 'playing nervously with his glasses and some coloured pencils . . . he was the only one who sat, hunched on a stool, while the field marshals stood.'

His nerves stretched to breaking point, dog-weary from lack of sleep, Hitler was relying on his last reserves of energy to stop himself from falling apart. Arguments raged around the success of the allies — the British were moving towards Caen and the Americans were preparing to capture Cherbourg — and the disposition of vital reserves. Neither Runstedt nor Rommel appeared to have a proper appreciation of the need for counter-measures or of the danger of a major allied breakout.

Cherbourg, said the Fuhrer, must be defended and the peninsula cleared of the enemy.

Cherbourg, contended Rommel, was a lost cause.

Hitler lost control and began pounding the table, his voice rising. 'Will someone please tell me what is going on here? In every situation report I made it absolutely clear that Cherbourg must not be isolated; that sufficient batteries had to be installed to protect the entire area. I was told these instructions had been implemented.'

Why were the allies not being forced back; pinned down in Normandy?

Runstedt suggested a regrouping of his battalions inland rather than a suicidal attempt to hold ground.

Rommel was for fighting on the run; for freedom of movement.

The Fuhrer glared at both field marshals. 'I gave categorical orders. Yes, yes, you said. And when I look into the matter nothing has been done. Are you too cynical, too corrupt to care? Do you not realise that I, your leader and supreme commander, still have some cards to play? I tell you the spirit of my soldiers will be the deciding factor. And, given time, the flying bombs will destroy London.'

He ordered Rommel to hold Cherbourg and committed eight panzer divisions to hold a twenty-mile line between Caumont and Caen.

On his return to Obersalzberg, Hitler relapsed into an almost constant state of deep depression continually criticising the lack of initiative of the generals; reviewing the failures; instancing Goring's inability to use the Luftwaffe to maximum advantage. 'In the spring of 1943, I was promised a thousand serviceable aircraft by 1944. There is a desperate need for fighters, but where are they? On the day of the invasion there were only sixty fighter aircraft on stand-by. Half of those were in action defending German cities from enemy bombers. We should have had hundreds of aircraft in readiness.'

Linge understood. Goring was out of favour once again.

The Fuhrer turned his attention to the launching sites for the flying-bomb project. Unfortunately there was still some way to go before full production could get under way. What was the problem? There were many but the primary one was an insufficient labour force.

Hitler, as was his custom in such situations, called in the SS. The relatively simple matter of speeding up production was left to a particularly forthright gruppenfuhrer named Kammer.

Linge had known him in the old days and during a confidential chat Kammer told him later how things had developed. In charge of the programme he found more than 700 engineers and technicians — all highly paid and most of them hoping the flying bomb project would be a permanent, pensionable occupation. None of them was keen on speeding things up — not even for the SS.

Kammer combed the concentration camps for labour; then thinned out the executives and introduced new measures to ensure the unhampered manufacture of the V-bombs. As an incentive, the food rations for prisoners engaged on heavy work were increased.

In the mornings they each received half a litre of ersatz coffee and a bread ration of 350 gr. At lunch, cabbage or noodle soup and in the evening, 20-30 grams of sausage or cheese with ¾ litre of ersatz tea.

Rommel failed to hold Caen and his forces were repulsed at Cherbourg. Reports reached the Fuhrer of soldiers fighting on until the last cartridge, with many of the cream of the Hitler Youth perishing in the storming of Cherbourg.

That upset the Fuhrer even more than the news of the allied victories. Because his orders had been ignored; because his crack divisions had been held back; because his forces had been cut in two at the base of the Cherbourg peninsula, his boys had been sent into a fight that was lost long before the first rounds had been fired.

On June 23 Stalin, having seen his long-called-for second front succeeding, began a summer offensive. By the middle of August the Russians had reached East Prussia. On August 22, Rumania surrendered. Three days later, the Finns asked for an armistice.

Zeitzler, who had been briefed to assess the position on the South-eastern front, returned to the Berghof at the end of June to make his report. He believed the initiative was very much in the Red Army's favour. This led to sharp differences of opinion between the chief and himself. Zeitzler was unable to reconcile Hitler's assessment with the reality: divisions hopelessly outnumbered; commanders unable to contain their own battle groups; coming up against endless columns of Russian infantry.

In this climax of the war, Hitler adopted a stance of blind arrogance, refusing to listen to Zeitzler's voice of reason.

More tantrums, louder arguments, heavier table poundings eventually culminated in the unfortunate 'Thunderball' Zeitzler experiencing a sudden agonising pain in his chest.

It was, seemingly, a heart attack.

Linge summoned an ambulance and stood anxiously by as the general was rushed away unconscious, strapped to a stretcher. He was never seen again.

Within hours of the defeat at Cherbourg, Runstedt and Rommel were called to the Berghof to explain themselves.

Runstedt, with stony-faced determination, asked for a free hand in the future.

Rommel suggested a withdrawal of the entire Seventh Army to the Seine.

The Fuhrer refused to listen.

On July 1 Keitel, without two strategic ideas to rub together, spoke to Runstedt on the phone. 'What shall we do?'

'End the war, you fools,' snapped Runstedt. 'What else can you do?'

Keitel relayed the conversation to the chief.

'The old man has lost his nerve,' said Hitler, 'and is no longer master of the situation. We will have to let him go.'

On July 3 Runstedt, relieved of his command, was succeeded by Field Marshal von Kluge. He lasted a total of forty-four days. Replaced by Model on August 17, Kluge was ordered to report to FHQ without delay. Unable to face the Fuhrer, he sent a letter instead and took poison.

Model held the job for eighteen days. The command passed back to Runstedt on September 4.

* * *

During that summer of 1944 a picture emerges of the Fuhrer turning from a close study of the battle of Normandy, to observe the fresh Russian counter-attacks. He resembled a man who, backing away from a rampaging elephant, treads on the open jaws of a crocodile.

He was fighting on his own territory with an enemy who demanded unconditional surrender. His determination to resist to his last breath had to be the only answer. He indulged in long spells of introspection, staring moodily at campaign maps, functioning on a lean mixture of bewilderment and hope, and spared details of the worst disasters by Keitel and Jodl.

Hitler stayed at Obersalzberg until the worsening situation to the East in mid-July sent him back to Rastenberg.

'When we leave the Berghof this time,' he said to his stalwart valet — a silent witness to his struggle to hang on to his sanity, 'it will be with a heavy heart. Fraulein Eva has done everything possible to persuade me to stay. You and I know I can't stay here now, surrounded by enemies, beset by petty treasons. On two fronts, the generals are crying out for more: more tanks, more aircraft, more fuel, more men. I must go where this war takes me; accept whatever fate destiny has in store for me. I have explained the situation to the Fraulein and thank providence that she, at least, understands.'

Linge was shocked at the bleak tone of despair and at the utter weariness. His face gave the appearance of one who could barely tolerate the pain of being alive. His left hand trembled more violently than ever and he walked as though he was held together by rivets.

The valet felt totally inadequate; caught in the arbitrary horror of the nightmare, he was unable to offer anything in the way of comfort.

God was with the bigger battalions and the Fuhrer's season in hell was just beginning.

When he was only fifteen, in the closing months of World War II, Helmut Kohl, the West German Chancellor, was drafted into the infantry at a time when the desperate Nazi regime was calling up teenagers to fill the depleted ranks of the once mighty Wehrmacht. He went through basic training in Berchtesgaden near Hitler's mountain retreat. But the war ended before he was thrown into combat. In his ill-fitting uniform, with no money in his pocket, Kohl trudged back home 150 miles to Ludwigshafen.

Time Magazine, March, 1983

On Friday, July 20, 1984 Helmut Kohl attended a ceremony to mark the anniversary of the July Plot. He visited the Berlin courtyard where Colonel Claus von Stauffenberg was shot.

Of the 7,000 of von Stauffenberg's sympathisers who were rounded up by the Gestapo, 5,000 were executed. The key conspirators were hanged by piano wire strung from meathooks at the Plotzensee Barracks, Berlin. The killings were filmed so that the Fuhrer could play back the hangings at his headquarters.

News Item, July, 1984

CHAPTER TWENTY-ONE

Six weeks after the Normandy invasion Colonel Claus von Stauffenberg landed at Rastenberg airfield with a briefcase containing details on the newly formed Volksgrenadier divisions. Hitler's Home Army Commander had been ordered to report to the Fuhrer at the midday conference.

Seriously wounded in Tunisia a year before, von Stauffenberg had only one arm and wore a black eye-patch over his left eye. Two fingers were missing from his left hand.

Inside his briefcase, concealed in clean linen, was a plastic-explosive bomb of British make, primed by a glass capsule of acid. When the glass was broken the acid would corrode a fine wire, releasing a firing pin against the detonator, and the device would explode ten minutes after the mechanism was activated.

From the landing strip, a staff car conveyed Stauffenberg and his adjutant, Oberleutnant von Haeften, along a winding road through a dense fir forest to a red-and-black striped barrier manned by an SS platoon of men, submachine guns under their arms.

At a second observation point over a railway embankment, the Wehrmacht officers' passes were examined by the duty officer and their names noted in the duty daybook. The car then continued to the main gate, which was set in an electrified fence protected by pillboxes.

The inner compound was heavily camouflaged with netting, shrubbery and clumps of trees. Grassy banks concealed the flat-roofed barrack blocks. The whole area was extensively mined and patrolled night and day by guard dogs and a handpicked unit of assault troops.

A gravel drive led from the main checkpoint to the headquarters building — two wings connected by a roofed-in corridor. The wooden structure was in the process of being reinforced with toughened concrete cladding. The conference barracks lay some yards further on.

According to Linge, Hitler had been forced to take temporary accommodation in a guest house adjoining the barracks while his underground bunker was being strengthened. The conference room was no more than thirty feet by fifteen. It had ten casement windows and was dominated by a long table fashioned from heavy oak planks, with its underside supported at each end by solid uprights.

Despite the assumption that the daily conference almost invariably took place in the Fuhrer's bunker; and that it was only due to the alterations in progress that the July 20 meeting was held in the *lagebaracke* above ground, Linge confirms that the conference was always held in the *lagebaracke*.

Although it is doubtful Stauffenberg had eyes to notice, it was a beautiful summer's day that Friday. He was concerned with covertly setting the fuse in the ante room before being escorted into the Fuhrer's presence by Keitel. The OKW chief had explained why the meeting had started half-an-hour earlier at 12.30: Mussolini was due to visit Hitler at 2.30 pm.

Hitler was seated halfway down the table, studying a map. Stauffenberg, his heart sinking, noticed that all the windows were wide open because of the heat. He moved to the far side of the Fuhrer, next to Colonel Brandt, carefully placing his briefcase underneath the table inside the support and roughly six feet from the leader. After a moment, he quietly left the room, murmuring an excuse about an urgent phone call to Berlin. Brandt shifted the briefcase sideways.

At 12.42 the bomb exploded, flinging bodies in every direction.

Hitler, an armoured steel vest beneath his shirt, was thrown through the door opening, hair alight, both ear-drums perforated.

*　　*　　*

Linge later declared that although he had an idea a number of people were disenchanted with the progress of the war, he found it difficult to believe that so many high-ranking officers had actually gone to the lengths of attempting to assassinate their supreme commander. He recalled how, during a meeting between the Fuhrer and his Balkan allies — held at the Schloss Klessheim at Salzburg a few days previously — Fegelein, Eva Braun's brother-in-law, had buttonholed him.

'You'd better keep a sharp look-out, Linge,' the Gruppenfuhrer suggested. 'There've been so many officers sacked because of inefficiency, I have heard they're gunning for the Fuhrer. I've told Himmler and he's beginning an investigation. You see anything, hear anything suspicious, report to me right away. That clear?'

The valet hummed and hawed and nodded sagely. He had the measure of the boozy Fegelein, with his indiscretions and love of the dramatic. For God's sake, hadn't it always been a matter of personal pride, the way he'd protected the chief over the years?

Of course there'd been the malcontents, the negative thinkers all creeping out of the woodwork since the Normandy landings, but he'd never met a professional soldier yet who didn't enjoy a good moan at someone else's expense. It was true that, over the past weeks, he'd heard a few generals voicing their doubts about the Fuhrer's capabilities. They were human; and their lives would be part of the price of defeat. But since their future and that of Hitler's was inextricably bound together, he found it difficult to believe any of them would openly rebel, never mind attempt an assassination.

There'd also been some rumblings of discontent among fringe party members — the very ones formerly earmarked for advancement. Their loving loyalty had evidently paled since that laurel-wreathed day in 1933, when they feted their leader's rise to the echo and raved among themselves about the ascendancy of national socialism.

And that English-born head of the foreign section of the party, Ernst Bohle, had dared to write a memo to the Fuhrer suggesting it was time to begin peace negotiations with the English and Americans. Privately, many of the party hierarchy were, by 1944, disillusioned, and contemptuous of Hitler, whom they had seen as a piece of clay which could be shaped to their purpose.

* * *

At 12.30 on July 20, Linge was strolling outside the *lagebaracke*, enjoying the warm sunshine and breathing in mouthfuls of an air fragrant with the scent of wild flowers. He had stopped about a hundred metres from the conference room to discuss security arrangements for Mussolini's visit with one of the guards, when he heard an explosion. The two men, thinking it was just another mine touched off by a clumsy guard dog, continued talking. Linge remembered looking at his watch. It was just after a quarter to one. Seconds later an orderly rushed out of the conference block, shouting his name.

'Hauptsturmfuhrer Linge! You must come at once. Come quickly, please!'

Realising that something terrible had happened, Linge ran towards the *lagebaracke*. As he neared the door Keitel appeared, face bleeding and dirt-streaked, his uniform in ribbons, shouting, 'Attentat! Attentat!' Jodl had been blown through a window and flung violently to the ground.

'What has happened in there?' shouted Linge. He almost collided with Von Freyend, Keitel's adjutant, who came staggering out, blood running down his face. He veered around, staring blankly at the valet for a minute. 'It's all right,' he stammered, 'the Fuhrer is safe.'

Linge experienced a cold stab of fear followed by a measure of relief at the news. As long as the chief's life had been spared, nothing else mattered.

Puttkamer was carried out, mortally injured; Schmundt followed, unconscious on a stretcher, one leg completely severed. Then came Hitler, assisted by two officers, right arm hanging limp, a trouser leg torn away. Despite everything he seemed to be taking the outrage calmly.

His stenographer, Berger, had been killed. Brandt, Schmundt, the adjutant and General Korten died from their wounds. Apart from Keitel, most of the other officers present had been severely injured.

Linge led the way to the Fuhrer's quarters and with Hitler lying on a table, Morell and Surgeon Hasselbach began a searching examination to determine the extent of his injuries.

His hair had been badly burned and scores of splinters were later removed from his legs. His right arm was badly bruised and temporarily paralysed, his back lacerated by falling debris.

At the end of the examination, as he rose painfully to his feet, Linge made a move towards him to lend a helping hand. Hitler told him to summon half-a-dozen guards and check his quarters thoroughly in case more explosives had been planted.

Once the block had been cleared, Linge returned. For the first time since he had begun serving the Fuhrer he helped him undress, carefully peeling away the ruined clothing before bringing a fresh uniform.

Half-an-hour later Hitler was ready to meet Mussolini. He explained that he had just had the greatest piece of luck in his life and described how the bomb had exploded six feet away from him.

It was only later, after he had discussed the event with Goebbels, that he realised the full significance of what had occurred.

Linge, once he was no longer needed by the chief, quickly went to assist in tending the wounded, who were arranged in a line outside the *lagebaracke*, with medical orderlies attempting to comfort the officers bleeding to death. Both Berger's legs had been blown off — he had been standing across the table from Hitler when the bomb exploded. Brandt, Zeitzler's adjutant, had also lost a leg. He died in agony a couple of hours later. Schmundt was in a terrible condition, his face torn open, an eye destroyed, and the lower half of his body completely shattered. He died in hospital two weeks later.

The conference room looked as if a malevolent colossus had lowered a hand into the place and crushed it. The roof had caved in, a wall was demolished, there were gaping holes where the windows had been, and chairs had been reduced to matchwood. Linge found it difficult to believe that one small bomb could have done so much damage.

It was the blessing of providence that the sturdy table and the officers gathered around it had protected the chief from the worst of the blast. He heard the full details from Hitler that night.

'A moment before the blast,' he said, 'I remember supporting myself on top of the table, with all my weight resting on my right arm. As the bomb went off, the table lifted, striking me a severe blow on that arm. Then I was flung clear. The swine who did it must have thought the conference would be held in the bunker. If it had been, not one of us would have come out of it alive.'

When the valet was told it was Stauffenberg who had placed the bomb, he felt relieved to know that none of the workers employed in strengthening the buildings had been involved.

'I won't forget,' Hitler went on, 'that it was not simply a botched murder attempt, but an organised conspiracy aimed at destroying everything I have built up over the years. If Stauffenberg had pulled out a gun and shot me at close range he'd have proved himself a soldier. His action was the work of a coward.'

Ribbentrop, Goring and Himmler, having reaffirmed their loyalty, vehemently stated their determination to get to the bottom of the matter. Goebbels, reached by phone in Berlin, told the Fuhrer that his guard commander, Major Remer, had already drawn up plans to prevent an uprising in the city.

Hitler spoke directly to Remer, ordering his immediate promotion to Colonel and instructing him to arrest every last traitor and show no compunction.

He finally left his quarters to go out and talk to the workmen who had been engaged on reinforcing the underground bunkers. 'I knew from the beginning,' he said, 'that no conspiracy, either directed against me personally or against the party, could have originated from you. I've known for a very long time that most of my enemies are arrogant swine who have "von" before their names and with a disreputable body of blue-bloods behind them. Please continue with your work as before, friends, the worst is over.'

Eventually, details of the plot came to light. In the aftermath, two generals and two colonels committed suicide; one general, two colonels and another officer were executed by courtmartial; a field marshal, five generals, two colonels and five more officers were thrown out of the army and sentenced by a people's court to be hanged. They had all planned to negotiate peace terms with the allies over the Fuhrer's dead body.

Hitler followed the purges closely, asking to see transcripts of all the proceedings, as well as the related documents and photographs.

Refusing to believe that Stauffenberg had been shot, he ordered the body to be exhumed to prove it was the right man. He even doubted that von Kluge had killed himself. His driver, his staff, his widow were subjected to lengthy interrogation and his corpse was also disinterred for identification.

But it was the revelation that Rommel was also involved in the conspiracy that really shocked Linge. The Desert Fox had had talks with General von Stulpnagel, the commander of Paris, in April 1944. Like Kluge, he had been in touch with the British — in response to offers of a safe haven after the war and large sums of money. He had sent Hitler an ultimatum on July 15 demanding the start of peace negotiations. Hitler had ignored it.

Two days later, while checking his front line, Rommel was

travelling along the road from Livarot to Vemoutiers, not far from the village of Ste Foy-Montgomerie when his car was machine-gunned by two low-flying RAF fighters. Rommel was critically injured, suffering a skull fracture, broken cheekbone, an injured left eye and concussion.

In October, Rommel was convalescing at his Herlingen home near Ulm, when Burgdorf contacted him with a different kind of ultimatum. As the Field-Marshal had been implicated by Stulpnagel in the July plot, he could choose death by poison, which would mean a state funeral with full military honours and a generous pension for his wife and family; or a people's court trial with reprisals against Frau Rommel and his sixteen-year-old son Manfred.

At 1.25 pm, October 14 a staff car containing Rommel, Burgdorf and General Maisel drew up to the front entrance of Ulm Hospital. Rommel was already dead. Maisel stated later that on a deserted stretch of road, he and the SS driver were ordered to leave the car for a few minutes. When they returned, Rommel was dying.

At the state funeral on October 18, the reinstated Runstedt delivered a eulogy to the Field-Marshal on behalf of the Fuhrer.

*   *   *

It was soon apparent to Linge that his chief was affected more severely by the explosion than he was prepared to admit. While keeping up a pretence that he was in good condition, the valet often had to support him when he was on his feet, for he had difficulty maintaining his balance. Reluctantly, he submitted to exhaustive X-rays. The surgeons were optimistic about his hearing, telling him it was a temporary impairment. But as Hitler himself put it: 'No other part of my body is as important as my head.'

Advised by Morell to stay in bed for at least a week — with Linge fully prepared to keep him wrapped in blankets and feed him hot soup — he rested for three or four days, leaving administrative details to Keitel. Throughout a testing train of events, the OKW chief had demonstrated an unexpected energy and efficiency.

On his feet again, and accompanied by Linge, Hitler was able to enjoy brief walks as part of his convalescence. He spoke a great deal about the plot and the fact that despite so many attempts on his life, Providence continued to spare him; and that the ultimate good of Germany was still safe in his hands. 'It has to be the best of all omens, Linge, that I am here, living and breathing and able to enjoy these walks with you. The future of the nation rests with me. With the enemy pushing forward to the west and with our central eastern front overrun by the Russians, it is necessary for me as Fuhrer to retain control. We will halt the Russians, our flying bombs will inflict serious damage, Runstedt will hold the west wall and we will prepare a counter-attack against the armoured spearheads of the allies.

'Let it be known among the staff that I will not tolerate defeatism. I will not countenance talk of capitulation or negotiation. There must be an end to such foolishness.'

He visited the survivors of the bomb outrage several times and was full of sympathy for their suffering. He said, 'These are the brave ones who took the full force of a malignant outrage aimed solely at me. I will never forget their sacrifice.'

As a result of the purge, Himmler was appointed commander in chief of Home Forces.

* * *

Now, more than forty years on, the ghosts of Stauffenberg, the handsome aristocrat and his fellow-conspirators have been brought in from the cold.

Referred to as traitors for so long, Berlin is spending a million pounds on transforming their Wehrmacht offices into a museum. The Plotzensee prison, where hundreds of thousands of people were hanged or guillotined during Hitler's reign has become a memorial.

Stauffenberg's son, Count Franz Ludwig, is a Christian Social Union representative in the West German Parliament.

'The July Plot,' said Professor Lowenthal, formerly lecturer in political science at Berlin University, 'has been misunderstood for too long. In England it's perpetrators were seen as a group of slightly eccentric, ineffectual army officers — whereas the civilian participation has always been underrated. Today, there is a desire to see the plot in perspective. There is a revival of the sense of German identity and an interest in German history; and I don't mean nationalism.'

* * *

Had Hitler died as a result of the plot, the collapse of Germany would have occurred before the winter of 1944. The generals, according to Goring, were convinced the war was lost. Hitler, even after the surrender of Paris, refused to accept this point of view.

The loss of Paris after four years of occupation was a devastating blow to the Fuhrer. He had ordered that the city should never be re-taken by the enemy, for it was the one city he was most proud of having occupied. In a meeting with General Choltitz, the new commandant of Paris, he had ordered all the city's bridges and important state buildings and monuments to be destroyed.

Choltitz received written confirmation of this instruction on August 23, the very day that an allied tank division was entering the outskirts of Paris. Having no intention of obeying the Fuhrer, he ordered a few perfunctory shots to be fired before surrendering. For him, the war was over and he was taken to an American P-O-W camp.

*   *   *

At the end of August, General Burgdorf — Schmundt's successor as chief military adjutant — was ordered to call a conference of field commanders. The Fuhrer would address them personally at headquarters.

Burgdorf, an egregiously heavy drinker, shared the views of his chief. A true man of the people, he hated the arrogance of the old Prussian traditions.

Hitler agreed. 'We need natural leaders from now on,' he said. 'Graduates from the Hitler Youth with the kind of qualities essential to success. We must begin a series of courses aimed at supplementing military theory.

'In future, we will look to young men from ordinary backgrounds. Pick the best and brightest; train them to function like machines and we will still be able to hold our place among the great nations of the world.'

'If necessary,' he told the generals, 'we'll fight on the Rhine. It doesn't make any difference. Under all circumstances we'll continue this battle until as Frederick the Great said, one of our damned enemies gets too tired to fight any more.

'We'll fight until we are in a position to negotiate a peace . . . a peace securing the life of the nation for the next fifty or a hundred years . . . for a settlement which above all does not besmirch our honour a second time, as happened in 1918. I live now solely for the purpose of leading the fight; if there is no iron will behind it, the battle will be lost.'

While superficially the Fuhrer appeared to have recovered from his injuries, even with Linge's strong right arm he found walking increasingly difficult, shuffling along like a land crab for most of the time, taking slow, measured, painful steps. Hair completely grey and puffy-faced, his scaly skin took on a translucent quality. He complained of stomach pains and suffered severe throat trouble. He was oyster-eyed from lack of sleep. Stricken with an attack of jaundice, he used the illness to delay decisions, sitting alone, staring at maps, going without solid food for days at a time. Whereas, formerly, his pronouncements had been remarkably sound, indifferent health gravely affected his judgement. He spoke like an old man who had exhausted his last reserves of strength.

In November, under the usual conditions of absolute secrecy, Professor Blaschke, Hitler's dental surgeon, was called to Rastenberg. He found the Fuhrer's teeth, like the rest of his body, in poor shape; his right cheek was morbidly swollen; his breath was obnoxious.

Blaschke located a badly decomposed wisdom tooth. Aware of how much Hitler hated anaesthetics, he injected a minuscule amount of cocaine into his upper jaw. The extraction, which involved sawing through an existing plate, took forty minutes.

'Throughout the operation,' Linge remembered, 'the chief sat in his chair without showing by the tremor of an eyelid how much agony he was suffering.'

Afterwards, Blaschke was instructed to begin work on another secret project: a gold-plated denture for Eva Braun, whose teeth were also in need of treatment.

*   *   *

Under pressure from his medical advisers Hitler, on the morning of November 20, left the freezing fog of Rastenberg for the last time. It was proving to be one of the hardest winters in living memory. He remained in Berlin until the second week of December, studying dispatches from agents based in Belgium, Holland and France. The information was so accurate that the Fuhrer was able to identify and place every allied division in the west. It was

259

obvious that the Americans had concentrated all their eggs in the Ardennes basket — right on or just behind the front line there. Why not let Runstedt and his men break through in a surprise counter-offensive, then there'd be nothing to stop him reaching the coast. Runstedt, poised at that classic gateway out of Germany, knew every inch of the terrain.

Once he had neutralised the western front, Hitler knew his chances of holding off the Russians in the east for the winter would be considerably improved. The summer of 1945 could be the turning point for Germany. And with thousands of rockets, jet aircraft and U-boats about to be mass produced, he might look to Stalin and suggest a separate peace.

On December 10, temporary headquarters were set up at the Adlerhorst at Ziegenberg, near Frankfurt — a manor house enlarged in 1939 to accommodate the Fuhrer during his western campaign. It was from there, surrounded by SS bodyguards, that Hitler decided to launch the final attack against the allies.

It would be his trump card, and with the help of Runstedt and his commanders, he would play it boldly.

On December 14, the Fifth Panzer Army moved south-west towards Luxembourg. The Sixth Panzers took their place the following day. On December 16 both armies attacked simultaneously on a line less than forty miles wide.

During the campaign, Hitler appeared to recover some of his old fire. Disregarding physical infirmities, sustained by hefty doses of amphetamines, he took on fresh energy. His armies went forward as planned and he was confident the attack would split the allies and change the course of the war.

It is a fact that the significance of the counter-offensive in the Ardennes was not immediately apparent to the allies, mainly because the ferociously bad weather had precluded the necessary air reconnaissance. By Christmas Eve, the Germans had penetrated as far as Dinant, forty miles into Belgium. And then, after a week of fog, the weather broke clear and sunny. Five thousand allied aircraft were able to take off and flatten the panzers' supply lines into the ground. The Germans were driven back.

The air attacks were so intense, reported Runstedt, that his men — already freezing to death in their foxholes — were unable to lift their heads for fear of having them blown off. By New Year's Day the offensive had passed back to the allies.

Goring was summoned to the Adlerhorst. Where was the promised air cover? The Luftwaffe chief, eyes blazing with determination, a wide, almost shy smile on his face, went into his blustering act. At the centre once again of a fast-moving, potentially ruinous credibility crisis, he quickly discarded distasteful facts and figures. The point was, as he unctuously reminded his Fuhrer, the people were still for him; there was still grounds for hope. Who had, after all, transformed the passive character of German docility into an aggressive single-mindedness? 'The impossible could yet become the possible,' he claimed.

'Maybe,' Hitler retorted, 'but only as long as people continue to listen to my orders and do as I say.'

The counter-attack had proved to be more costly than he could have imagined. Eleven divisions, five of them armoured, were destroyed; 400 tanks out of action; fuel stocks severely depleted; a quarter of a million men wounded, killed or captured — many of them transferred from Guderian's defence force in the east.

On January 9, Guderian's intelligence sources reported an imminent Russian offensive on a front stretching from the Baltic Sea to the Carpathians.

'I begged the Fuhrer for more troops,' said Guderian later. 'It was useless. He was incapable of grasping the dangers we were facing by then.'

Three days later the Soviet army, moving forward like an avalanche, poured through the German lines. By January 23, they were on the river Oder near Breslau. Hitler, irresolute, despondent, finally returned to Berlin to set up his thirteenth and last field headquarters in a concrete bunker beneath his Chancellery.

With the combined forces of the three most powerful nations in the world hungry for Caesar's blood, the question was whether his people would continue to fight stubbornly to the death or go swiftly under.

Three years ago, Hitler had Europe under his command from the Volga to the Atlantic Now he's sitting in a hole under the earth.
General Heinrici, 1945.

CHAPTER TWENTY-TWO

At the end of January, 1945 Linge had something to celebrate. He had been serving his Fuhrer for ten years. And 'in spite of insurmountable problems,' said the valet, 'Hitler did not forget me.'

He was instructed to present himself in the Fuhrer's office one morning just before noon. Hitler, in a formal field grey tunic, white shirt, black tie, sporting his Iron Cross, First Class (with black wound ribbon) above the left breast pocket, solemnly presented his valet with an engraved gold watch. After Linge had thanked him profusely and accepted a celebratory glass of schnapps, his chief discussed more pertinent matters.

With the situation on the eastern front becoming daily more fraught it seemed that Hitler would be forced to spend more and more time in the underground bunker. He asked Linge to take over the provisioning for those members of the staff who would be working there. 'I want you to make sure the ordinary workers get decent meals,' he said. 'The Scheisskerl party officials can take care of themselves.'

Linge immediately went into action, content to have something to occupy his time, even though he was downcast to see his beloved chief in such unsettled circumstances.

It troubled Linge deeply that the Fuhrer — he who had single-handedly rebuilt a broken nation; who had restored hope and strength to a people fragmented and troubled in the aftermath of World War I — was reduced to skulking deep in the bowels of the earth as his enemies triumphantly destroyed every trace of his accomplishments: Germany's fine cities, Hamburg, Dortmund, Essen, which were now simply targets for saturation bombing. Dresden and Cologne were in ruins; and the savage barbarian hordes that constituted the Red Army were moving remorselessly, kilometre by kilometre, nearer to Berlin. And whatever was left would, according to custom and the familiar pattern of decisions

264

made by victorious powers, be viciously dismembered. Russia and America had already completed preparations for tearing the heart out of Germany and for dividing the helpless remains among the allied powers.

It saddened the valet to watch the Fuhrer feeling his way slowly along the corridors of the Chancellery, his once powerful body debilitated and wracked with pain. He was no longer able to stand upright; the left side of his body seemed to be out of control; and his left eye continued to plague him. Frequently Linge heard him crying out in distress because of it. Finally, Linge urged Morell to prescribe something for the soreness. Special eye-drops were made up and the valet was the only one trusted to administer the treatment. 'You have such a steady hand,' said Hitler, 'and I know you will never cause me unnecessary pain. I often think if you had gone on to study medicine you'd have made an excellent physician.' But his eye remained badly bloodshot and his sight became increasingly impaired. Despite it all, he would acknowledge neither failure nor defeat. He would admit only to betrayal.

There remained a glimmer of hope — put into words during the January 27 strategy meeting.

Jodl was asked for his opinion on the allied reaction to the phenomenal progress of the Russian offensive. He believed its impact had not yet hit home as far as the British, at least, were concerned. 'Later, the full realisation will dawn.'

Goring was inclined to agree. 'They underestimated our ability to hold them back in Normandy while the Russians broke through our defences to the east.' In any event the British traditionally regarded Russia with suspicion and he was sure there would be overtures quite soon by the allies. Like Germany, they were no more willing to allow the heart of Europe to succumb to bolshevism. By then, the Red Army was less than a hundred miles from Berlin.

For some time the Fuhrer clung to a slender hope — that the British and the Americans would join his armies to repel the Russian invaders. As he saw it, the powder keg in the hold was the generals' protracted inability to obey orders.

He instructed Linge to find minutes of the last five conferences; particularly those with the paragraphs relating to the Russian breakthrough in Poland and Upper Silesia — the only remaining source of oil, steel and coal. Hitler planned to visit Goebbels and wanted to take the papers with him. Having skimmed through them in his car en route, he attached a note to the file, written in green ink: 'Is it not time we disposed of these unreliable generals?'

The Fuhrer took tea with Goebbels and his family; although it was his own tea poured by Linge from his personal vacuum flask. Some time was spent going over earlier, happier memories — January 30 was the tenth anniversary of the party's rise to power — before the current situation was reviewed.

Goebbels went through the conference reports with Hitler and when he finally spoke he was direct and to the point.

'When you can see for yourself the disastrous way things have turned out, why on earth don't you issue every order to these swine personally?' He was no longer quite the obsequious lickspittle of former days.

Hitler sighed heavily. 'Look at the minutes again and you'll see I've done little else for weeks. It seems impossible to convince my field commanders that I have always been intuitively correct in my strategic planning.

'Perhaps I've relied too heavily on their ability to grasp the whole picture, to comprehend the leadership concept. But for God's sake, they're supposed to be professional soldiers. And yet whenever I issue directives without adequate explanation, such as the vital need to stabilise defensive lines before striking back in counter-offensive, they seem unable to build up a strong front. All I ask is that every soldier does his duty. If the generals would carry out orders, the Russian assault would soon collapse — just as the allied initiative in the west will ultimately fail. Our tanks are far superior to those of the enemy; new weapons are evolving the whole time, and these will influence the whole course of the war.

'If you asked one of the generals for an honest opinion, what will he reply? That he has always been in the right and my way was wrong. There is nothing I can do to counteract such deep-seated resentment.'

*   *   *

From the beginning of February there was a change in the weather: the skies cleared, the earth dried out and the forecast was for warm, sunny days ahead.

Linge realised that Hitler, wholly or partly as a result of heavy sedation, had withdrawn almost completely from reality. Bored with the endless discussions, he also found tedious the constant quarrelling at meetings.

Occasionally he'd try to take hold of himself and issue orders or write directives; or attempt a joke with the staff in an effort to restore morale. Then, as if it was all too much, he'd lapse back into a brooding silence again.

Late at night after his guests had been dismissed, he would detain his valet on some excuse or other, simply to have an audience for his introspective soliloquies. In a detached, world-weary manner he meditated aloud on the tragedy of failure and physical decline; on the gulf that stretched between his public and private self; on the fate of Germany at the mercy of 'the Jewish Bolshevik mortal enemy'. The young and the old would probably be slaughtered or shipped off to Siberia, the women and girls reduced to the level of barrack whores. It would be better, he felt, for the nation to be wiped off the face of the earth rather than be subjected to such humiliation.

'So many times,' he said one night, 'I've been forced to permit wholesale massacre and savage oppression myself. Not because I wanted it, but only in order to retain a grip on the party; sometimes out of desperation and for the good of Germany. I've been forced so often to close my eyes; to allow unspeakable practices to take place — many times against my better judgement. No one knows better than I that starvation, exhaustion and cold can destroy physically and psychologically. That is how the strong gain the upper hand.'

Hunched deep in the chair, he allowed his head to sink down on his chest. He seemed to be asleep.

Linge spoke his name softly, but Hitler was wide awake, an almost palpable clamminess about him, like a cold sweat. It took a great effort to control the tremors, the ague racking his whole body.

'Always so much pressure on me,' he murmured, 'what could I do? And they'll say I was indifferent to misery. They'll be after me like a mad dog.'

The valet said nothing. He had heard the rumours and he had no wish to learn the truth.

'I still believe, whatever happens, that everything in life is preordained . . . Goodnight, Linge.'

'Goodnight, my Fuhrer.'

*　　*　　*

From the beginning of March, Linge spent most of his time cheek by jowl with his chief, either below ground in the bunker or in the Reichskanzlei offices, having previously shared a chalet in the garden with SS Colonel Kempka and one of the secretaries, Johannes Hentschel. Tormented by doubts as to the Fuhrer's safety, he decided to seek the help of Krebs, Guderian's chief of staff out at High Command headquarters, located eighteen miles from Berlin along the Reichsstrasse 96, close to Zossen.

Krebs suggested that in the interests of security the Fuhrer should move permanently to Zossen. The OKW HQ was a warren of underground installations, well-camouflaged, concealed by a thick forest, seventy feet below the surface. It had a large, efficient telephone exchange, its own kitchens, water supply and air conditioning, and a special filter system to cope with possible enemy gas attacks.

Reporting back to Hitler, Linge met with stubborn resistance to his suggestion.

'The people of Berlin wouldn't be too pleased,' the Fuhrer told him, 'to learn that I was miles away at Zossen while they go through hell every night. I know you had the best of intentions and Krebs has a point, but I have decided to remain here.

'Supposing I decided to move out there? I'd be disturbed at the thought of all those generals barking at my heels. That'd be more than my nerves could take. You know how it used to be: how they used to come cringing and fawning, snouts sniffing the air for promotion, for honours. Now they keep out of my way and prefer to cause endless mischief with their lying and lack of simple tactical ability. Those of them, that is, that haven't absconded to the west and given themselves up.'

Linge states that, apart from the visit to the Goebbels family, the Fuhrer broke cover just once more. At the end of March, he journeyed to Army Group Vistula's headquarters, then at Prenzlau, fifty miles from Berlin.

Linge confessed himself to be shocked at the situation there. He was doubtful whether the army, which appeared to be composed mainly of raw recruits, would put up much of a defence once the Russians began an attempt to cross the river Oder. The commander, General Heinrici, had less than 500,000 troops and no reserves of any kind. He was also desperately short of tanks, guns, ammunition and fuel.

The Fuhrer waved aside the appalling problems facing Heinrici. 'Issue every man you have here with the lightest of arms,' he ordered, 'so they can operate at speed. Remember you are not only defending this side of the Oder; you are defending Berlin.'

Heinrici pointed out that he had very few rifles to issue.

Hitler continued to speak in a mechanical, almost bored tone of voice, utterly lacking in enthusiasm. 'Training is no longer important; physical fitness doesn't matter now. Your men have no combat experience? Put them up against the Russians and that will cease to be a problem. Cut off the Soviet armies by encircling them; push the stragglers back into the Baltic Sea. Isolate their armoured divisions and you will render them useless. Then you will be able to march south and relieve Model. His Group is bottled up in the Ruhr.'

Heinrici shrugged and turned away, purportedly to study a map. He was finding it difficult to control his temper. Although the spring thaw was late, the ice was rapidly melting and the Russians — three million of them, according to reports — had regrouped in preparation for their drive across the river.

Returning to the Chancellery the Fuhrer's car carefully threaded its way through Berlin with Hitler crouching low in the back seat, staring unseeingly at the ruins.

Linge, sitting beside him, wondered what his thoughts were. Suddenly, Hitler's body jerked violently and he began to tear at the buttons on his jacket, gasping that his collar was choking him, his clothing was too tight. Unable to breathe properly, his complexion took on an alarming bluish tinge. The valet quickly unbuttoned his coat and opened the car window. Then he massaged the Fuhrer's chest until, gradually, he began to breathe normally again.

As the Mercedes continued at a snail's pace along the potholed streets Hitler started talking at a machine-gun pace. He gave Burgdorf, sitting on his other side, instructions on the manner in which Berlin should be defended; then contradicting them, gabbling furiously in a nonsensical manner, complaining of dizziness, thirst; that the interior of the car was far too hot, there was no air; and that he was feeling sick.

One or two people passing in the street recognised the Fuhrer but, Linge noted, none of them seemed overjoyed at the sight of him. Their faces merely showing a dull apathy. Maybe, he thought, they were wondering why their leader, who of all of them could have been miles away, was staying in Berlin.

The car stopped momentarily at a bomb crater and a woman, standing on the pavement close to it, broke into tears.

Kempka looked up from the wheel at her and laughed. 'Christ, you'd have thought the sight of her Fuhrer would have cheered her up at least; and given her the courage to dry her eyes.'

Hitler gave no indication of having heard anything. He stared straight ahead, eyes glazed and protuberant, the entire lefthand side of his body trembling in a transport of frenzied agitation.

* * *

Once back in the Chancellery, the Fuhrer moved permanently down to the bunker, occasionally emerging above ground for a stroll in the gardens or to take a meal in the only part of the Chancellery left undamaged.

Morale began to decline sharply among those personal cronies — Goring, Ribbentrop, Bormann and others — who now spent more time quarrelling among themselves than thinking up constructive ideas for the defence of Berlin.

Hitler's attitude fluctuated. Like a man in a swamp searching for a way out, he appeared to sink deeper into the mud. Sometimes he was remote and his mood would turn to desperation, as he cursed everyone he had ever known, particularly every general who had dared to question his tactical superiority.

He brooded for a long time on the treachery of Himmler — the house-trained Reichsfuhrer had dared to turn round and bite the hand that fed him. Hitler realised he had 'overestimated his abilities, just as I did with Goring. I placed a heavy load on their shoulders and they failed me miserably.'

Fegelein believed that Himmler suffered from throat trouble: he was prepared, he said, to do anything to win the coveted *Ritterkreuz* to hang round his neck.

Bormann sneered openly at Himmler's cranky theories; at his

strange beliefs; at his cunning in being able to placate those whose sense of propriety was ruffled by his deeds. Yet Himmler was so puritanical, he accepted no money other than his official salary of 2,000 marks a month, supporting a wife, daughter, an ailing mistress and two bastard sons on it.

Hitler turned against Goring, all wheeze and froth and maundering grandeur, proclaiming him innately lazy. Speer would not obey orders and as for Ribbentrop: 'He is just a stubborn man I set against the stubborn English. I have no wish to speak to him again. There is no foreign policy left to discuss, is there?'

* * *

At about this time, the Fuhrer's voice failed him temporarily, which required the removal of a polyp from his vocal chords. Linge carried a writing pad for him on which he scribbled instructions. It was absolutely intolerable, thought the valet, that a man who loved talking so much should be unable to use his voice.

On the rare occasions that the generals were called to the conference table, Hitler sat mostly in silence. Or, when he had recovered from the operation, he would break into bitter denunciations, accusing them of plotting against the party. Then, just as quickly, he would change the subject, describing grandiose schemes for rebuilding Germany, paralleling events of 1918 with 1945.

'The Kaiser disregarded his responsibilities,' he said, 'by slinking into exile. Who supported him? His army? The people? I, the Fuhrer, will never let my people down. They trust me absolutely. They have always trusted me. I will not choose the easy way out. Unlike Wilhelm, the possibility of surrender does not exist for me.'

His own room in the bunker, according to one of his secretaries, Christa Schroder, 'was very cramped, accommodating no more than a small desk, a sofa, a table and three chairs. It was a cold, uncomfortable room. The door to the left led into a bathroom and the one on the right into his equally small bedroom.' There was also a portrait of Frederick the Great, and Linge noticed his chief spent a great deal of time studying it.

Not addressing the valet directly he said: 'He knows what I am thinking. Those expressive eyes, that masterful forehead! He loved his country too. The poor and the old were his people. And when

271

things went wrong after his death, he was blamed — as I will be. But he did what he could, as I have done. His wisdom and his strength sustain me, giving me the resolve to hold on.' He uttered these words many times, until in the end, it became a kind of compulsion.

Attempts by his military advisers, Keitel or Jodl, at reasonable discussion on the course of the war inevitably disintegrated into shouting matches. The Fuhrer refused to allow his remaining forces to withdraw from untenable defensive positions until they were overrun by the enemy.

On March 28, Guderian was ordered to the Fuhrerbunker for a personal briefing. It was quickly obvious to everyone present at the meeting that the Chief of OKH was out of favour. The conference had begun quietly, but as the tension mounted accusations were hurled across the room. The force of the Fuhrer's invective, Linge says, was unusual even by acrimonious standards stretching back over ten years.

Hitler accused Guderian of negligence and of rank incompetence. Guderian angrily pointed out that the reason for his failure was that his men had been called to fight with insufficient ammunition and no artillery support worth speaking about. As for the promised air defence, it never showed up.

Burgdorf and Keitel exchanged glances, stunned by his insolent attitude.

Guderian, temper mounting, pointed out the vast number of lives already lost.

The Fuhrer yelled at him: 'They failed! They failed!' All his bitterness and resentment poured from him. In the next few minutes the two men were engaged in a furious shouting match. Guderian short of breath, purple in the face; Hitler hoarse, ranting, beside himself with fury. Finally he lifted his right hand, demanding silence. Then he dismissed everyone from the room except Guderian and Keitel.

Somewhat calmer, he spoke directly to Guderian. 'It seems from your reaction that your nerves are in a bad way. I doubt you are in a fit state to continue in command. What you need is some time to recover your common sense. You must get some treatment and rebuild your strength. The situation will shortly become more critical and we will need your tenacity.'

Guderian cleared his desk at Zossen HQ, bade farewell to his staff and travelled south to a sanatorium near Munich. For him the war was over.

The monocled Krebs, one time military attache to Moscow, replaced him as army chief.

That same night, when Linge knocked on the Fuhrer's door, he was sitting behind his desk, lost in thought, head moving from side to side. When he spoke it was as if he were alone.

'The things that happen to a man depend in the last resort upon himself. I've known about the disruptive element for a long time; about the discontent in the army. I've been well aware that a kind of bloodlust has pervaded so many of the Reichsleiters; of the manner in which the Waffen SS has regressed to brutality and mass murder.'

The valet stood in the doorway, helpless, expressionless, staring at his chief. Hitler showed no sign of recognition.

'At the beginning I had to employ every means, simply to hold the party together. If violence was necessary for order and discipline, for a nationalist revolution, then it was brought into play; against communists, the Jewish press, any enemies of the party. Defeatists were ruthlessly eliminated. It was the only way we could achieve power — without compromise. And we finally reached our goal, a new Reich, acclaimed by the people, sanctified with blood.

'The people knew; they believed in me and I lived for Germany. Everywhere they were full of enthusiasm and that gave me inspiration. When I started to win, I won all along the line. The force and compulsion of my beliefs intimidated any opposition. The communists, the reds, almost destroyed the nation. If we had not taken control, everything would have ended in a terrible catastrophe.

'If we *were* extreme in our methods, well, a revolution is a revolution.

'There is no doubt what is in store for Germany if we go under now. As for the leader, every act will be weighed against me alone. I'll be the one held responsible for every criminal act, for every death. Yet if we had been victorious, extremist measures would have been dismissed as justifiable. If I had conquered Russia, I would have gone down in history as one of the greatest leaders of the twentieth century.

'The war is reaching its climax. When it ends, I'll be condemned as a man lacking common decency; as the living personification

273

of evil. Had providence provided me with success I would freely have acknowledged the heroism of our enemies. I would also have welcomed the opportunity to have singled out those who have over the years shown selfless devotion to the good of Germany.

'After the war, Germany will cease to exist.'

Linge realised he was listening to a man aware that his days among the living were numbered. Yet the valet was convinced his chief wasn't simply speaking out of a sense of guilt. He seemed more like a man who had come face to face with reality; knowing finally the price that had to be paid for allowing acts to be performed without regard to the consequences. The Fuhrer would bear the brunt and suffer the contempt of the world. The one man, in the valet's view, more gifted and intelligent than any other.

Out of respect for what he had been Linge declined to join in the chorus of recrimination.

*　　*　　*

Linge's memories of the last days in the Fuhrerbunker are somewhat disjointed. He was, for the first time, obviously in fear of his life, existing in a condition of sustained urgency; clinging to routine as the one sane thing in a mad world, barely able to grasp the significance of what was happening.

Odd incongruities remained fixed in his mind.

For instance, one morning, Hitler received a member of the Berlin fire brigade, a withered little man who had saved countless lives by disconnecting timing devices from more than 700 land mines dropped during air raids. Promoted to officer status, he was awarded the *Ritterkreuz*.

A few hours later, word reached the Fuhrer that the same fireman had performed a further act of heroism. Lowered by a rope into a cellar packed with ammunition, he had defused another mine just before it was due to detonate. Had it exploded, it would have devastated half of Hindenburgstrasse.

Brought down to the bunker a second time, the Fuhrer awarded him a set of oak leaves to add to his medal. The newly appointed lieutenant emerged from the bunker into the daylight suddenly aware that Hitler had promoted him to the rank of full captain. Unfortunately, he had no chance to draw his salary as a commissioned officer: he was shot by the first Russians to enter Berlin.

274

On another occasion, the Fuhrer learnt that a group of his soldiers had stubbornly held on to a bridgehead across the Oder in the face of massive Russian attacks, simply refusing to retreat. Standing to attention midway along the bridge, they were blown to bits by a well-aimed grenade.

Hitler insisted that their relatives should be awarded generous pensions. On the same day, Russian shells began to rain down on Berlin.

The Fuhrer, hauling himself along the corridors of his sub-terranean fort, weighed down by Bormann's tales of treachery, gross errors of judgement and outright cowardice, was never still.

Bormann told him how a Wehrmacht pioneer unit had failed to demolish the Ludendorff Bridge at Remagen just as an American armoured division was about to roll across it.

Without bothering to investigate the facts, the Fuhrer decided the engineers had been at fault. As there was no time for a court martial, he ordered the officers in charge to be executed on the spot.

When he was told that Sepp Dietrich — the former commander of his personal bodyguard — and his Sixth SS Panzers had fallen back, driven by the Red Army into Vienna, Hitler radioed a message:

'The Fuhrer believes the troops have not fought as the situation demanded and therefore orders that the SS Divisions Adolf Hitler, Das Reich Totenkopf and Hohenstauffen be stripped of their armbands.'

'It will be their responsibility,' he told Bormann, 'if we lose the war. Their nerve has failed and they no longer have the right to bear my name. Did you know that Frederick the Great removed battle standards from those regiments that did badly in battle? Yet his men probably loved him more than life itself. They were proud to fight under him.'

As one of the party old guard, Sepp replied that he would rather shoot himself than obey the order. He then suggested to his men that they conceal their armbands until the heat had died down.

With the Russians nearing Berlin, the remaining SS members of Hitler's staff, as part of the Leibstandarte SS Adolf Hitler, wondered whether they too would suffer the disgrace of being stripped of their armbands.

Linge, as spokesman for those in the bunker, went to Goring for advice. He suggested they should take them off for a couple of the days while he talked to the Fuhrer about the matter; Dietrich, after all, was one of his oldest friends.

Hitler heard him out before explaining that the measure was a punishment for the Sixth SS Panzers for failing to hold their positions. Naturally, his personal staff were absolved from any disgrace.

Such was the atmosphere of uncertainty, several SS men attached to the Fuhrer decided to make an issue of it and removed their armbands.

One evening in April, Goebbels sat with the Fuhrer, reading aloud from a favourite book, Carlyle's *History of Frederick the Great*. He was describing Frederick's predicament at the end of 1761, the most critical period of the Seven Years' War. The King's army was forced to hold the Russians back on one side, the Austrians on the other; most of the state was occupied by the enemy and there was precious little food and a desperate shortage of ammunition.

On January 5, 1762, Frederick, considering suicide as the only way out, stated boldly that in his opinion 'the age of miracles was over'.

That same day, Empress Elizabeth of Russia died and a miracle occurred. The Russian army came over to Frederick's side and the King was able to record that 'with the Messalina of the north dead, we are rid of the people whom the Hyperboreans (people of the extreme north) vomited over us'.

'At that point in the story,' said Goebbels, ' there were tears in the Fuhrer's eyes.'

Linge was sent to retrieve two horoscopes: one completed on September 9, 1918 which forecast the future for the German government, and Hitler's personal horoscope that had been drawn up in 1933.

Both had predicted World War II, promising victories for the Reich up to 1941, followed by a series of setbacks — until the beginning of April, 1945. Then there would be final victory, followed by peace in August, 1945. A difficult three years would follow until 1948, when the Fatherland would again emerge triumphant.

Goebbels, stressing the striking parallel between 1762 and 1945, urged the Fuhrer to hold on, to have faith in the predictions.

'Everything,' he said, 'will work out in the end and in the Fuhrer's favour and providence will then hold out all kind of possibilities.'

It was all Hitler had and it was almost enough. It had worked for Frederick the Great and there was a still, small hope inside him that something would happen, a last-minute gift from providence to save his skin.

On April 12, 1945, as President Roosevelt was at his home in Warm Springs, Georgia, sitting for a portrait artist, he suddenly fainted. He died that afternoon.

As soon as the news reached Goebbels, he was convinced that a miracle had happened. He immediately contacted Hitler.

'My Fuhrer, I congratulate you. President Roosevelt is dead. You remember the horoscopes? Today is Friday, April 13; it must be the turning point.'

Alternating between optimism and despair, Hitler believed, if only for the next couple of days, that the allies might break with Russia, precipitating a head-on clash between the two attacking forces on the Elbe.

On April 14, Harry S. Truman succeeded Roosevelt. General Eisenhower halted his forces on the banks of the Elbe. Berlin, in his view, was no longer a military objective. The Russian High Command was told on April 21 that the Americans had no intention of advancing east of the Elbe. Eisenhower had studied the disposition of German forces, which were dispersed along a line from the shores of the Baltic down as far as Dresden and the Czechoslovakian border, with particular concentration in the southern area stretching from Prague to the north of Italy. This was the famous Southern Redoubt. The Americans, leaving Prague to the Russians, would occupy the Redoubt, intending 'to subdivide the remaining German forces and capture those areas where they might form a last stand effectively'.

In Eisenhower's view, reported later, the military factors were more important than political considerations involved in the allies being the first to take Berlin. His plans put an end to the German High Command's last-ditch hopes of continuing to operate in the southern mountains after major operations were concluded.

And the Fuhrer's miracle fizzled out. He changed his original plan — to stage a glorious Gotterdammerung in Bavaria — and decided to stay in Berlin until the end.

On the night of April 15, Eve Braun arrived from Munich. Linge escorted her through the bombed-out Chancellery and down the stairs from the butler's pantry leading to the Fuhrer's quarters located at the end of a central passage. She had been given a bedroom adjoining Hitler's suite. It was small, cramped and uncomfortable. 'She was determined,' recalled the valet, 'to share whatever fate had in store for Hitler.' He found it difficult to conceal his admiration for her immense courage, however misplaced. Like the Goebbels', she had no wish to continue living in a Germany without the Fuhrer.

*   *   *

As the Russians approached Berlin, and the allies penetrated deeper into Germany, they found themselves faced with the awful realities of the death camps.

War correspondent R. W. Thompson wrote 'I do not know how to begin to describe something beyond the imagination of mankind.' He was in Belsen on Friday, April 20, 1945.

'When they told me that the women SS guards tied a live body to a dead one and burned them together while dancing and singing around the blaze, it did not shock me. It didn't shock me because life and death have ceased to have meaning. Because, in fact, the living were dead. In this terrible camp, where thousands have been reduced to bestiality each month by a cold, systematic process and then reduced by the same process to the ultimate release of death, all normal standards change . . . This Nazi concentration camp of Belsen is one of many. It is the expression of Adolf Hitler and Nazi Germany. It is the thing you read about and refused to believe from 1933 onwards.

'They are burning some of the filth now, some of the bedding; the place is thick with fumes as creatures that were once men and women squat, cooking old pieces of swede or potato.

'There is no sanitation. People just excrete when they must, where they are. This hut built to hold fifty at a pinch, held seven hundred. Here they are now. Some of the living are lying with the dead and the floor is thick with human excrement mixed with clothing and straw and bedding. As they sweep some of it, there are what were once people in it. There is a dead woman in this litter of muck here.

'I cannot go on. I can only tell you that the sight has lit such a flame in the soldiers who have seen it that this flame must light the whole world and must never die out.'

'In the camp at Ohrdruf,' reported Cornelius Ryan, 'General Patton . . . walked through the death houses, then turned away, his face wet with tears, and was uncontrollably ill. The next day, Patton ordered the population of a nearby village, whose inhabitants claimed ignorance of the situation in the camp, to view it for themselves; those who hung back were escorted at rifle point. The following morning the mayor of the village and his wife hanged themselves.'

*   *   *

Simon Wiesenthal is frequently asked how it could have happened that millions of people — Jews, Poles, Yugoslavs and others — let themselves be dragged away like cattle to the slaughterhouse without trying to resist. Hundreds of thousands walked into the gas chambers, guarded by just a few SS men. Why didn't the vast majority of victims at least make an attempt to revolt against the tiny minority of executioners?

'The victims' he says, 'had been numbed by shock long before they stepped into the gas chambers. The SS had succeeded in killing their victims' instinct of survival. Many of them no longer wanted to live; they were tired of torture . . . In the concentration camp society ruled by the SS, the weaker species was reduced to sub-animal species. They registered our gold teeth. They stripped us naked. They branded our wrists. They shaved a strip in the centre of a man's hair; they called it *Freiheitstrasse*, Freedom Street.

'They did many other things until they had squeezed out of us the last reserves of dignity.'

Why didn't the Jews 'do something' about it after the war?

He admits the historical chance of moral retribution was missed. 'The survivors were too weak, too apathetic for any concerted action. We were hardly able to walk; some of us were more dead than alive when we were liberated . . . Later on, when we were physically stronger, everybody wanted to get away from the horror of the past as quickly as possible . . . Life was cruel but life had to go on. And so the job of retribution was mostly left to those who never suffered in a concentration camp, the lucky ones who got out in time. They were our spokesmen — and they didn't care about moral restitution; they were only interested in material restitution. They talked about money, not about bringing to justice the men responsible for the apocalypse.

'Our critics have a point. It's too late now. Many murderers will remain among us.'

For years, Berliners would remember that April 20 for still another reason. Whether in celebration of the Fuhrer's birthday or in anticipation of the climax to come, no one knew, but that day the government gave the hungry populace extra allocations of food called 'crisis rations'. As Jurgen-Erich Klotz, a 25-year-old one-armed veteran, remembered the extra food allocation, it consisted of one pound of bacon or sausage, one half pound of rice or oatmeal, 250 dried lentils, peas or beans, one can of vegetables, two pounds of sugar, about one ounce of coffee, a small package of coffee substitute and some fats. Although there were almost five hours of air raids on Berlin this day, housewives braved the bombs to pick up the extra rations. They were to last eight days, and 'With these rations we shall now ascend into heaven'. The same thought apparently occurred simultaneously to Berliners everywhere; the extra food came to be known as Himmelfahrtsrationen — Ascension Day rations.

Cornelius Ryan

'It was a relief that Hitler didn't fall into our hands alive. What on earth could have been done with him?'

Lord Ismay

CHAPTER TWENTY-THREE

Living every moment in a state of high tension, the gradual disintegration during the last days in Berlin stood out vividly in Linge's mind.

Like the rest of the staff he fluctuated between hope and despair as the end drew near, trying to brace himself for death.

The Fuhrer, shattered in health though he was, pushed to the edge of endurance, continued to display cold courage and lack of concern for his own skin. He surprised everyone by stating his determination to go ahead with the parade planned for his fifty-sixth birthday: April 20, 1945. Linge helped him make his way up to the gardens where cabinet members, surviving officials and a detachment of SS men waited to congratulate their leader. The remaining party heavyweights, Goebbels, Bormann, Ribbentrop, Speer and Goring trailed respectfully a pace or two behind.

The Luftwaffe chief was seeing Hitler for the last time. He was going south almost immediately after the parade. Before leaving Karinhall, he had supervised the loading of twenty-four trucks with furniture, silver and paintings. The convoy would carry the most valuable items to Bavaria. When everything was ready, Goring walked down the road from the castle to join some officers standing by a detonator. Panting from the exertion, he bent over it to push the plunger home. With a deep roar his magnificent mansion crumbled to dust. Goring grinned, wiping his hands together.

'That's what you have to do sometimes,' he said, 'when you're a crown prince.'

In the gardens, Hitler limped along the line, nodding to familiar faces in what was left of the Frundsberg SS Division. He came to a halt midway, stepping back a couple of paces before speaking.

At first his voice was almost inaudible, the words coming slowly. He paused for several seconds and then — as Linge had seen happen many times over the weeks — he took a deep breath, making a visible effort. And as he spoke, harshly, enthusiastically, the parade appeared to gather fresh strength from his words. Every man there stood a little straighter.

With his eyes striving to pierce the veil of sooty disorder, he reached out for the medals carried by an adjutant. Awards were made to twenty members of Axmann's Hitler Youth, all of them orphaned by the war.

'One day,' he said, 'you, the Fuhrer's boys, will be able to hold your heads high and walk with pride again. You will remember for the rest of your lives that you were here during the final struggle for the fatherland. I urge you to hold in your hearts the thought that whatever may be in store, eventually it will be better than anything you have ever known.'

After the inspection, with Linge guiding him along the path, he made his way back through the ruined Chancellery.

'Self-sacrifice,' he seemed to be saying to himself, 'they understand that. And like all good soldiers, they'll remain steady under fire. They'll hold out bravely to the end, for me, for Germany.'

Most of the old comrades attended the birthday celebration in the bunker: Goebbels, Ribbentrop, Himmler, Goring and Bormann as well as the surviving military executive: Keitel, Jodl, Krebs and Donitz. There wasn't one of them who didn't promise the Fuhrer to stay by his side until the death. All of them urged him to quit Berlin for the Berghof, before it was too late.

The following morning the city radio announced that Hitler and Goebbels were remaining in Berlin, despite the presence of the Russians in the northern suburbs.

Reports came through that one of the ten aircraft flown out of Berlin the previous evening had crashed. All attempts at contacting it had been unsuccessful. It was Hans Bauer who had supervised the loading of the aircraft with documents and when he informed the Fuhrer that the Junker 352 carrying party archives was missing, Hitler was most upset and spoke of 'important files'.

Bauer himself disappeared when the war ended but unlike so many others he didn't manage to make it to South America. As a prisoner of the Russians, he was detained in a prison camp for nine years. When at last released — under an agreement between West Germany and the Soviets — he wrote his memoirs. In them he mentioned the missing aircraft and loss of important documents.

When Linge was interrogated by the Russians, it seemed they

were anxious to know exactly where Hitler had hidden his treasure trove. They had it fixed in their heads that somewhere a massive hoard of gold had been stowed away.

Linge found it impossible to convince them that his Fuhrer had never owned any gold. All gifts containing jewels or precious metals were exchanged for money. Everything of value had gone to the Reich bank to help purchase military materials.

Furnishings and antiques in the Chancellery had been shipped to Stuttgart early on in the war. Hitler's library of rare first editions had been packed in wooden crates and sent by road to Bad Aussig for storage. The State china and silver — infrequently used throughout the war — was in safe keeping at Bayreuth.

* * *

In May, 1980 some people from West Germany visiting a cemetery at Boernersdorf, a remote village south of Dresden, East Germany, solved the mystery of the missing aircraft.

Six named members of the air crew of the Junker-352, an unknown Wehrmacht soldier and an un-named woman, possibly a Chancellery secretary, had been buried in a line beneath simple wooden crosses. The date on each cross was the same: 21.4.1945.

Two villagers who witnessed the crash, a thirteen-year-old boy, Helmut Schmidt and an ex-soldier, Richard Elbe, now in his eighties, recalled what had taken place.

'The aircraft was on fire,' said Schmidt, now a quarryman in his fifties, 'and when it hit the ground I ran towards it in the wood. It had broken into pieces but there was one survivor, half sitting, half lying on the ground. He had a piece of flesh the size of your hand torn out of his backside.'

This was probably Franz Westermeier, the rear-gunner. According to Schmidt, he was 'clutching a large wooden case'.

Elbe cycled to the crash and remembered the man with the case. 'There was a rumour that some papers were handed over to the mayor, Erwin Goebel; and that when the Russians came, he handed them over and they burnt them.

Gertrud, Erwin Goebel's daughter-in-law, runs the village store. As far as she knows 'the aircraft was destroyed; there was nothing left. I don't think my father-in-law (he died in 1951) had any papers in 1945.'

It is understood that in 1980, *Stern* magazine writer Gerd Heidemann also visited the cemetery. The forged 'Hitler Diaries' appeared three years later.

*   *   *

Goring, having done his duty by attending the birthday parade, was anxious to get out of the city. In a brief broadcast, he made one last effort to reassure the unfortunate citizens left behind. The old outpourings of optimism were no longer there as he told them that 'your Fuhrer remains among you. He has taken the defence of Berlin into his own hands and has given his word to defend the city to the end. Either he will win the battle for Berlin or fall as the symbol of Germany.' Then it was into the car and off as fast as possible to the comparative safety of Bavaria.

Two other faithful friends of the Fuhrer also hurriedly left town: Himmler and Ribbentrop.

The dentist Blaschke packed his bags at his office in Kurfurstendamm and, before locking the door, phoned his secretary, Fraulein Heusermann. He told her to send the dental equipment south, as he expected to be leaving with the Chancellery party any day.

Fraulein Heusermann said she had decided to stay in Berlin. He asked had she any idea what would happen to her when the Russians arrived: 'First you'll be raped. Then they'll tear you apart, you have no idea what they're like'.

Before he hung up he urged her to get out. No, she would not leave Berlin. Afterwards, she phoned Blaschke's colleague, SS dental surgeon Grawitz with a coded message, to let him know that the party élite were getting out.

Soon afterwards, Grawitz — as Himmler's surgeon he had participated in unsavoury medical experiments on concentration camp inmates — joined his family at dinner: 'When everyone was seated, Grawitz reached down, pulled the pins on two hand grenades and blew himself and his family to oblivion'.

The day following the Fuhrer's birthday, Saturday, April 21, Berlin, beaten, battered, cluttered with corpses, suddenly found itself the front line.

As Cornelius Ryan described in *The Last Battle*: 'Shells now began to strike everywhere. Tongues of flame leaped from rooftops all over the centre of the city. Bomb-weakened buildings collapsed. Motor cars were upended and set afire. The Brandenburg Gate was hit and one cornice crashed down into the street. Shells ploughed the Unter den Linden from one end to the other; the royal palace, already wrecked, burst into flames again. So did the Reichstag. The girders that had once supported the building's cupola collapsed and pieces of metal showered down. People ran wildly along the Kurfurstendamm, dropping brief-cases and packages, bobbing frantically from doorway to doorway. At the Tiergarten end of the street a stable of riding horses received a direct hit. The screams of the animals mingled with the cries and shouts of men and women; an instant later the horses stampeded out of the inferno and dashed down the Kurfurstendamm, their manes and tails blazing.'

The first Russian artillery shells had reached the city.

Many citizens prepared themselves for suicide. Vast quantities of capsules had been handed out over the preceding weeks. They contained a concentrated hydro-cyanic compound which guaranteed instantaneous death, and the addition of acetic acid made the capsules work even faster.

In the outer suburbs, catch-as-catch-can SS units attempted to stage ambushes from wrecked buildings while ten-year-old boys defended streets with light artillery guns. Refusing to surrender, they fought to the death for their Fuhrer in bitter, prolonged battles.

Underneath the Chancellery, in the comparative safety of his low-ceilinged bunker, Hitler was doing all he could to prolong the full agony of the climax. He was still the supreme commander — even if his strategy dealt with imaginary forces whose effectiveness existed only in his febrile imagination. It was Burgdorf who encouraged his attempts at futile planning. It was the blunt-snouted Bormann who reminded him that he was still the Fuhrer.

Hitler listened through a fog of melancholia, studying his war maps with the intensity of hallucination. A last stand, that was the thing. Were there, he asked Burgdorf, commands outside Berlin capable of coming to the assistance of the beleaguered city?

When Burgdorf told him that SS General Steiner's panzer divisions were still holding out, the Fuhrer grabbed at the map showing Steiner's position. 'Steiner! That's the answer. He must lead a counter-attack by heading south. That'll cut off the Russians. We must send Fegelein to him with the order.'

286

The order read: 'It is expressly forbidden to fall back to the west. Officers who do not comply unconditionally with this order are to be arrested and shot at once . . .'

One of the officers who did not comply with the order was the luckless Fegelein, Himmler's liaison officer in the Fuhrerbunker (and husband of Gretl, Eva Braun's sister). He failed to report back the result of his mission.

Hoegl's men, sent to bring in, found him lying across the bed in his Charlottenburg apartment, dead drunk, a trunkful of money and jewellery spilling over the floor. On the point of deserting he had foolishly decided to drink two more bottles of brandy for the road. Returned to the bunker, he was placed under close arrest.

On Sunday, April 22, Himmler phoned to report that Steiner was beating the Russians back. The counter-attack was proving successful. Encouraging messages from Jodl and Keitel helped sustain the delusion.

No one yet realised it was far too late. Steiner no longer possessed an army of sufficient strength even to fight a losing battle. And Marshal Zhukov's armoured troops were already at the gates of Berlin.

At dinner that night — served as usual by Linge between 9 and 10 o'clock — Hitler talked optimistically about the counter-attack. There was a certain amount of head-scratching and muttering and doom-laden earnestness among the company, which included Gunsche, Bormann, Jodl, Keitel and Linge. Since his promotion to Sturmbannfuhrer (Major), the valet first supervised the serving of the meal and then took his place at the foot of the table.

Later, Bormann tried to persuade Eva and Frau Goebbels to leave Berlin for the mountainous security of Berchtesgaden — just in case Steiner failed to pull it off.

Both women expressed their determination to stay close to the Fuhrer; they were prepared to face the worst with him. Somewhat unwillingly, they agreed to carry the revolvers Bormann handed over — as a precaution. A bullet might prove a better option than falling into the hands of vengeful Russian rapists.

Over coffee, Goebbels became involved in a dispute with Ambassador Hewel, who was deeply concerned about the outcome of Steiner's attack.

Goebbels, ever the master of shining-eyed lucubrations, waved

287

away such doubts. He could leave the day-to-day strategy in the Fuhrer's hands.

'My own feeling,' said Hewel quietly, 'is that this is now the time to begin to attempt something on a diplomatic level.'

'Such a traitorous statement in front of our Fuhrer shows a lack of faith in his ability as military commander.' Goebbels stood up. 'We must never negotiate. If the Soviets capture Berlin, I intend taking my rifle up into the street to shoot as many of them as I can before putting the last round through my own head. Believe me, whatever happens, when we finally take our leave, the earth will shudder.'

Bowing to Hitler, he clumped noisily through the narrow metal door leading to the exit.

Hitler, ignoring the outburst, was explaining his reasons for remaining in the city.

'My friends and assistants are naturally worried about the situation. But there is no question of my leaving here. I shall defend Berlin to the end. Either we win the battle or I fall as a symbol of the end of the Reich.'

The following morning Linge, called to Hitler's room, found him pacing the floor looking very concerned indeed.

A telegram had arrived from Goring stating that he wished to take over leadership 'in accordance with the decree of June 29, 1941.'

Hitler, trying to flex his neck muscles in order to trumpet his rage, was rendered temporarily speechless. Breathing in a laboured manner he collapsed into a chair and began drumming the fingers of his good hand on the end of the table. The false optimism, the firecracker vitality of the previous evening had seeped away.

When he had regained his voice it was harsh with anger. 'This Goring, this decadent, corrupt drug-addict dares send me, his Fuhrer, an ultimatum. What kind of people were they who were supposed to be supporting me all these years?' He sent for Bormann, and that really upset Linge. The portly Bavarian, in his opinion, liked nothing better than stirring an already boiling pot. The valet felt the chief had enough of a stew to digest as it was.

Bormann naturally revelled in the chance to knock the absent Luftwaffe Reichsmarshal, becoming articulate to the point of effrontery. 'Obviously, this wire was intended as an insult to our Fuhrer. He wants a reply by 10 o'clock tonight and yet he must know it's not possible to contact him in time.'

He stood in the centre of the room, feet wide apart, gesturing with both hands; longing, thought Linge, to take over command himself. When he spoke again his remarks had all the subtlety of a knee in the crotch. 'God knows but I've said it time and time again. That Goring is nothing more than a moral weakling, a dissolute neurotic, a . . .'

His alcohol-moist face shone with the effort of searching for stronger epithets, but Hitler stopped him in mid-insult.

The Fuhrer, considerably calmer, adopted a tone of resignation. 'That is how it is. Having failed abysmally to achieve mastery of the air with his precious air force, he has finally taken upon himself the role of arch traitor to his Fuhrer.' He paused, glaring balefully first at Bormann, then at his valet. There was a steely undertone in his voice. 'No doubt there will be others.'

Goebbels hurried into the room to offer sympathy. 'It is lamentable,' he said, 'that this should happen. Our old comrade, Goring, of all people. When I think of all his extravagant speeches about honour and faith and sacrifice I can't help feeling disgusted by his treachery.'

Both Bormann and the propaganda minister appeared to relish the downfall of the once-powerful Goring. Bormann was instructed to see that the Reichsmarshal was placed under house arrest in Bavaria. Hitler wanted him held by the SS until a general court martial could be arranged.

As the day advanced every dispatch brought more bad news. By the hour, the Russians drew closer to the centre of Berlin. Steiner had not counter-attacked. The beige walls of the bunker itself trembled under the impact of the incessant shelling. Frantic queries were transmitted from the one remaining radio link to the new army headquarters at Rheinsberg, fifty miles northeast of Berlin: 'Where are the armies able to relieve the city? What has happened to Wenck's Twelfth Army?'

Keitel and Jodl replied optimistically. They had no wish to add to their Fuhrer's difficulties at the moment.

For those who wished to leave the city, just one escape route remained. This was the road to Dresden in the south, although by nightfall this last exit would be blocked by the enemy.

A final evacuation was hastily arranged. There was a series of somewhat maudlin partings, with messages for relatives relayed and with personal valuables pressed on those getting out by the ones left behind. By then, the thin crust of discipline and orderly behaviour was crumbling and a great deal of drinking heralded the departure of the officials, secretaries and minor party members preparing to make a run for it.

Eva Braun handed over a letter intended for her parents. Linge scribbled an encouraging message to his wife, which was her last news of him until he surfaced later in the Russian prison camp.

*   *   *

By Wednesday, April 25 the Russians were in Berlin, a few streets away from Chancellery.

As Linge prepared Hitler's bed that night the Fuhrer spoke. It was as if there was no more spirit left in him. 'You could say I'm almost alone now, Linge. The Third Reich is finished and Berlin is undergoing its blackest hour; the worst in its long and proud history.' He paused, eyes fixed on the portrait of Frederick the Great. 'Well, the orders to subordinates must also apply to the commander. I can do nothing now but remain here and await the end.'

Before the chief bade him goodnight, he spoke again. 'Linge, I have given the matter a great deal of thought and if it is at all possible I would like to think you will be able to rejoin your family. There will be nothing left down here shortly . . . nothing at all.'

The valet found it difficult to reply. 'My Fuhrer, during the last ten years I have been privileged to share the good times. It is right I should share the bad too.'

Hitler smiled, reaching out a hand. 'I don't believe I expected to hear you say anything else.' His eyes clouded over. 'Fraulein Eva and I will be ending our lives quite soon. I have discussed the matter with the others and I urge you to listen closely.

'You must do everything possible to prevent our bodies from falling into the hands of the Soviets. You can imagine how they'd gloat over the idea of putting us on show in that Moscow Panopticum. Schaub has disposed of most of my unwanted papers; you will see that my body is completely destroyed. There must be no trace left of me, of Fraulein Braun or any personal possessions. As to the portrait of Frederick, give it to Bauer. He might be able to take it to Southern Bavaria.'

Linge assured the Fuhrer he would do his utmost to follow

instructions to the letter. With an effort, he held himself in control, presenting his usual impassive face.

Needing to talk to someone about the business ahead he made his way along the corridor, looking for police chief Hoegl. He noticed bottles strewn everywhere; he heard the noise of people shouting and laughing hysterically above the music of gramophone records. It was the last of the faithful, trying in their own way to come to terms with the imminence of death; living by moments, dulling fears with brandy, savouring each segment of whatever existence remained.

On the following day, General von Greim and the courageous woman pilot, Hanna Reitsch, crash-landed on the strip that had been prepared along the East-West Axis avenue near the Brandenburg Gate. The General's foot was shattered by shrapnel in a blast of shelling.

After his wound had been dressed by Stumpfegger, von Greim was accommodated in quarters close to the Fuhrer and the two spent some time talking together. At the end of the talks Greim had been promoted to Field Marshal and appointed by Hitler as the successor to Goring. He was also supplied with cyanide pellets for Hanna Reitsch and himself.

That night, the first Russian shells landed in the grounds above the bunker — the enemy was less than a mile away.

It was during a discussion on the night of Saturday April 28 that a message arrived which finally brought home to Hitler the futility of clinging to any last-minute hopes. A Reuter dispatch from Stockholm had been intercepted. 'It struck a deathblow to the entire assembly. Men and women alike screamed with rage, fear and desperation, all mixed in one emotional spasm.' Hitler was the worst of the lot, said Hanna Reitsch, 'He raged like a madman.'

Himmler had secretly contacted Bernadotte, head of the Swedish Red Cross, suggesting that he was willing to surrender the Third Reich unconditionally in the west while continuing the fight against the Russians in the east.

The offer had been rejected. Hitler's *treue Heinrich* had finally betrayed his Fuhrer. It was the unkindest cut of all. 'He was prostrate and broken,' said Linge. 'There was no more spirit left in him.'

The rest of the news was an anti-climax: Schoener's forces had been pinned down in the mountain region of Bohemia; the naval detachment under Donitz was suffering terrible losses trying to defend the Chancellery.

Later, most of the talk centred on the relentless approach of the Russians: what would happen when they broke in? Should those left in the bunker to try to shoot it out or kill themselves first?

The Fuhrer's secretaries, Traudl Junge and Gerda Christian, feared the Russians but were plainly terrified at the prospect of swallowing cyanide. They both clung desperately to the possibility of survival. Most of the others began making preparations for a final military operation — a breakout.

The turmoil reached fever pitch when a number of civil defence leaders and a quantity of civilian refugees sought refuge in the bunker. Some members of the German Girls' League, hysterically begged to be allowed admittance.

Hitler shrugged his shoulders, as if to dismiss the threat hanging over his own head. 'Just be careful about them,' he advised. 'The Russians are sure to try to smuggle in a number of spies. We must all be on our guard. There is nothing on earth they would like more than to capture me alive. In their peasant minds, they imagine I would become a laughing stock for the whole world to despise.'

Through all the confusion, the Goebbels' children — Helga, Holde, Hilda, Heide, Hedda and Helmuth, played innocently in and out of the corridors, sublimely unaware of the mortal danger they were in. Magda Goebbels had no intention of allowing them to fall into the hands of the Red Army. Stumpfegger promised to help her 'if the worst came to the worst'.

As the Russian artillery began to concentrate its fire on the Chancellery, the bunker began to shake beneath the thunderous explosions. Linge was told that every metre of ground above them was being savagely fought over, with the young defenders showing an utter contempt for death. They lost their defensive position in the Anhalt station briefly, but although the losses were horrendous they recaptured it again — and then were blown to bits by an armoured unit.

Everyone realised that the situation was hopeless. The wounded, dragged down into the bunker, were tended by exhausted, shocked medical assistants, their faces showing the gruesome experiences they had undergone in the final spasms of a city succumbing to the chaos and carnage of total war.

Despite everything, the Fuhrer spared the time to decide the fate of the miscreant Fegelein, accusing him of being an accomplice to Himmler's act of treachery. He ordered the SS man to be taken upstairs and shot. Fegelein, in his last desperate hour, spoke to Linge over an internal phone, pleading to be allowed to talk to Hitler.

The Fuhrer refused to see him.

Breaking down completely Fegelein urged Linge at least to ask Eva Braun to intercede on his behalf. She locked herself in her bedroom, refusing to open the door. Deeply depressed on account of her brother-in-law's behaviour, she firmly told Linge there was nothing she could do. 'Fegelein was a deserter, and even worse, had betrayed his Fuhrer.'

Fegelein was handed over to the Gestapo shortly afterwards and shot.

The valet recalls that one of the most tranquil people in the bunker in the last hours was Eva. With no longer any hope in the future, her one regret was that she could not stroll in the gardens one last time with her beloved Fuhrer. 'I know,' she said, 'there will be no miracles. Life isn't like that. I will die with the Fuhrer and please God I will do so as his wife. That is my greatest wish.'

Her wish, born of destruction and despair, was surprisingly granted.

Early in the morning of April 29, Hitler and Eva were married as Russian shells showered down on the undefended bunker.

Linge prepared the conference room adjoining Hitler's bedroom for the brief ceremony, which was conducted by Councillor Walter Wagner, called in by Goebbels. The Fuhrer and his bride declared they 'were of complete Aryan descent . . . and had no hereditary disease to exclude the marriage.' And in a voice low with fear, Eva pleaded with God to bless the union.

The wedding, as Linge recalled ten years later, was much discussed and criticised as soon as the news reached the outside world. He confessed that as one of the witnesses, he thought it more than a little bizarre himself.

Having had a decent interval in which to think about it, he felt that from Hitler's point of view, with his political life at an end, it was simply an honourable gesture, a measure of his respect for the girl's feelings. Eva was a fundamentally respectable girl who had, for a number of years, cherished the hope that the relationship would some day be officially sanctioned — if only for the sake of her family.

293

When people asked Linge what was the point in the Fuhrer marrying the girl when his time on earth was numbered in hours, he replied that it was a straighforwardly selfless act born of respect and gratitude, the end result of mutual perceptions not possible to define in everyday language.

At the end of the ceremony the couple celebrated the union with a weird wedding breakfast. Linge, pen in hand, noted the guest list: The Goebbels, Krebs, Burgdorf and Bormann, Stumpfegger, the remaining secretaries and Fraulein Manzialy, the Fuhrer's vegetarian cook. Champagne was produced and the last delicacies from Linge's much depleted store of provisions. Hitler held the floor for most of the time, finding comfort in remembering past glories.

After the celebration, Frau Junge was called and Hitler dictated his last will and testament. The final paragraph read: 'My wife and I choose to die in order to escape the shame of overthrow or capitulation. It is our wish that our bodies be buried immediately in the place where I have performed the greater part of my daily work during the course of twelve years service to my people.'

Looking back on it, Linge felt the whole event was unreal — almost like a dream. Overhead, the city had been reduced to a pile of jagged rubble; deep underground, protected by reinforced concrete, a brief, near-hysterical gaiety prevailed with the survivors going through the motions, toasting their leader, joking with his bride and finally slipping away, one by one, before the awful grief of their situation overwhelmed them.

Then, just as Hitler had finished dictating his 'political last will and testament', striking the names of Goring and Himmler from the party's roll of honour, and nominating Donitz as successor, details of Mussolini's shameful end reached him.

*   *   *

Unsuccessful in his attempts to negotiate with Italian resistance fighters, Mussolini had joined a German convoy led by a Major Kritz, hoping to make a dash for Switzerland with Clara Petacci. She had arrived at the Duce's quarters outside Como the night before with her brother, Marcello. She also carried with her in a red leather suitcase every single piece of jewellery given her by the Duce since the beginning of their relationship.

Mussolini, for his part, had with him millions of pounds in

assorted currencies and gold, together with a quantity of the crown jewels, the property of the Italian royal family.

At Musso, a few hours from the border, the convoy was held up by a unit of partisans attached to the 52nd Garibaldi Brigade. Kritz might have bulldozed his way through but, disenchanted with the war he offered his Italian passengers as bait if the partisans would allow him to continue on to Austria.

Mussolini and Clara were bundled out of a lorry and locked in the bedroom of a nearby farmhouse. When a communist partisan leader came to question him early the next morning, the Duce was prepared to promise him anything if he would spare his life. As the two men talked Clara, still in bed, began writhing around under the clothes as if in pain. When the officer asked her what was wrong she replied, 'It's all right, I'm only looking for my knickers.'

The couple were taken out on the road and placed against a wall. As the firing squad raised their rifles, Clara, huge stricken eyes taking in every line of the Duce's features, courageously tried to shield her lover's body with her own. They were both shot, along with the seventeen other captured fascists.

On the night of Saturday, April 28, the two bodies, together with the corpses of other fascists, were driven into Milan and dumped in the Piazza Loreto, where next morning, they were strung up by their heels outside a petrol station for some hours before being cut down.

Throughout the rest of the day, Mussolini's body lay sprawled on top of Clara Petacci's — in the gutter. They were buried in plain coffins in a communal grave in the Cimiterio Maggiore in Milan, although some time later, the Duce's body was removed by fascist sympathisers and handed over to a religious order for safe keeping.

When Mussolini was taken by the partisans at Dongo, near Lake Como, the contents of his luggage were taken to the town hall and carefully inventoried. After the executions, all trace of the money, gold and jewellery carried by Mussolini and Clara Petacci mysteriously disappeared. Part of it — mostly currency notes — was reported to have financed the postwar political activities of the partisan members of the Italian communist party. The hoard of gold, known as the 'Treasure of Dongo', was rumoured to have passed into the hands of the Catholic church.

* * *

In 1956, an Italian fund, The Balzan Foundation, was set up to make awards for work contributing to international progress or world peace. Recipients included the late Pope John XXIII. The fund was administered by Father Zucca, Mussolini's reputed confessor, who was imprisoned in 1946 for hiding the Duce's body. He was implicated in efforts in 1957 and 1967 to sell forged diaries attributed to Mussolini. All rumours that Father Zucca was connected with the 'Treasure of Dongo' were strongly refuted.

According to A. E. Hotchner — writing in 1969 — Mussolini's body was handed over to two monks of the Ambrosian Order, who agreed to care for the corpse and pray for the peace of the Duce's soul.

When, in the 1950s, the Italian government finally traced the body to the Ambrosian monastery, it was removed and eventually laid to rest in the Mussolini mausoleum at Predappio.

Many theories have been propounded as an explanation of the mystery concerning the final disposal of Mussolini's treasure. Without comment, the author offers the following as his contribution to the search for the truth.

On Sunday, December 2, 1984 the body of a top Italian industrialist was found dead in a bedroom at the Grosvenor House Hotel, Park Lane, London. He was alone and there were no signs of violence.

Yugo Niutta, aged 63, was an associate of Roberto Calvi, chief of the failed Ambrosiano Bank, whose body had been discovered, trussed and hanging from London's Blackfriars Bridge, two years earlier.

Niutta, believed to be a cashier for P2, the Catholic masonic lodge — whose links with the Vatican have been the subject of Italy's biggest scandals since World War II — was officially in London on business as president of the Montedison International chemical company. He had previously been investigated by an Italian parliamentary commission inquiring into the activities of P2, to whom he had admitted that, while acting as cashier, he had received money supplied by a P2 front organisation.

It has been suggested that Roberto Calvi was killed because he threatened to reveal the whole truth of what was going on. Was Niutta's apparent suicide linked with the unsolved death of 'God's banker' Calvi? And could either of them have thrown fresh light on the 'Treasure of Dongo'?

296

Who was in a better position than the church to hold valuables for a long period of time without exposing them to the market?

Did the treasure find its way from the religious order of St Ambrose to the coffers of the Ambrosiano bank?

Perhaps the Church of Rome, through the grace of gold, has been able to absolve the soul of the faithful departed dictator from the bonds of earthly sin, allowing him to escape the judgement of heaven.

Mussolini had, after all, come to terms with the Vatican. He signed a treaty of conciliation in February 1929, thus establishing its independence, and this 'Lateran Agreement' became part of the Italian constitution in 1947.

The Duce had, in 1942, knelt before the Pope and received holy communion. An ardent atheist at the beginning of his political career, during the war, despite deriding many aspects of the church, he had become increasingly religious. As a wedding gift, he presented his daughter, Edda, with a solid gold rosary and his youngest child was given a religious name, Anna Maria. When Anna Maria married in June 1960 — to a professional entertainer known as Nando Pucci — Pope John XXIII sent a telegram of congratulations. As informed people in Rome used to say in the 1960s, 'Italy will never have a dictator again — not a man on horseback. What we might well have is a man in a cassock.'

*   *   *

As soon as Hitler had finished reading the account of Mussolini's death, he called in Linge and repeated his instructions concerning his body. 'It must be completely destroyed, understand? Completely.'

After lunch, he rapidly skimmed through a digest of news on the Russian advance. It looked as if the Chancellery would be in their hands by May 1, so he had very little time left.

Late that night, Linge was instructed to call everyone to Hitler's quarters. The Fuhrer wished to say goodbye. When they were all lined up along the corridor, Hitler shook each one of them by the hand. No words were exchanged.

Before he retired to his room some time before dawn, Hitler had his dog, Blondi, poisoned and gave orders for the destruction of any remaining documents in his files. At about 4.30 am, he stretched out on his bed for an hour or two, fully dressed.

In the staff canteen, some kind of a party was in progress. More bottles were opened, dance music blared out from a gramophone, uniform tunics were discarded and staid senior officers danced wildly around the room with some of the women — or with each other. A polite request from Hitler's quarters for less noise was ignored and the dancing went on well into the morning.

Bormann, Burgdorf and Krebs took some bottles and easy chairs into the conference room. Expecting the Russians to burst in on them at any minute, they sat drinking and dozing for a couple of hours.

Other members of the staff slept on mattresses on the floor, loaded pistols by their sides. 'We did not,' said Linge rather pompously, 'intend to sell our lives cheaply without making some kind of fight for them.'

Shortly before 5.30 am, some inner anxiety prompted the valet to check the Fuhrer's bedroom, but just as he was about to enter, the door opened.

Hitler, raising a finger to his lips to indicate that the sleepers should lie undisturbed, stepped carefully over the bodies to make his way to the telephone exchange. He wanted a final word with SS General Mohnke, who was manning the command post in the Chancellery cellar. He was told that the Russians were in the Tiergarten, preparing for the final assault. Any attempt at defence was pointless.

At the usual noon conference Hitler had a few words to say on the theme of treachery; on the generals' disloyalty; the lack of faith of his former comrades and of the worthlessness of so many of his advisers. He had spoken in a dead voice, drained of emotion.

'My chiefs of staff have left me in the lurch and my soldiers are no longer able to fight. I no longer want them to do so.'

He had spent some time talking to Bauer, Hewel and Doctor Haase. Linge suspected the doctor may have given him a final injection — possibly of morphine.

Bormann, Burgdorf and Krebs, greyfaced and hungoever, spent twenty minutes with Hitler. In his farewell message he told them: 'In this city I was able to dictate orders; now I am at the mercy of the dictates of providence. Even if it proved possible to save my skin I would not. The captain must go down with his ship.'

Linge stood by, gloomily aware that this was to be the last meeting. For him it was a poignant, unforgettable moment.

'Quite soon,' continued the Fuhrer, 'there won't be a single hair on my head that will not be reviled and cursed. There is an impossible time ahead for the German people. Our enemies will delight in our downfall. That is why I want you to remember this: history must eventually realise that I did what I could for Germany.

'It is possible you will find out many new facts about me — things of which you are at present ignorant. You must understand — as the world must one day accept — that what I did was all for Germany.' He had begun talking conversationally but suddenly he began to shake, as if from anger and frustration. 'Germany has always been a great nation, yet her legitimate demands were never given proper consideration. But the efforts and sacrifices of the people must not have been in vain. The aim must still be to win territory in the east for the German people.'

Shortly before one o'clock, Linge was called into Eva's apartment. He found her pale but in control of herself — although her voice was husky, her words somewhat slurred, as if from drink. She explained that she would not be lunching with the Fuhrer but she wanted to express her gratitude to the valet for all he had done on her behalf. 'And if you should ever see my poor sister, Gretl, again, I beg you, dear Linge, don't tell her how her husband Fegelein lost his life.'

For the valet, it was one more forlorn farewell. This time, however, to a compassionate, plucky girl.

Lunch was served shortly before two o'clock. The Fuhrer, through sheer force of will, ate the spaghetti and salad with apparent enjoyment. The others at the table, Traudl Junge, Gerda Christian and the 'mousy but pleasant little *Innsbruckerin*', Fraulein Manzialy, picked at the food, unable to provide much in the way of small talk. Linge, who was assisted by an SS orderly, Corporal Schweidel, was conscious of one thought running through his mind. This was the last meal; he would never prepare the table for his chief again.

The final farewells were said at the end of the meal and Linge stood by the door of Hitler's bedroom. The Fuhrer waited until the others had gone before grasping Linge's hand. He momentarily lost his balance, slumping against the wall; then taking his cue he was onstage again, alive to the moment.

'Linge,' his voice steady, 'faithful friend, I've given orders for those left in the bunker to attempt to break out. You must join

299

one of the groups heading for the west.'

'My Fuhrer,' replied the valet, 'what point is there in my trying to escape once you've gone?'

Hitler released his hand. 'You must. For the sake of your children; for the man who will succeed me; for the future.'

Linge vainly tried to express his feelings. There was a need to say something moving or significant but through training and custom, he didn't know how. His lips moved but no sound emerged. The words eluded him. The door closed and it was too late.

It took him some time to collect himself, to realise what was about to happen, and to remember his promise. No one was to be allowed near the chief's quarters for at least ten minutes. Suddenly, Magda Goebbels appeared and began arguing with Adjutant Gunsche, pleading to be allowed a last word with Hitler. Gunsche, growling at her like a bulldog defending his master, reluctantly tapped on the door and asked if she should be admitted for a few moments. The request was curtly denied, stopping the distraught woman in her tracks. She hurried back down the corridor, tears pouring down her cheeks.

For Linge, the next few minutes passed in a kind of a haze. Perhaps it was the pressure of events, a sense of ever-increasing dread, that proved too much for him. Trying to stifle his fear, he dashed wildly up the stairs and through the emergency exit. The fresh air hit him like a blow, and the deafening noise of an artillery shell exploding on Wilhelmstrasse brought him back to reality. Under the callous sneers of the SS guards, he retraced his steps. Gunsche looked at the valet through half-closed eyes, no expression on his face.

'Check your watch,' suggested Linge.

It was half past three.

Linge, a finger to his lips, strained to hear the sound of a shot, but found it impossible to distinguish anything above the sound of gunfire overhead.

In a 1945 testimony, he reported that he heard 'a single shot' before going into the room ten minutes later. According to Gunsche, none of those outside the door, Goebbels, Bormann, Krebs, Burgdorf, Axmann, heard a shot — only Linge.

He claims he was the first to enter the room, followed by Gunsche and the others. They started back in horror from the smell of death, the stench of cordite and of cyanide.

Hitler, sitting at one end of the sofa, had shot himself in the head. Blood had dripped from the wound, staining the carpet. His stocky body was slumped forward, his right hand on his knee. What was left of his face was the colour of clay and his mouth was clamped shut. The poison had done its work efficiently; the bullet had not been necessary.

Eva sat nearer the middle of the sofa, shoes kicked off, feet curled trimly beneath her dark blue dress. There were no visible wounds, but the deep lines around her eyes and the firmly closed lips had set in a cyanide mask of death.

Linge, almost choking from the fumes of the poison, noticed that a vase containing fresh tulips had fallen from the table. Mechanically he picked it up and replaced the flowers before setting it neatly on the table alongside Eva's small pistol and a bright red silk scarf. The others stood watching in silence.

Gunsche broke the spell. Calling for blankets, he ordered Linge to spread them on the floor. At that point Stumpfegger, the cyanide king, appeared. He carefully examined both bodies before pronouncing them dead.

Then Linge, assisted by an SS orderly, carried the Fuhrer's blanket-wrapped body out into the conference passage and up the stairs to the exit. Rattenhuber staggered along the corridor, soaked in brandy and was stupefied to learn that the Fuhrer had shot himself. Hearing Linge's account of the manner of death, he decided that someone must have fired the shot — on Hitler's orders, in case the poison proved ineffective.

Later, the Russians were only too ready to believe his version: that Gunsche or Linge helped Hitler take the coward's way out.

Among all the conflicting accounts of the last hours, perhaps writer James O'Donnell's conclusions are nearest the mark. In *The Berlin Bunker* — published while Linge was still alive — he voiced the opinion that the only shot fired was fired by the Fuhrer and that no one in the bunker heard it. In other words, the eye-witnesses spoke the truth and Rattenhuber did not. At the same time it was possible, he felt, that Linge and Gunsche might have lied. Both of them, even in 1979, remained loyal to the Fuhrer. Neither wished to go down in history as 'the man who shot the Fuhrer'. He believed the same was true of Axmann. Kempka he dismissed as 'a crude and unreliable braggart'.

In his testimony, Kempka related how — as Linge was carrying

301

Hitler's body up to a shallow grave a few metres from the emergency exit — he attempted to wrest Eva's corpse from 'the lout Bormann'.

'He was carrying her,' said Kempka, 'by clutching her breasts with his apelike paws . . . as if she were a sack of potatoes. I grabbed her body from Bormann to carry it up the stairs myself. If Bormann had resisted, I'd have clobbered him there and then. But he made no protest.'

Both Kempka and Gunsche, said O'Donnell, knew how much Bormann and Eva Braun hated each other and both men resented Bormann's fake concern at her death.

Halfway up the stairs, the body of Eva Braun Hitler passed from Kempka to Gunsche. He in turn handed it over to a couple of SS officers waiting by the exit door.

Both bodies, still wrapped in army blankets, were placed side by side in a kind of shallow ditch, close to the bunker entrance, under the shadow of an abandoned cement mixer. 200 litres of petrol, supplied by Kempka, were poured over the corpses.

Linge later testified that the first attempts to set the fuel ablaze were unsuccessful. Finally, he ran back downstairs to the bunker and grabbed a handful of intelligence reports.

Up in the open air again, he quickly twisted the papers into spills and using his lighter to ignite them, began flinging them like darts towards the ditch. A huge flame belched into the sky and the funeral pyre was under way.

The SS officers, Linge, Bormann, Goebbels, and Kempka stood stiffly to attention, their arms raised in the final Nazi farewell.

Their war lord, their Fuhrer, the ultimate born-again Siegfried, having watched the real life Gotterdammerung and witnessed the collapse of Valhalla, had left them on their own — and taken his Brunhild with him.

And Eva, having stayed throughout the graphic violence, the self-destructive furies and the torments of sexual ambivalence — in the rapture of her love for the noble savage — had sacrificed the gods and the world.

Wotan's ravens could go back home. The master race was left without a leader.

'What I don't understand,' said the woman, screwing up her face so that it looked more wrinkled than ever, 'is how they can all go on marching like this. They must have had enough by now. There was the first war and there was Hitler and there was the second war and there was the occupation and the Russians and now they're all marching up and down again. I don't understand how they can do it. Everybody,' she went on calmly, 'tells us how bad Hitler was. But at least Unter den Linden looked a little more respectable then than it does now'.

Ian McDougall : German Notebook : 1953

The West German government was yesterday urged to ban a rally by Nazi veterans timed to clash with the 40th anniversary of VE Day.

Opposition Social Democrats condemned the reunion of the most notorious SS units — the Death's Head division, the Hitler Youth and one formed from Hitler's bodyguard.

The rally, planned for the first week of May in Nesselwarg near Munich, will coincide with ceremonies to mark the end of World War Two in Europe on May 8, the world economic summit in Bonn, and a visit by President Reagan.

News Item. April 19, 1985

Silvi Negri, grand-daughter of Benito Mussolini has been elected to the council of the Italian city of Forli. She is a member of the Neo-Fascist Italian Social Movement.

News Item. May, 1985

CHAPTER TWENTY-FOUR

It had rained briefly just before daylight. Against a sky streaked with black and orange, the trees still standing in the bare expanse of the Tiergarten were like cardboard cutouts covered in dust.

Peering across the pile of rubble that had once been the Unter den Linden, Linge spotted the line of tanks, squat, menacing, blocking the escape route over the Weidendamm Bridge. Every now and then, he could hear the crackle of machine gun or rifle fire.

*   *   *

Having disposed of Hitler's body on the Monday evening, the manservant felt released from all further responsibility. It was time to leave the bunker.

Unfortunately, the getaway planned for that night, April 30, had to be postponed for twenty-four hours. The Russians, in a flood of tanks, artillery and infantry, had reached the East-West Axis, sealing off any hope of escape through the Tiergarten.

The next day at noon, Linge was told to present himself to the Reich Propaganda Minister. It seemed that Goebbels felt the valet might have done more to persuade the Fuhrer to stay alive.

'I know,' said Goebbels, his face even more gaunt than usual, his movements ponderous and weary, 'that I have no need to remind you that Der Chef was a man of superlative qualities; of great courage. His presence would have continued to be an inspiration for those who remain.'

'With respect, Herr Doctor, you, an outstanding orator, tried to reason with the Fuhrer. You were not able to influence him. What could I, a servant, say to make him change his mind?'

Goebbels looked at him and nodded. They both remained silent for a few moments.

'Well, if you come through,' said Goebbels, 'never forget what a privilege it was to serve such a leader; so gifted with political genius. Other people wished for things to happen. He willed them. Do you understand me?' His voice was harsh and penetrating.

'Yes, sir.'

That night, some time after eight o'clock, Werner Naumann, Goebbels' assistant, sat drinking champagne with the little doctor and his wife. Goebbels had made the rounds, saying goodbye to everyone. When he spoke to the two secretaries, Gerda Christian and Traudl Jung, who were preparing to join one of the ten escape groups, they begged to be allowed to take the Goebbels' children along.

No, said Goebbels, it was not possible. His mind was made up.

Linge laid the responsibility for the deaths of the six children at Stumpfegger's door. Other somewhat unreliable sources believed that Magda alone was responsible.

Naumann later testified that she had been sitting for some time, drinking and chain-smoking. 'Suddenly she got up and headed for the children's bedrooms. After a short while she returned, ashen-faced and shaking.'

Goebbels then spoke to his adjutant, Schwagermann, handing him his signed portrait of the Fuhrer. Schwagermann in turn promised to carry out his last wish and burn the bodies of the doctor, his wife and family.

Shortly after 8.30 pm on the night of May 1, Goebbels escorted his wife up the stairs and into the Chancellery garden. As Magda quickly crunched a cyanide capsule between her teeth, he put a bullet in the back of her head. Then he bit into his own ampoule, almost simultaneously shooting himself in the right temple.

The bodies were soaked in petrol and set ablaze.

However, according to the subsequent testimony of Kempka, Axmann and Schwagermann, the cremation was badly bungled. The following morning the Russians occupied the Chancellery gardens and were able to identify the charred remains.

All in all it was an ending perfectly in tune with what had gone before.

*   *   *

Linge, making a detour to the Friedrichstrasse subway, came up against more Russian tanks pumping out shells in sequence. He flung himself to the ground, praying for a lull in the firing. As he tried to take stock of the situation, he saw a familiar figure, a dark leather coat covering his SS uniform, crouching in the wake of a German tank.

It was Martin Bormann. His group, including Kempka, Axmann, Naumann and Stumpfegger, had been the first to leave the bunker. Using the tank and a number of other vehicles as a shield, he was going to make an attempt to bulldoze through the Russian line.

The valet watched Bormann follow the tank as it headed for the Weidendamm Bridge. Suddenly, there was a direct hit on the tank. Bormann's body vanished behind a pall of black smoke. Linge decided that that was the end of the burly Reichsleiter.

Kempka also saw the tank explode. 'Where Bormann had been standing, there was nothing but flame.'

But Axmann had a different tale to tell. He too saw the tank blow up, but claimed that the group, including Bormann, took cover in a bomb crater. Shortly afterwards, as he crossed the bridge leading to Lehrter station, he spotted the bodies of Stumpfegger and Bormann below on the embankment. He assumed then, and was quite certain later, that both of them had taken poison.

To Simon Wiesenthal, the fate of Martin Bormann remains the biggest unsolved Nazi mystery. In 1966, he still believed that Bormann had escaped to South America and 'was probably living near the frontier of Argentina and Chile'.

General Gehlen, in his memoirs published in 1971, wrote that Bormann had acted as a secret agent for Moscow throughout the war. In May 1945, he had crossed to the Russians and was taken to the Soviet Union.

In 1972, some building contractors were at work on a new exhibition park across from the site of the former Lehrterstrasse station. During the course of excavations, two skeletons were revealed; one of an extremely tall man (Stumpfegger was over 6'6") and the other somewhat shorter. Glass splinters that might have remained from ampoules of cyanide were lodged in both jawbones.

Dental records, said O'Donnell, later identified the remains as those of Bormann and Stumpfegger.

*   *   *

Down in the subway Linge, fighting for breath, made towards the tracks that would take him to Stettiner station on Invalidenstrasse. Suddenly there was a stir of activity and screams rose in crescendo. Someone yelled out that the Russians were overhead, about to flood the subway. People surged in a panic towards the street exit.

Using fists and boots and his superior height, Linge fought his way to the front of the crowd and doubled back upstairs. Outside the station, a tank clattered to a halt.

'It's all right!' a voice called, 'we are German soldiers. You can safely show yourselves.'

Linge stumbled out of the entrance to find himself looking straight into the barrel of a gun mounted on the olive green turret of a Russian tank. He automatically clicked his heels and stood to attention. For him it was *kaput*, the finish.

Two weeks later, lounging dispiritedly behind barbed wire at Posen, Linge was recognised by a former SS colleague. Hoping to curry favour with his captors, the obersturmfuhrer buttonholed the nearest Russian guard and the valet's true identity was revealed.

The Soviets were not displeased. Hitler's personal flunkey was a catch worth preserving. And as one of the officers who had been with the Fuhrer at the end, his evidence could be of great significance.

A week later, in Berlin, Major Ivan Nikitine, deputy chief of the Soviet Security Police, surprisingly announced that Hitler had neither shot himself nor been cremated, as was generally believed. Indeed, he said there was doubt that he had perished at all.

It was that event which started the rumours that Hitler was not, after all, dead.

At the Potsdam Conference in July, 1945, Stalin insisted that Hitler was still alive and probably living in Spain or South America. Later, a Russian newspaper suggested that Hitler and Eva had found sanctuary in the British Zone of Occupation and were living comfortably in a Westphalian castle.

Hugh Trevor-Roper, now Lord Dacre, was sent to Berlin in 1945 by the British government to verify the circumstances of Hitler's death in the bunker. He is the author of *The Last Days of Hitler*, for years regarded as the definitive account of the Fuhrer's final hours.

He is also the eminent historian who stated in April, 1983 that he believed the Hitler Diaries were genuine. He later explained that his endorsement was based on the evidence of the mass of the material available and a link he believed was established between the material and the aircraft that had crashed in the

Heidenholz pine woods, near Boernersdorf, in April, 1945.

Later, he became convinced that the diaries 'were forgeries until the opposite is proven'.

Has Hitler's body ever been positively identified?

It wasn't until 1963 that Marshal Sokolovsky — who had examined the badly charred remains in the Chancellery garden — admitted to Cornelius Ryan that he believed Hitler had died on April 30, 1945.

The official Russian line is that Eva's body was never recovered and that Hitler's body was cremated 'outside Berlin'. They have never named the location.

Soviet writer Lev Bezemenski affirmed that Hitler's body had been identified by his dental X-rays, which were obtained by the Russian Security Police from Fraulein Heusermann in Berlin. Her employer, Dentist Blaschke, escaped to Bavaria but Kathy Heusermann was arrested by the Russians on May 7, 1945. She was able to recognise the dental work that Blaschke had performed on the Fuhrer in November, 1944. Released after the identification, Fraulein Heusermann was picked up by the NKVD. Despatched to Russia, she was kept in a Soviet prison, most of the time in solitary confinement, until she was released in the summer of 1956.

Doctor Lester L. Luntz, dentist and professor of oral diagnosis at the University of Connecticut Dental School, has spent eighteen years studying the evidence. In September, 1984 he presented the results of his research to the International Association of Forensic Sciences, meeting in Oxford, stating that, in fact, Hitler's dental records have never been discovered.

Blaschke, eventually run to earth by the American forces in Bavaria, testified that all his records, including those of the Fuhrer, Eva Braun and party officials, had been aboard the Ju-352 aircraft — together with all the other important documents — that crashed on April 21, near Boernersdorf.

And what of the X-rays of Hitler's skull which are stored in the National Archives in America?

According to Luntz these are merely duplicates with the dates handwritten in ink. The originals were undated, whereas the word 'October' appears on the duplicates. Had the plates been genuinely dated at the time they would have carried the word *Okt* — an abbreviation for the German word *Oktober.*

'Such doubtful ante-mortem evidence,' said Luntz, 'is unacceptable for making a positive dental identification. It appears there were several sets of original and duplicate X-rays, adding to the confusion of what happened to the originals.'

The professor offered two further powerful submissions to support his belief that the identity of the body remained in doubt. Gunsche, Hitler's personal adjutant, released from Russian captivity in 1955, emphatically declared that the Soviets had never discovered the Fuhrer's body. Their post mortem report stated that Hitler died of cyanide poisoning and that there was no sign of lethal injuries.

*   *   *

Heinz Linge, sentenced by the Soviets to twenty-five years hard labour, was also released in 1955 and returned to Germany. He died in Hamburg in 1981.

The brief history of a united Germany which lasted only seventy-five years and which died in the rubble of Berlin in 1945, demands the attention of reflective men, not only for what it has to teach about the role of fear and cupidity and obtuseness in human affairs, about the seductions of power and the consequences of political irresponsibility, and about the apparently limitless inhumanity that man is capable of inflicting upon his fellows, but because also it has much to say about courage and steadfastness, about devotion to the cause of liberty and about resistance to the evils of tyranny.

Gordon A. Craig

500 veterans of one of Nazi Germany's most brutal SS Divisions marched again yesterday in procession through Marktheidenfeld, a small Bavarian town, on their way to a memorial service. The 4th SS Police Armoured Grenadier Division was blamed at the Nuremberg war crimes trials for murdering up to 2,000 civilians in occupied Greece.

News Item. October, 1984

Michale Kuhnen, 29, founder of a West German neo-Nazi movement, was jailed for three years and four months in Frankfurt for printing and distributing pamphlets glorifying Hitler. He was stripped of his civil rights for five years.

News Item. January, 1985

311

EPILOGUE

The sentencing began just before noon.

Fritzsche, Schacht and von Papen were acquitted. It was a letter Pope John XXIII had written to the Tribunal that may have saved von Papen. 'I do not wish to interfere with any political judgement on Franz von Papen. I can only say one thing: he gave me the chance to save the lives of 24,000 Jews'.

Von Papen later gave evidence on oath to the tribunal dealing with the beatification of Pope John — who had been Papal Nuncio in Istanbul when von Papen was German ambassador there.

Rader, Funk and Hess received life sentences; Speer and von Schirach twenty years; von Neurath fifteen years; Donitz ten years.

The tribunal adjourned for lunch — a breathing space for the remaining eleven accused.

In the afternoon, in handcuffs, they were called one by one. It took about twenty minutes to sentence each of them to death: Goring, Ribbentrop, Keitel, Jodl, Kaltenbrunner, Frank, Frick, Streicher, Sauckel, Seyss-Inquart and Rosenberg; the death sentence on Bormann was announced to an empty dock.

Ribbentrop and the other men condemned to death were hanged by Master Sergeant John Woods between 1.14 am and 2.57 am on Wednesday, October 16, 1946.

Goring, after his plea to be shot had been rejected, bit into a cyanide capsule at 10.30 pm on the night of October 15. He had concealed two capsules: one in his rectum, one in his navel.

After the executions had been completed, the bodies of Goring and the ten who had been hanged were photographed, clothed and unclothed, from various angles by a US Signal Corps photographer.

The United States Surgeon General had asked for the brains to be removed and sent to Washington for research but the application was turned down.

At 4 am the corpses were placed in packing cases, loaded on to two US army trucks and, under heavy escort, taken via Munich to Dachau. Journalists who attempted to follow the vehicles were stopped and forcibly prevented from doing so. The convoy arrived at Dachau at daylight, the crematorium ovens were ignited and the bodies cremated. That night their ashes were dropped into the Conwentz river on the outskirts of Munich.

Donitz, Rader, Funk, von Schirach, von Neurath, Hess and Speer were forced to clean the gymnasium in the Palace of Justice where the hangings had taken place.

After his return from the executions and cremations, Colonel Burton C Andrus, the Nuremberg jailer, was handed a telegram from the United States: 'A big businessman was prepared to give me $25,000 for the rope that had hanged Goring' (sic).

*   *   *

On May 21, 1945 British sentries on a bridge at Bremervorde, north-western Germany, questioned a man with a black eyepatch, wearing the uniform of a field security policeman and carrying papers in the name of Heinrich Hitzinger. Taken to Luneberg, his true identity was revealed.

Himmler escaped judgement at Nuremberg by clamping his jaws together and crushing the cyanide capsule hidden behind his teeth. Next morning, US Army officers located the place at Berchtesgaden where Himmler had hidden over a million dollars in banknotes of twenty-six different countries — beneath the floor of a barn.

On October 6, 1945, in his cell at Nuremberg, Dr Leonard Conti — who had conducted experiments on concentration camp inmates — tied a towel around his neck, attached it and knotted it securely to the window bars and jumped from his chair.

*   *   *

On October 25, 1945 Robert Ley looped the zip-fastening of the old American GI jacket he had been given around the handle of the lavatory cistern. He then wound a towel soaked in water around his neck and, having torn up his underpants and stuffed them into his mouth, finally flung himself down on the seat of the water-closet.

313

Since 1946, the authorities in West Germany have been tracking down wanted Nazis — their efforts hampered by lack of extradition treaties, legal formalities and, in the case of South American countries, pure pigheadedness.

At the end of World War II, 600 wanted Nazis escaped to South America; another 600 went to the US and Canada.

Two major figures have been extradited: Treblinka camp commandant Franz Stangl, in 1967 (he died in prison in West Germany) and more recently, Klaus Barbie, the Gestapo chief, at Lyon, France.

A handful of American citizens were stripped of their citizenship when it was discovered they had entered the US illegally by hiding their true identities. Canada has handed back only one suspected Nazi. Simon Wiesenthal claims there are six former Nazis living openly in Canada.

Gustav Wagner was arrested in Brazil in 1979. He was the commandant jointly responsible for at least 150,000 deaths at the Sobibor death camp. Four countries: West Germany, Poland, Austria and Israel have asked for Wagner's extradition. He attempted suicide twice and was transferred from prison to a mental hospital, remaining in Sao Paulo owing to an error in the translation of the German extradition request.

After a third attempt to kill himself by throwing himself in front of a car, Wagner finally succeeded in ending his life, on October 4, 1980, by stabbing himself with a knife.

*   *   *

Walter Rauff, in charge of the Gas Truck Department at the Central Security Offices in Berlin, was responsible for the deaths of 250,000 people. In the gas trucks, the victims were asphyxiated by the fumes funnelled into the interiors. Rauff was held in a war criminals camp in Milan in 1945 but managed to escape to Chile. He explained the reason for the gas trucks: mass shootings became too much of a psychological strain for the SS. Wiesenthal sent a telegram to Chilean President Augusto Pinochet, asking for Rauff's extradition. Pinochet never replied.

Robert Mildner, as Gestapo chief for Katowice, was responsible for the deaths of large numbers of Germans and Poles he despatched to Auschwitz. A native of Linz, he was in the same SS group as Eichmann and Kaltenbrunner. Imprisoned after the war, he escaped with the help of a Nazi underground movement. His family still live in Austria, but he is believed to be living in Argentina under a false name.

*   *   *

And finally, Dr Mengele, who in 1944 personally selected 400,000 people for death in the Auschwitz gas chambers - 200,000 of them children. As camp doctor, he conducted vivisection experiments on children in an attempt to breed a blonde, blue-eyed super race. Thousands of his victims died in agony.

After the war, he went back home to Gunzburg, on the banks of the Danube, where the family firm Karl Mengele & Sons is the main employer. Gunzburg was in the American Zone and he remained there for five years, until his former SS driver threatened to expose him. Using the Odessa escape route, he fled in 1951 to Italy.

In 1952 he was in Buenos Aires.

After three days of speculation about a body exhumed in June, 1985 from a cemetery at Embu, Sao Paulo police produced a statement which purported to fill in the gaps about the fugitive Mengele.

Mrs Gitta Stammer, a 65-year-old Hungarian immigrant, claimed that she and her husband had sheltered Mengele from 1962 to 1975; she knew the doctor as Peter Hochboicket, a Swiss who worked for the Stammers as a farm manager.

In 1975, a mutual friend, Wolfgang Gerhard, arranged for Mengele to move to a bungalow owned by an Austrian couple, Wolfram and Liselotte Bassert.

When Gerhard died in Austria, say the police, Menegel assumed his identity and was buried as Gerhard when he died in 1979. The body was exhumed from the Gerhard grave at Embu on June 14, 1985.

Police also claimed that Mengele's son, Rolf, twice visited Sao

Paulo, the second time in 1979 to collect his father's personal effects. A photograph of Rolf Mengele found at the Bassert's home has been identified by the West German authorities.

*   *   *

Nini Rascher   *Munich. April 13, 1942*
                                                   Trogerstr. 56

Highly esteemed der Reichsfuhrer!

You have given us great pleasure once again! So many good things! The children's evening porridge will be enriched now for quite a while. Heinrich Peter always fidgets with excitement when a parcel arrives. He guessed who had sent it and was of course given some chocolate immediately.

Dear Reichsfuhrer, I thank you from the bottom of my heart for the presents and the pleasure which you have given us all. My husband is very fond of chocolate and took some with him to the camp.

We thought you would allow yourself a little peace and quiet after so many strenuous weeks but you had to leave again today.

Thank you very much, dear Reichsfuhrer, for the letter which you enclosed.

My husband is very pleased at the interest which you have shown in his experiments. At Easter he conducted the experiments for which Dr Romberg would have shown too much restraint and compassion on his own. My husband will discuss all these matters with Mr Sievers at the end of the month.

My husband takes the liberty of sending his humble good wishes and of expressing his gratitude for everything.

With most sincere wishes for your wellbeing, I remain Always gratefully yours

Nini Rascher

*   *   *

316

Dr Rascher was removed from his post at Dachau in April, 1944, imprisoned and then shot by the SS shortly before the liberation. His wife, Nini, who had stolen several children and pretended she had given birth to them, was sent to Ravensbruck and shot there.

*   *   *

Those who cannot remember the past are condemned to repeat it
                                        Santayana

THE END

BIBLIOGRAPHY

Andrus, Burton C, *I Was the Nuremberg Jailer*. New York: Coward-McCann, 1969.

Angell, Norman, *The Great Illusion*. London: Heinemann, 1933.

Boothe, Clare, *European Spring*. London: Hamish Hamilton 1941.

Bowyer, Chaz, *Air War Over Europe*. London: Kimber 1981.

Browne, Lewis, *Something Went Wrong*. London: Gollancz 1942.

Bullock, Alan, *Hitler: A Study in Tyranny*. London: Odhams, 1952

Burgess, Alan, *Seven Men at Daybreak*. London: Evans Bros 1960

Cerruti, Elisabetta, *Ambassador's Wife*. London: George Allen & Unwin 1952

Churchill, Winston S, *The Second World War* (vols.1-6). London: Cassell & Co 1955

Ciano, Galeazzo, *Ciano's Diary 1939-1943*. London: Heinemann 1947

Collins, Larry and Lapierre, Dominique, *Is Paris Burning?* London: Gollancz 1965

Conot, Robert E, *Justice at Nuremberg*. London: Weidenfeld & Nicolson 1983

Cowles, Virginia, *Looking For Trouble*. London: Hamish Hamilton 1941

Craig, Gordon A, *Germany 1866-1945*. London: O.U.P. 1981

Distel, Barbara and Jakusch, Ruth, *Concentration Camp Dachau 1933-1945*. Brussels: Comité Int. de Dachau 1978

Everett, Susan, *Lost Berlin*. London: Hamlyn 1979

Fest, Joachim C, *Hitler*. London: Weidenfeld & Nicolson 1974

Flanner, Janet, *Paris Was Yesterday*. New York: Viking Press 1972

Fleming, Peter, *Invasion 1940*. London: Rupert Hart Davis 1957

Fredborg, Arvid, *Behind the Steel Wall*. London: Harrap 1944

Fuller, Maj-Gen J F C, *The Decisive Battles of the Western World* (vol.3). London: Eyre & Spottiswoode 1956

Garrison, Omar V, *The Secret World of Interpol*. Glasgow: Maclellan 1977

Gehlen, Reinhard, *The Gehlen Memoirs* (trans: D Irving) London: Collins 1972

Gibbs, Philip, *European Journey*. London: Heinemann with Gollancz 1934

Gibbs, Philip, *The Pageant of the Years*. London: Heinemann 1946

Gilbert, Martin, *Final Journey*. London: George Allen & Unwin 1979

Goebbels, Joseph, *My Part in Germany's Fight*. London: Hurst & Blackett 1935

Gromova, T, *Steeled in the Storm*. Moscow: Progress Publishers 1968

Gun, Nerin E, *Eva Braun: Hitler's Mistress*. London: Leslie Frewin, 1968

Gunther, John, *Inside Europe*. London: Hamish Hamilton 1936

Gunther, John, *Inside Europe Today*. London: Hamish Hamilton 1961

Hitler, Adolf, *Mein Kampf*. London: Hutchinson 1933

Hotchner, A E, *Treasure*. New York: Random House 1970

Hughes, H Stuart, *Contemporary Europe*. New Jersey: Prentice-Hall Inc 1961

Huss, Pierre J, *The Foe We Face*. New York: Doubleday, Doran Inc 1942

Jackson, J Hampden, *The Postwar World*. London: Gollancz 1935

Kempka, Erich, *Ich habe Adolf Hitler verbrannt*. Munich: Kyrburg Verlag (No date)

Kessel, Joseph, *The Magic Touch*. London: Rupert Hart Davis 1961

Kielar, Wieslaw, *Anus Mundi*. London: Allen Lane 1981

Kohn, Hans, *The Mind of Germany*. London: Macmillan 1962

Krausnick, Helmut and Broszat, Martin, *Anatomy of the SS State*. London: Collins 1968

Lajos, Ivan, *Germany's War Chances*. London: Gollancz 1939

Langer, Walter, *The Mind of Adolf Hitler*. London: Secker & Warburg 1973

Lennhoff Eugene, *X-Ray of Europe*. London: Hutchinson 1939

Lorant, Stefan, *I Was Hitler's Prisoner*. London: Penguin 1935

Maser, Werner, *Nuremberg, A Nation on Trial*. London: Allen Lane 1979

McDougal, Ian, *German Notebook*. London: Elek 1953

Moorehead, Alan, *Eclipse*. London: Hamish Hamilton 1946

Neave, Airey, *Nuremberg*. London: Hodder & Stoughton 1978

O'Donnell, James P, *The Berlin Bunker*. London: Dent 1979

Oechsner, Frederick, *This is the Enemy*. London: Heinemann 1943

Olden, Rudolf, *Hitler the Pawn*. London: Gollancz 1936

Paul, Elliot, *The Last Time I Saw Paris*. New York: Random House 1942

Poller, Walter, *Medical Block, Buchenwald*. London: Souvenir Press 1961

Pryce-Jones, David, *Unity Mitford: A Quest*. London: Weidenfeld & Nicolson 1976

Read, Anthony and Fisher, David, *Operation Lucy*. London: Hodder & Stoughton 1980

Roth, Jack J, *World War I: A Turning Point in Modern History*. New York: Alfred A Knopf 1967

Ryan, Cornelius, *The Last Battle*. London: Collins 1966

Sava, George, *A Tale of Ten Cities*. London: Faber & Faber 1942

Salter, Arthur, *Personality in Politics*. London: Faber & Faber 1947

Schacht, Hjalmar, *My First Seventy-six Years*. London: Wingate 1955

Shirer, William L, *End of a Berlin Diary*. London: Hamish Hamilton 1947

Shirer, William L, *The Rise and Fall of the Third Reich*. New York: Simon & Schuster Inc 1960

Skorzeny, Otto, *Special Mission*. London: Robert Hale 1957

Speer, Albert, *Inside the Third Reich*. London: Weidenfeld & Nicolson 1970

Strategicus, *The Tide Turns*. London: Faber & Faber 1944

Taylor, A J P, *The Second World War*. London: Hamish Hamilton 1975

Thomas, Hugh, *The Murder of Rudolf Hess*. London: Hodder & Stoughton 1979

Thompson, Dorothy, *Goodbye to Germany*. New York: Harpers Magazine, December 1934

Thompson, R W, *Men Under Fire*. London: MacDonald 1945

Tolischus, Otto D, *They Wanted War*. London: Hamish Hamilton 1940

Trevor-Roper, Hugh, *The Last Days of Hitler*. London: Macmillan 1947

Tuchman, Barbara W, *Practicing History*. New York: Alfred A Knopf Inc 1981

Viorst, Milton, *Hostile Allies*. New York: Macmillan 1965

Ward Price, G, *I Know These Dictators*. London: George G Harrap 1937

Wheeler-Bennett, *Knaves, Fools and Heroes*. London: Macmillan 1974

Wheeler-Bennett, *Friends, Enemies and Sovereigns*. London: Macmillan 1976

Whitehead, Don, *The FBI Story*. New York: Random House 1956

Wisenthal, Simon, *The Murderers Among Us*. Paris: Opera Mundi 1967

Wilmot, Chester, *The Struggle for Europe*. London: Collins 1952

Documents

Despatch submitted by Field Marshal Montgomery; British Information Services. New York 1946

Documents Concerning German-Polish Relations. London: HM Stationery Office 1939

Documentation Centre Bulletins, Simon Wiesenthal, Vienna 1979-1985

Journal of Historical Review, Keith Stimely, Editor, Torrance, California, USA 1984

KZ-Gedenkstatte Dachau Archives, Barbara Distel, 8060 Dachau-Ost West Germany

INDEX

326

337

THE HOLY BLOOD AND THE HOLY GRAIL
BY MICHAEL BAIGENT, RICHARD LEIGH AND HENRY LINCOLN

The subject of this book could constitute the single most shattering secret of the last two thousand years.

The first publication, in 1982, of THE HOLY BLOOD AND THE HOLY GRAIL, sparked off a storm of controversy, reverberations of which are still resounding throughout the Western world. The book's conclusions are persuasive, and to many will be shocking, perhaps profoundly dangerous. Whatever your own views, it is a book that you will truly not be able to set aside.

"Probably one of the most controversial books of the 20th Century."
U.P.I.

"A book that cannot easily be dismissed."
Neville Cryer, The Bible Society

"Their quest for knowledge possesses all the ingredients of a classic 19th Century mystery novel . . . a book that will be hotly denounced and widely read."
Financial Times

"A very extraordinary story . . . if you like this sort of detective work on the past you will like the book very much."
Anthony Powell, Daily Telegraph

0 552 12138 X   £3.50

TRANSIT POINT MOSCOW
BY GERALD AMSTER AND BERNARD ASBELL

When Gerald Amster was offered $24,000 to fly to Kuala Lumpur and collect a package, he should have said no. But, short of cash and eager for adventure, he agreed. With two friends, he took off for Malaya. There, they realized that they were in very bad company, and when ordered to take three extremely heavy suitcases to Paris via Moscow, they were in no position to argue.

They were assured that everything would go smoothly — but it didn't, and they were arrested at Sheremet' yevo Airport in possession of 62 pounds of heroin.

Thus begins a true story that takes the reader inside the Gulag where Amster served four and a half brutal years; then to Moscow, to which he escaped, posing as a deaf mute for six lonely, terrifying months; and finally to the breathtakingly daring bargain he struck with the Soviets, which won him his freedom in 1980.

0 552 12698 5 £2.50

IN GOD'S NAME
BY DAVID YALLOP

"Was John Paul I murdered? He may have been. To the extent the Vatican does not address itself to a responsible discussion of the evidence Mr Yallop has gathered, the probability of murder goes up. It is time that all Catholics face the unpleasant truth of the present condition of the Vatican, a condition which makes it possible to think a Pope could have been murdered."
— *Andrew Greeley*

IN GOD'S NAME

AN INVESTIGATION INTO THE MURDER OF POPE JOHN PAUL I

On September 28, 1978, thirty-three days after his election, Pope John Paul I, "the Smiling Pope," was declared dead. No official death certificate has ever been issued. No autopsy ever performed. His body was hastily embalmed. Cause of death: Unknown. And Vatican business continues.

This extraordinary book, product of more than three years' intensive investigation, unfolds a story so powerful in its revelations, so shocking in its inescapable conclusions, that it has made a stunned world take note. The facts are here in meticulous detail, documenting widespread corruption within the Vatican and presenting a compelling case that six powerful men, to protect their vast financial and political operations, decided on a shocking course of action — *Pope John Paul I must die.*

0 552 12640 3   £3.50

A SELECTED LIST OF NON FICTION
AVAILABLE FROM CORGI BOOKS

THE PRICES SHOWN BELOW WERE CORRECT AT THE TIME OF GOING TO PRESS. HOWEVER
TRANSWORLD PUBLISHERS RESERVE THE RIGHT TO SHOW NEW RETAIL PRICES ON COVERS
WHICH MAY DIFFER FROM THOSE PREVIOUSLY ADVERTISED IN THE TEXT OR ELSEWHERE.

☐	12698 5	TRANSIT POINT MOSCOW	*G. Amster & B. Asbell*	£2.50
☐	12138 X	THE HOLY BLOOD AND THE HOLY GRAIL		
☐		*Michael Baigent, Richard Leigh & Henry Lincoln*	£3.50
☐	99065 5	THE PAST IS MYSELF	*Christabel Bielenberg*	£2.95
☐	12712 4	ISLAND OF BARBED WIRE	*Connery Chappell*	£2.50
☐	12610 1	ON WINGS OF EAGLES	*Ken Follett*	£2.95
☐	12368 0	THE ANATOMY OF POWER	*John Kenneth Galbraith*	£2.95
☐	12389 7	INDECENT EXPOSURE	*David McClintick*	£2.50
☐	99158 9	BRENDAN BEHAN	*Ulick O'Connor*	£2.95
☐	99143 0	CELTIC DAWN	*Ulick O'Connor*	£4.95
☐	99247 X	THE FORD OF HEAVEN	*Brian Power*	£3.50
☐	12577 6	PLACE OF STONES	*Ruth Janette Ruck*	£2.50
☐	13058 3	THE MARILYN CONSPIRACY	*Milo Speriglio*	£2.50
☐	12589 X	AND I DON'T WANT TO LIVE THIS LIFE	*Deborah Spungen*	£2.50
☐	12640 3	IN GOD'S NAME	*David Yallop*	£3.50

*All these books are available at your book shop or newsagent, or can be ordered direct from the publisher.
Just tick the titles you want and fill in the form below.*

Transworld Publishers, Cash Sales Department, 61-63 Uxbridge Road, Ealing, London, W5 5SA.

Please send a cheque or postal order, not cash. All cheques and postal orders must be in £ sterling and made
payable to Transworld Publishers Ltd.
Please allow cost of book(s) plus the following for postage and packing:

UK/Republic of Ireland Customers:
Orders in excess of £5; no charge. Orders under £5; add 50p.

Overseas Customers:
All orders; add £1.50.

NAME (Block Letters): ....

ADDRESS ....

....